JESUS THE CHRIST AND RELIGIOUS PLURALISM

Rahnerian Christology and Belief Today

JOSEPH PANDIAPPALLIL

A Herder and Herder Book
The Crossroad Publishing Company
New York

The Crossroad Publishing Company
481 Eighth Avenue, New York, NY 10001

Printed in the United States of America

Library of Congress Cataloging-in-Publication Data

Pandiappallil, Joseph.
Jesus the Christ and religious pluralism : Rahnerian Christology and belief today / Joseph Pandiappallil.
p. cm.
"A Herder and Herder book."
Includes bibliographical references and index.
ISBN 0-8245-1917-5 (alk. paper)
1. Theology of religions (Christian theology) 2. Rahner, Karl, 1904- .—Contributions in theology of religions. 3. Jesus Christ—Person and offices. 4. Rahner, Karl, 1904-—Contributions in Christology. I. Title.
BT83.85 P33 2001
261.2'092—dc21

2001002506

1 2 3 4 5 6 7 8 9 10 05 04 03 02 01

Contents

Foreword

Cardinal Walter Kasper
Pontifical Council for Promoting Christian Unity

The theme of religious pluralism is discussed quite often in the Catholic, non-Catholic, and non-Christian theological circles. It seems that in the twenty-first century this theme will gain further theological relevance. For Christians, it is Christian theology in the context of religious pluralism. In such discussions Christology is the center because Christianity is founded on the person, work, and teachings of Jesus Christ, the Son of God. In this context it is the duty of theologians to evolve theologies that, on the one hand, explain the teachings of the Catholic Church and, on the other hand, are understandable to the present-day generation living in a society of religious and cultural pluralism.

In *Jesus the Christ and Religious Pluralism,* Joseph Pandiappallil presents a Christology that is meaningful for our contemporary society of cultural and religious pluralism. He summarizes the main teachings of pluralistic theology and presents in detail the transcendental theology of Karl Rahner. He evaluates both pluralistic theology and transcendental theology in the context of the history of religions and against the background of the origin and development of the religious idea. The author concludes that pluralistic theology fails to provide a reasonable answer to the problem of religious pluralism; but a transcendental theology and transcendental hermeneutics can help us develop a Christology in the context of religious pluralism that accepts other religions without sacrificing the Christian experience and Christian claims. The author affirms that a Christocentric and an ecclesiocentric transcendentalism developed in the light of the Christology of the Bible, the fathers of the church, the documents of the church councils, the encyclicals, and the teaching authority of the Catholic Church and together with the help of contemporary philosophy will help to develop a Christology understandable to a humanity that experiences pluralism in religion and culture.

The readers of this book will be particularly pleased by the manner in which Joseph Pandiappallil deals with the fact of religious pluralism and absolute revelation. The author argues convincingly, philosophically, and systematically. What makes the book important is the relevance of the author's conclusions in relation to Christology, ecumenical and interreligious dialogue, missiology, and theology in the context of cultural and religious pluralism. The valuable contributions of the author will surely be a landmark for Christology in this century and thereafter.

ROME
9 SEPTEMBER 2000

Preface

I HAVE BEEN INSPIRED TO INVESTIGATE the relevance of Karl Rahner's theology for a Christology in the context of religious pluralism by my own personal experience of Christian faith in the context of religious pluralism in India, the study of Indian philosophy, participation in interreligious dialogues, and an awareness, while I was engaged in my pastoral work in the Archdiocese of Freiburg, that Karl Rahner's theology may well have greater influence in the Catholic Church in the twenty-first century. My neighbors in my village belonged to different castes and religious faiths (Kerala-aborigines, Dravidians, Brahmins, Kshetrias, Vaiśyas, Sudras, Syrian Catholics, and various Protestant and Orthodox denominations), and my studies, pastoral work, and missionary activities in different states of India (Kerala, Karnataka, and Maharashtra) have also inspired me to start this inquiry.

It is a pleasant task to acknowledge those who have helped in different ways to bring this project to completion. First, I gratefully acknowledge the valuable guidance of Prof. Peter Walter. The numerous conferences with him and his suggestions and corrections and the discussions in the doctoral colloquium inspired me greatly. I express my thanks to Dr. Eva-Marie Faber, who agreed to be the second reader. There are many people who inspired and supported me one way or another. Here I should like to mention Dr. Albert Raffelt, Dr. Alfons Knoll, Dr. Michael G. Parker, Prof. Dr. Günter Biemer, Dr. Roman Siebenrock, Prof. Dr. Gerhard Oberhammer, Prof. Dr. Joseph Neuner, Prof. Dr. Daniel P. Jamros, Dr. Hilary Mooney, Br. Edward Daily and Dr. Francis Kodiyan. My study tours to the Karl Rahner Archives, Innsbruck, the Gregorian University, Rome, the Catholic University, Louvain, and to the Institut Catholique de Paris were also very useful. I am thankful for the support and encouragement of Msgr. Oskar Saier, archbishop of Freiburg, Msgr. Dr. Robert Zollitsch, Mr. Andreas Lerbs, Dr. Hermann Herder, Dr. Gwendolin Herder, Mr. Franz Johna, Msgr. Thomas Elavanal, bishop of Kalyan, and my superiors and confrères in the Missionary Congregation of the Blessed Sacrament. I thank them and those whose names I have not mentioned.

I dedicate this study to my grandfather Ulahannan (1900–1998). In discussions with him in his old age I experienced the presence of God, the loving Father who makes himself available also to "our brothers and sisters of other faiths."

Abbreviations

Abbreviations of Old Testament and New Testament books are taken from *The Holy Bible. Revised Standard Version. Catholic Edition* (London, 1966). Abbreviations other than those below are taken from *Theologische Realenzyklopädie. Abkürzungsverzeichnis*. Compiled by S. Schwertner (Berlin/New York, 1976).

AAS	*Acta Apostolicae Sedis*
B.G.	*Bhagavadgīta*
CCC	*Catechism of the Catholic Church*
DZ	Denzinger, H., ed., *Enchiridion symbolorum definitionum et declarationum de rebus fidei et morum* (Freiburg, 1976)
FABC	Federation of Asian Bishops' Conferences
Foundations	Rahner, K., *Foundations of Christian Faith: An Introduction to the Idea of Christianity*, trans. W. V. Dych (London, 1978)
Gk.	Rahner, K., *Grundkurs des Glaubens: Einführung in den Begriff des Christentums* (Freiburg/Basel/Vienna, 1976)
GW 1939	Rahner, K., *Geist in Welt: Zur Metaphysik der endlichen Erkenntnis bei Thomas von Aquin* (Innsbruck, 1939)
GW 1957	Rahner, K., *Geist in Welt*, 2. Auflage, ed. J. B. Metz (Munich, 1957)
GW	*Geist in Welt,* ed.

HTTL	Rahner, K., *Herders theologisches Taschenlexikon* (Freiburg, Bd. 1–3, 1972; Bd. 4–8, 1973)
HW 1941	Rahner, K., *Hörer des Wortes: Zur Grundlegung einer Religionsphilosophie* (Munich, 1941)
HW	*Hörer des Wortes*
HW1	Rahner, K., *Hearers of the Word*, trans. Michael Richards (New York, 1969)
HW1963	Rahner, K., *Hörer des Wortes: Zur Grundlegung einer Religionsphilosophie*. Neubearbeitet von J. B. Metz (Munich, 1963)
HW2	Rahner, K., *Hearers of the Word: Laying the Foundation for a Philosophy of Religion*, trans. Joseph Donceel (New York, 1994)
Investigations	Rahner, K., *Theological Investigations* (London, Vol. I, 1961; Vol. II, 1963; Vol. III, 1967; Vol. IV, 1966; Vol. V, 1969; Vol. VI, 1969; Vol. VII, 1971; Vol. VIII, 1971; Vol. IX, 1972; Vol. X, 1973; Vol. XI, 1974; Vol. XII, 1974; Vol. XIII, 1975; Vol. XIV, 1976; Vol. XV, 1977; Vol. XVI, 1983; Vol. XVII, 1983; Vol. XVIII, 1983; Vol. XIX, 1983)
LThK	Höfer, J., and K. Rahner, eds., *Lexikon für Theologie und Kirche* (Freiburg, Bd. I, 1957; Bd. II, 1958, Bd. III, 1959; Bd. IV, 1960; Bd. V, 1960; Bd. VI, 1961; Bd. VII, 1962; Bd. VIII, 1963; Bd. IX, 1964; Bd. X, 1965; Bd. XI, 1967; Bd. XII, 1, 1966; Bd. XII, 2, 1967; Bd. XII, 3, 1968)
$LThK^3$	Kasper, W., with K. Baumgartner, H. Bürkle, K. Ganzer, K. Kertelge, W. Korff, and P. Walter, eds., *Lexikon für Theologie und Kirche* (Freiburg/Basel/Rome/Vienna, Bd. I, 1993; Bd. II, 1994; Bd. III, 1995; Bd. IV, 1995; Bd. V, 1996; Bd. VI, 1997; Bd. VII, 1998)
N-R	Neuner-Roos, *Der Glaube der Kirche in den Urkunden der Lehrverkündigung,* Neubearbeitet von Karl Rahner and Karl-Hainz Weger, 13. Auflage (Regensburg, 1992)
QD	Quaestiones disputatae
RV	*Rig Veda*
Schriften	Rahner, K., *Schriften zur Theologie* (Einsiedeln/Zurich/Cologne, Bd. I, 1962 (6. Auflage); Bd. II,

1960 (4. Auflage); Bd. III, 1962 (5. Auflage); Bd. IV, 1967 (5. Auflage); Bd. V, 1962; Bd. VI, 1965; Bd. VII, 1966; Bd. VIII, 1967; Bd. IX, 1970; Bd. X, 1973; Bd. XI, 1972; Bd. XII, 1975; Bd. XIII, 1978; Bd. XIV, 1980; Bd. XV, 1983; Bd. XVI, 1983)

SM Rahner, K., A. Darlap, G. Weigel, C. Ernst, F. Keer, J. Daniélou, H. Crouzel, J. Alfaro, J. Fonderila, C. Colombo, A. Bellini, P. Fransen, and P. Schoonenberg, *Sacramentum Mundi: Theologisches Lexikon für die Praxis* (Freiburg/Basel/Vienna, Bd. I, 1967; Bd. II, 1968; Bd. III, 1969; Bd. IV, 1969)

SW Rahner, K., *Sämtliche Werke,* Hrsg. von der Karl-Rahner-Stiftung, Bd. 2, *Geist in Welt: Philosophische Schriften,* Bearbeitet von Albert Raffelt (Düsseldorf/Freiburg, 1996); Bd. 4, *Hörer des Wortes,* Bearbeitet von Albert Raffelt (1997); Bd. 8, *Der Mensch in der Schöpfung,* Bearbeitet von Karl-Heinz Neufeld (1998); Bd. 19, *Selbstvollzug der Kirche: Ekklesiologische Grundlegung praktischer Theologie,* Bearbeitet von Karl-Heinz Neufeld (1995); Bd. 3, *Spiritualität und Theologie der Kirchenväter,* Bearbeitet von Andreas R. Batlog, Eduard Farrugia und Karl Heinz Neufeld (1999); Bd. 26, *Grundkurs des Glaubens: Studien zum Begriff des Christentums,* Bearbeitet von Nikolaus Schwedtfeger und Albert Raffelt (1999)

Wagnis Vorgrimler, H., ed., *Wagnis Theologie: Erfahrungen mit der Theologie Karl Rahners, Festschrift für Karl Rahner,* (Freiburg/ Basel/Vienna, 1979)

Introduction

CHRISTIAN THEOLOGY TODAY is theology in the context of religious pluralism. We can gauge the importance and relevance of this trend from the increase of the publications about theology in the context of religious pluralism. The presence of "our brothers and sisters of other faiths" in Europe and America, those who come from Europe and America in search of religious experience in non-Christian Ashrams, and the elaboration of indigenous theologies likewise contribute to this trend. The encounter that Indian Christians have experienced with other religions, cultures, and ideologies in the last twenty centuries has become a universal reality today. A theological response to this pluralistic religious and secular context is a task facing us all today. The process of globalization in technology, trade, and industry has its impact also on the fields of culture, civilization, philosophy, art, religion, and worship. The tremendous development of possibilities of communication and their accuracy speed up this process and its impact. In this context, we are challenged to abandon the dominant and colonial attitudes of any one national, cultural, or confessional community vis-à-vis others, and to maintain tolerance, acceptance, and recognition, allowing the Spirit to work, guide, and reveal the truth. At the same time, any theology that abandoned one's own convictions and faith-experience would cease to be a theology at all.

The Centrality of Christology

In his recent encyclical *Fides et Ratio,* John Paul II formulates the concept of revelation in Christ in the following way:

> The truth communicated in Christ's revelation is therefore no longer confined to a particular place or culture, but is offered to every man and woman who would welcome it as the word which is the absolutely valid source of meaning for human life. Now, in Christ, all have access to the Father, since by his Death and Resurrection Christ has bestowed the divine life which the first Adam had refused (Rom. 5:12–15). (12)

The Asian bishops encourage and develop a theology in the context of religious pluralism and the social situation of Asia. They believe that their insights are important contributions to a Christian theology in the context of religious pluralism:[1] "To present Jesus Christ as the one and the only savior for all humankind and to emphasize the uniqueness of his mediation of salvation to all peoples cannot be the starting point for talking about Jesus Christ in the multicultural and multireligious conditions in most Asian countries." This does not mean that Asian Christianity adopts the pluralistic and relativist theology that developed in the context of European postmodernism. But it may mean that "the statement 'Jesus Christ is the Lord and only Saviour' is a confession of faith that stands at the end of a long process of becoming familiar with the person of Jesus Christ."[2]

Today, Christology has become the focus of every theological discussion. Christians can never forget that the uniqueness and universality of Jesus Christ are the core of Christian faith. On the other hand, this dogmatic conviction was formulated out of the experience of the early Christians of Jesus Christ. There is a reciprocity here, which theology must maintain in the multireligious and multicultural context, without offending the convictions of "our brothers and sisters of other faiths." Accordingly, Christology is central to every theological discussion.

Why Rahner's Christology?

Karl Rahner (1904–1984), who formulated his Christology in the context and categories of the transcendental idealistic philosophy and transcendental scholasticism of his time, is a very important theologian of the twentieth century whose primary concern was to establish logically and philosophically the uniqueness and universality of Jesus Christ.

Karl Rahner was a theologian of his time, with a historical consciousness.[3] His commitment to philosophizing and his openness to the world did not lead him to neglect the traditions of the church. He was aware of the secular religious philosophies and the spiritual traditions as well. This is why we find in Rahner's transcendental anthropological theology the influences of a number of theological, philosophical, and spiritual traditions. The transcendental Thomism of Joseph Maréchal (1878–1944) and the Thomistic metaphysics of knowledge, Aristotelian scholastic philosophy, neoscholastic theology, the theology of the church fathers, the philosophy of Maurice Blondel (1861–1949), the theology of Duns Scotus (1265–1318), the spirituality of Ignatius of Loyola (1491–1556), German idealism, especially the transcendental philosophy and idealism of Immanuel Kant (1724–1804) and Johann Gottlieb Fichte (1762–1814), Friedrich Wilhelm Joseph Schelling's (1775–1854) concept of freedom, Georg Wilhelm Friedrich Hegel's (1770–1831) phenomenology, the phenomenology and existential ontology of Martin Heidegger (1889–1976), the thought of Pierre Rousselot (1878–1915), the German Protestant Christology from above and from below —all these influenced the "anthropologically orientated theology" of Rahner. Bonaventure (1217–1274) influenced the mystical direction of Rahner's thought and Suarez (1548–1617) the scholastic nature of his thought. Rahner's knowledge of the mystical doctrine of Origin and Bonaventure, his interest in the mystical side of St. Thomas Aquinas (1224–1274), his appreciation of St. John of the Cross and St. Theresa of Avila,[4] and his understanding of the empirical studies on mysticism by Karl Albrecht, also played a role in shaping his thought. Theological consciousness of the changing history of the dogmas inspired Rahner to attempt to integrate Thomas Aquinas, as the authoritative theologian, and contemporary European philosophy.

Rahner says that he is more influenced by Heidegger than by Kant. Karl Lehmann considers the theology of Rahner neither an explicit nor an implicit philosophy, but a theology that employs the concepts of philosophical thought. The works of Rahner display not only a philosophical dimension but also original philosophical thought.[5]

Rahner wrote his theological discussions against the background of neoscholasticism, documents of the magisterium, renewal movements within the church and in Catholic theology, and the pluralistic society of natural scientists, atheists, Marxists, philosophers, literary writers, and so on. With genuine awareness of the need and the nature of society, Rahner uses the contemporary terminology of the philosophers and makes clear, without betraying the traditions of the church, that theology has something to say to the contemporary world. According to H. Vorgrimler, Rahner believed that theology should remain as a science;

it should develop like any other science and should not be imposed on the theologians.[6] Rahner was of the opinion that one should think in order to theologize; the thinking should begin from present-day philosophy and present-day life situations. Vorgrimler points out that one would misunderstand the writings of Rahner, if one viewed his theories as something that developed out of speculative philosophical interests: proclamation and pastoral theology were essential influences on Rahner's person and work.

The climax of the philosophical theology of Rahner is his transcendental Christology, that is, the concept of a transcendental Christ and of an absolute savior. We can observe a coherent development in the theology of Rahner, from his interpretation of the metaphysics of knowledge of St. Thomas in *Geist in Welt*—a totally abstract philosophy of the human being that understands the human being as spirit in the world with the capacity to transcend himself and God as Spirit—to his theology as reflected in his last talk in Budapest in 1984 on the meaning of dialogue[7] and in his last published text in 1985 on the history of dogma.[8] Although the early abstract philosophical Rahner[9] with deep spiritual insights[10] and a complicated style of writing evolves into a later Rahner who is theological, spiritual, clear, and understandable, his early christological theses are never contradicted or radically changed; they are developed like a gradual revelation of mystery. We can understand the entire theology of Rahner as a single whole, a mystery revealing the absolute through the historical culmination of the revelation of the person of Jesus of Nazareth, who is experienced as the transcendental and immanent absolute Being, who is God, the Mystery, the Experience, "really real" Reality.

The influence of the theology of Rahner on the documents of the Second Vatican Council, on the changed attitude of the church toward non-Christians and non-Christian religions, and on the present theology of religions proposed by Catholic and non-Catholic theologians cannot be denied. Translations of his works into many languages, the popularity of his philosophical theology all over the world, and numerous studies of Rahner's theology clearly manifest his significance for current theological thinking.

The theology of religions and the attitude of the church toward non-Christian religions are major concerns of the Catholic Church today at the dawn of the third millennium. The theological literature that finds its starting point in the few references and the brief declaration of the Second Vatican Council on this topic shows not only the interest of Catholic theologians and believers in this theme but also the urgent need to clarify the references in the conciliar documents. In *No Other Name?* Paul Knitter says,

> Theologians, reflecting the uncertainty within the Christian community, are asking whether and how Christ plays a unique role in the history of salvation, whether, as Rahner maintains, "salvation willed by God is the salvation won by Christ"—that is, whether Christ is the constitutive cause of salvation. Such uncertainty extends to questioning whether God really wills that all persons and all religions become Christian.[11]

Rahner's writings clarify some of the problems underlying these contemporary theological approaches, making clear both his own standpoint and that of the Catholic Church. Hence, our presentation of the theocentric Christology of John Hick (1922–) and the revised Christology of Stanley J. Samartha (1920–) in the first chapter of this book will show the challenges posed by the pluralistic trend of theological discussion. In an evaluative discussion of the transcendental Christology of Rahner in the fourth chapter in the context of theocentric and revised Christology, I will explore Rahner's answer to the "problem of religious pluralism."

Many Catholic theologians believe today that the Catholic theology of religions has gone much further than the theological position held by Rahner. Knitter says,

> These efforts to move beyond Rahner and beyond traditional understandings of Christ and the Church are no doubt significant. One must, however, ask how far they really go. In the end, they seem to amount to more of a remodeling than a radical change in Rahner's basic approach.[12]

It is relevant to ask how this remodeling of the approach of Rahner is elaborated, and how far it is successful. Has the attempt to develop Rahner's approach ended in a radical deviation from his theological position and from the theological position of the Catholic Church? Does Rahner's approach suggest any direction other than that taken in contemporary theologians' proposals concerning the problem of religious pluralism? Will such an approach lead to a more valid and acceptable solution to the problems of religious pluralism and the pluralistic social situation, and provide an answer to the challenge of pluralistic theology? Will a new approach based on Rahner's transcendental Christology solve the problems of extreme exclusivism, extreme inclusivism, and extreme pluralism? This book attempts to discuss these questions in the context of the theological positions of theocentrism, pluralism, exclusivism, and inclusivism. The historical, cultural, and religious situation of India provides the theological background to this interpretation, application, and "remodeling" of the theology of Rahner in the context of the religious pluralism of the society in which we live and in the context of the challenges of a pluralistic theology.

Method of Approach

The aim of my analysis of Karl Rahner's philosophy and theology is not to present the chronological development of Rahner's transcendental Christology, nor to identify the boundary between his transcendental philosophy and transcendental theology. Other studies have already analyzed this development, clarifying the different emphases at various stages of Rahner's writings. Our aim is to understand the structure of Rahner's thought and to summarize his transcendental Christology. For this purpose, we take the various writings of Rahner as a single unit, since they are the writings of a single person—though without overlooking the fact that his first and last publications are separated by fifty years.

Rahner considered the speculative and the philosophical aspects of Christology important. But he did not neglect the dogmatic traditions of the church and scholastic theology in this area; he attempted to present his own belief and church teaching through the medium of philosophy. Other studies concentrate on this aspect of Rahner's theology. The present study concentrates on two points. First, I present the philosophical concepts of Rahner and their importance and relevance to Christology, as well as the support which these philosophical concepts provide for Rahner's transcendental Christology, which seeks to make Christology comprehensible not only to Christians but also to secular philosophers. Second, I analyze the relevance of Rahner's transcendental Christology in the context of religious pluralism, to which the philosophical aspect of the transcendental Christology is more relevant than its biblical and documentary foundations.

John Hick and other pluralistic theologians analyze Christian concepts philosophically and arrive at a pluralistic theology. This study of their views concentrates on the challenges they raise to the Christian faith. But Rahner analyzes human experience and the support it offers for developing Christian concepts and arrives at a transcendental Christian theology. For this reason also the present study emphasizes Rahner's philosophy and its contribution to his transcendental Christology.

Structure of This Book

The first chapter of this work introduces the problem. Religious pluralism is a fact that everyone has to accept. A Christian believer and theologian should also recognize the faith and the religious life of the non-Christian believers, who also seek God in a valid way. But the attempt of pluralistic theologians to understand and accept this fact raises many serious challenges to Christian faith, Christian theology, and even to religious faith. The reality of the problem and the challenge of the attempts at a solution necessitate new approaches. In the search for models other than pluralistic theology, Rahner's transcendental theology proved a good starting point. The concept of the presence of Christ in non-Christian religions is the culmination of Rahner's transcendental theology: hence the importance of the second and the third chapter. The final chapter offers a synthesis showing the importance of Rahner's approach for a Christology elaborated in the context of religious pluralism and the possibility of doing parallel work, remodeling and developing this approach in a theology in the Indian context.

In selecting this theme my goal was not to discuss all the important themes of theology in the context of religious pluralism, or to arrive at a Christology that clarifies all the questions. The present work is an attempt to articulate my faith in Jesus Christ, God incarnate, in the context of religious pluralism and to point out the philosophical and theological support it gains from Rahner's transcendental Christology. I hope that this will contribute to the elaboration of a valid approach to Christology in the context of religious pluralism.

1

The Reality of Religious Pluralism and the Challenge of a Pluralistic Theology

BY MEANS OF THE DECLARATION of the Second Vatican Council on the "Relationship of the Church to the Non-Christian Religions," the church opened the door to theological responses to the important reality known as religious pluralism. This decree called for awareness of mutual interaction, influence, and enrichment in the historical process whereby Christian faith and life are brought to their perfection. At the same time, it encouraged collaboration and coexistence. This declaration intensified the growing interest of the local churches and the local theologians in indigenous Christian theology in all the continents, both Catholic and non-Catholic. This has been given many titles, for example, the theology of non-Christian religions, pluralistic theology of world religions, contextual theology, theology of interreligious dialogue, theology of inculturation, theology of aboriginal cultures and religions, tribal theology, *dālit* theology, and so on. This theology is associated with the concepts of Indian Christ, Amerindian Christ,[1] Pacific Christ, Melanesian Christ,[2] African Christ,[3] Black Christ,[4] Unknown Christ,[5] Hidden Christ,[6] Acknowledged Christ,[7] and so on. The focal point in such theologies is the attempt to establish the uniqueness of the Christian experience in the midst of religious, philosophical, cultural, and theological pluralism. Our task in this chapter is to identify the unity and continuity in cultural and religious development with special reference to India, in the face of the overwhelming experience of pluralism, and to evaluate two contemporary theological responses to pluralistic religious reality.

Continuity and Plurality: The Two Basic Characteristics of the Cultural and Religious Consciousness of India

Continuity and Unity of the Indian Religious and Cultural Reality

Historians of religion have postulated a relationship between religious concepts and cultural expressions of present-day Indians and the pre-third-millennium totemistic Proto-Australoid and Austro-Asiatic inhabitants of India. The relationship between the religion of the Hindus and the religion of the people of Mohenjo-daro and Harappa, which existed before 2500 B.C.E., is evident. Historians of religions also identify a relationship between the religion of the ancient aborigines and the people of Indus Valley, viz., the Dravidians. These relationships show a continuity of religious ideas from the early inhabitants of pre-third-millennium B.C.E. to present-day religious concepts. The unity and continuity of religious thought in India from ancient times onward, and its role in shaping the religious belief of contemporary India are very important when we consider how to make the Christian faith relevant in the Indian context. Such an awareness and rethinking are not experienced with the same urgency in the European situation, where Christian theology has always developed in a manner coherent with the local culture, philosophy, and religious practices, especially in Rome and Greece. Many twentieth-century European theologians, including Karl Rahner, consider humanity a single unity and try to interpret the Christian faith in the light of pluralism in experiences of the Divine. A similar approach is much more important when we try to make the Christian faith relevant to the Indian context.

Today we find philosophical and religious pluralism in India, but there is an underlying continuity and unity too,[8] the result of a long process of interaction, adaptation, integration, assimilation, and synthesis.[9] Just as the Hindu or *Āryan* culture and religion are spread today over the whole of India and influence the entire social and religious system, so too the aborigines of India, viz., the totemistic Proto-Australoid and Austro-Asiatic inhabitants of India, were spread over the whole of India before the third millennium B.C.E. and had a well-developed religion, social system, and democratic village government.[10] The religion and the culture of the totemistic Proto-Australoid and Austro-Asiatic inhabitants of India influenced the subsequent religion and culture of the Indus Valley people, that is, the Dravidians. Their religion and culture were taken over by the Hindu (*Ārya*) religion and culture. This is evident today in the religious beliefs and practices of various tribes in India.

The ancient population of India was divided into different races, villages, families, and tribes, with a religion of the people and a religion of the priests. The mutual influence, continuity, and unity of these different traditions paved the way for the later development of that religious idea whose centrality can be identified as the major stream of religious belief in the multicultural and multireligious society of modern India. This is due to the interaction, intermingling, and integration of different cultures and traditions. It is also due to the existence of a clear religious idea in the mind and traditions of the totemistic Proto-Australoid and Austro-Asiatic inhabitants of pre-third-millennium India.[11] This allows us to trace the origin of some of today's major religious concepts and cultural traditions to prehistoric times. The word *Brahma,* the central concept of the Hindu religion from the time of the *Vedic Samhitas*[12] up to contemporary Hinduism,[13] originally meant the supernatural power or influence (much like the Proto-Australoid *mana*), and derives from the magical spell of Dravidian times.[14] This shows how the religious concept and the system of the aborigines of the pre-third-millennium B.C.E. continued to exist during the Dravidian and *Āryan* periods.

Continuity and unity can be seen not only in the culture and the religious thought of India from the prehistoric period prior to the third millennium B.C.E. to the present day, but also in its relationship to European thought. This is the result not only of interactions and intermingling but also of common ethnic and ancestral factors. This continuity, integrity, and unity of culture and religion of the country, as well as the relationship between culture and religion in its origin, development, and expression, which is evident also in the Judeo-Christian, European-Christian, and Indian religions, should be taken into consideration when one preaches a new faith to the existing cultural and religious milieu.[15] This faith should be situated and integrated within the framework of the cultural and religious unity, continuity, and integrity of the country without destroying, disturbing, or replacing it, but integrating it so as to present

God as much nearer to the people. This is the core of the Christian faith and the Gospel message.

Religious and Cultural Pluralism in India

"Pluralism of all kinds, especially of religions is a fact. The need to live together as one community, in spite of the many pluralisms is also a fact," says M. Amaladoss.[16] Cultural, religious, linguistic, and ethnic pluralism characterize the land and the people of the Indian sub-continent. When Christ is preached to India, one must therefore be aware not only of the coherent unity and continuity of various cultures and religions from prehistoric times onward but also of the reality of a tremendous diversity and plurality.

Religious Pluralism and the Coexistence of Different Religions

India has given birth to many great religious mediators, such as Krishna, the God incarnate of Hinduism; Buddha, the founder of Buddhism; Vardhamana Mahavira, the founder of Jainism; Sankaracharya, the great philosopher and prophet of Hinduism; and Guru Nanak, the founder of Sikhism. In a population of 950 million people, 120,000 are Parsees,[17] 0.5% Jains, 0.7% Buddhists, 1.1% Sikhs, 2.4% Christians, 11% Muslims,[18] and 80.5% are generally called Hindus. The actual percentage of Aryans is less than 20% of the population. In 1948 there were 40,000 Jews in India; in 1988 they numbered only 8,000.[19] 15.75% of the population belong to officially listed castes and 7.76% to officially listed tribes. This microcosm of world religions and world cultures in India offers a unique context for presenting the uniqueness of Christ.

The Pluralistic Nature of Hinduism

Hinduism itself is pluralistic in outlook. Integrating the Dravidians and the Aborigines and recognizing other religions such as Islam, Christianity, Buddhism, Jainism, and so on as valid paths toward salvation, Hinduism accepts many foreign elements without losing its own predominance and influence. It also maintains the unity, continuity, and integrity of the religious history and the religious tradition of the country. The principles of tolerance, integration, and coexistence are seen at least in theory, even in the context of recent fanatical Hindu movements.

The sectarian and Protestant movements are not excommunicated, but accepted and respected as valid experiences and approaches. The *Vaishnavites*, a sect of Ramanuja,[20] the *Madhvās* of Madhvacharya, the *Chaitanyās* founded by Krishna Chaitanya in the sixteenth century, the *Saivite Āgamās*,[21] the *Ligāyats* of the twelfth century, the *Alvar Vaishnavites* of Tamilnadu, the *Adiyar Śaivites,* the *Śakti Tantrās,*[22] and the *Smartās* are just some of the Hindu sects who have a valid existence within Hinduism. Modern Hindu reform movements like *Brahma Samāj* of Raja Ram Mohan Roy (1772–1833);[23] *Prārthanā Samāj,* led by Dr. Atmaram Pandurang (1823–1898); the Church of the New Covenant of Keshab Candra Sen (1838–1884), based on his personal experience of Christ, who was identified with the *logos;*[24] Pratab Candra Mozoomdar's (1840–1905) attempt to interpret Christ in the light of oriental philosophy and spirituality; the Ramakrishna Mission of Sri Ramakrishna Paramahamsa (1836–1886) and Vivekananda (1863–1902), understanding Christ as *jīvanmukta;* the reforming attempts of Mohader Govind Ranade (1842–1901); Rabindranath Tagore (1817–1905), identifying Christ with suffering humanity; Sarvepalli Radhakrishnan (1888–1975), interpreting Christ in the light of *Vedānta* and considering him a mystic; and Mahatma Gandhi (1869–1948), accepting Christ as a *Satyāgrahi* were accepted and respected in Hinduism.[25] Influential modern Hindu religious movements like the Hare Krishna Movement, Transcendental Meditation, *Ānanda Mārga*, Divine Light, and so on popularize Hinduism and contribute to the multidimensional nature of Hinduism. They all recognize the different religions as valid paths of experiencing and realizing God (salvation). One of the major themes of Gandhi is that all religions are in the ultimate sense one, true, and equal.[26] Swami Abhedananda says that Hinduism accepts the fundamental principles of all religions. "If we understand the nature of that infinite Being as nameless, then we may say that it is Brahman of the Hindus, Vishnu of the Vaishnavites, Shiva of the Shaivaites or Sakti of the Saktas. It is also the Father in heaven of the Christians and the *Allah* of the Mohammedans, *Jehovah* of the Jews, and so on."[27] Therefore it is clear that Hinduism is pluralistic in the very nature of its theology, culture, and worship.[28]

Pluralism in all its dimensions is evident in India. Uniformity has never been demanded. Unity and continuity in the cultural and religious thought of India, and plurality in all its possible dimensions, constitute the Indian reality of human existence. But the experience of pluralistic religious reality prompts many Indian Christian theologians today to follow the pattern of pluralistic theology, viz., the theocentric model formulated by the religious philosopher John Hick and others. In this context we must consider seriously the pluralistic nature of Indian culture and religions and ask whether pre-sixteenth-century Christian theology in India was pluralistic in nature without compromising its Christocentric character. The attempt of the theocentric Christology of pluralistic theologians to respond to the multiple religious reality poses many questions. In suggesting another approach to the problem—though without denying the positive aspects of contemporary pluralistic Christology—I consider it appropriate to mention some of these questions here.

Theocentric Christology as a Contemporary Christian Theological Response to the Reality of Religious Pluralism

Aware of the reality and the theological richness of world religions and their current undeniable influence in Europe and the United States, the Declaration on the Relationship of the Church to the Non-Christian Religions of Vatican II affirms that "the Catholic Church rejects nothing of what is true and holy in these religions" (2,2). Several theological attempts to understand Christ in a wider perspective of universal religiosity, thus liberating Christ from the framework of Jewish religion, Western culture, and Greek philosophy,[29] prepared a solid background for a pluralistic Christian theology, or a theocentric model of Christian theology. This was initiated by the writings of Wilfred Cantwell Smith[30] and was propagated by John Hick, one of the most influential religious thinkers of the twentieth century.[31] The theocentric model of Christian theology proposes a global theology of world religions in its attempt to find a reasonable solution to the problems of religious pluralism. It attracted worldwide attention in the churches and among contemporary theologians, and its influence on both Catholic and Protestant Asian theologians is evident. This pluralistic theology has exercised a tremendous influence on Indian theologians. Since it is radically different from the traditional Indian understanding of religions and religious mysteries, I choose to study the challenges to Christology posed by this theocentric model of a Christian theology of the world religions and make this the theological background to my study of the relevance of Karl Rahner's Christology in the context of Indian religious pluralism of India. I pay special attention to the Christology of John Hick because of his prominent place among proponents of the theocentric model.

The Religious and Philosophical Background of the Christology of Hick

Hick's personal encounter with and study of world religions, and his interpretation of religions in the context of modern European philosophy and liberal theological thinking, form the background of his theocentric model of the Christian theology of world religions and hence of his Christology.

Hick's Encounter with and Experience of World Religions

John Hick experienced religious pluralism in Birmingham, England, because this city was racially, culturally, and religiously pluralistic. The presence of African and Asian immigrants in Birmingham, Hick's efforts to assist people of ethnic minorities, and his decision to include a Roman Catholic, a Jew, a Muslim, a Hindu, and a Sikh among the non-Anglican church representatives in efforts to form a multifaith syllabus for religious education contributed to his personal experience of religious pluralism and a growing awareness of the need to promote religious coexistence. Hick was confronted with believers of other religions: Hindus, Muslims, Sikhs, and Jews. He studied Hinduism and Buddhism and attended their spiritual services. A one-year stay in India and Sri Lanka and his study of Hinduism and Buddhism deepened his awareness of the immense spiritual depth and power of these oriental religions. He was involved in Buddhist–Christian dialogue and maintained personal contacts with people in India, Japan, and Sri Lanka. Hick also studied Wilfred Cantwell Smith's critique of the concept of religion.

Hick claims in *The Rainbow of Faiths* that the pluralistic idea has roots in the views of Nicholas of Cusa in the fifteenth century, Akbar in the sixteenth century, Ashoka in the third century, and so on.[32] His intention is to contribute to the ongoing development of Christian thought in the light of knowledge of the wider religious world.[33]

The Influence of Contemporary European Philosophy

Hick's pluralistic theology is situated in the historical context of the European Enlightenment and the pluralistic theology of the West. The contemporary discussion of religious pluralism is a product of post-Enlightenment rationalism influenced by Michel Foucault (1926–1984), Jacques Derrida (1931–), Jürgen Habermas (1924–), Immanuel Levinas (1905–1995), and Theodor Wiesengrund Adorno (1903–1969). The idealism of Immanuel Kant (1724–1804), the theories of religion of Ludwig Feuerbach (1804–1872) and Sigmund Freud (1856–1939), Kant's distinction between transcendental reality in itself and as experienced by human beings and his concept of "noumenon" and "phenomenon" were applied by Hick to his theology of religions. The pragmatic approach to religion in secular academic circles and in popular religious preaching influenced Hick's concept of religion.[34] Hick's pluralistic interpretation is influenced by analytic philosophy and the Wittgensteinian and neo-Wittgensteinian interpretation of religious language and of the philosophy of religion, although he is not uncritical of this approach. His thinking is influenced also by the philosophies of Alfred Julius Ayer, Dewi Philips, Antony Flew, Paul Edward, George Santayana, John Herman Randall, Julian Huxley, Richard M. Hare, and Max Weber. Hick interprets Christian theology in the light of the two main factors that are transforming Christian thought today, viz., contemporary scientific knowledge and technological power (which offer a nonreligious understanding of the universe) and the newly encountered fact of other world religions.

Liberal Theological Thinking

John Hick claims that his picture of Jesus falls within the tradition of the liberal interpretation of Christianity established by Friedrich Schleiermacher, David Strauss, Adolf Harnack and others; but he goes far beyond the interpretations and conclusions of these authors. Contemporary investigations of the origin of Christianity and the historical Jesus, the finding of the Qumran rolls, mid-twentieth-century progress in Catholic theology, and so on formed the historical context for the "Copernican revolution" in Hick's Christian theology.[35] He speaks of the connection between historical Christianity and continuing life in the Western world, where Catholic theological tradition reflects the Latin Mediterranean temperament and Protestant theological tradition reflects the northern Germanic temperament, whereas the Mediterranean temperament was basic to the development of the Indian religious tradition. The awareness of the interaction between religious and nonreligious factors in Christian theology and of their relation to ancient religious and nonreligious traditions influenced Hick's research, which aims at clarifying the mythological character of Christianity without, however, issuing any appeal to "abandon the traditional language of Christian devotion."[36]

A Christology Promoting the Equality of all Religions

Acceptance of the equality of all religions and the denial of many existing claims about Christ and Christianity are two important characteristics of the Copernican revolution in Hick's theology in general and in his Christology in particular. They aroused strong criticism from all quarters, alleging that his Christology denies the basic faith of the churches in Jesus Christ as Son of God: despite the many theoretical, philosophical, and historical reasons adduced by Hick, his arguments would amount to a contradiction of the Christian faith. I present here Hick's arguments for a Christology that accepts the equality of all religions.

Hick's Philosophical Argument

"The Real," "the ultimately Real," "ultimate Reality," "the Ultimate," and "Reality" are the terms Hick employs to signify God in his book *An Interpretation of Religion.*[37] In *God and the Universe of Faiths,* Hick says that God is not a phenomenon available to a scientific study, whereas religions can be objects of scientific study.[38]

> There can be a history, a psychology, a sociology and a comparative study of religion. Hence religion has become an object of intensive investigation, and God has perforce become identified as an idea which occurs within this complex phenomenon of religion.[39]

He speaks of a "transcendent theism," which means a belief in a transcendent God together with the major corollaries of this belief. In the context of Wittgenstein's concept of "seeing" as "seeing-as," Hick analyses "experience" as "experiencing-as."[40] He says, "The outcome in consciousness can be called 'experiencing-as'—developed from

Wittgenstein's concept of 'seeing-as.' . . . But in fact all our seeing is seeing-as and, more broadly, all conscious experiencing is experiencing-as."[41] Hick understands three human dimensions of meaning: the "ethical," a "meta-meaning" of a physical situation; the "aesthetic," an "aesthetic significance" of the physical meaning;[42] and the "religious," which is an experiencing of places and persons as divine, as in the case of Jesus, who was experienced by the disciples and by the Christians in the mode of "experiencing-as, Jesus as Christ."[43]

Another expression for ethical meaning is moral meaning. We experience it in the social and personal significance of a situation. The ethical meaning presupposes natural meaning. This is why the ethical meaning is described as the higher order of meaning, the "further meaning" or meta-meaning of a physical situation. The aesthetic meaning sometimes (but apparently not always) presupposes a physical meaning. Human beings are aesthetic as well as ethical creatures. They experience aesthetic significance in their environment. The human being is a religious animal, with the tendency to experience individuals, places, and situations as bearing a religious meaning. Throughout a good deal of religious life, individuals have been experienced as divine, and many places have been identified as sacred. In monotheistic religion, any human situation may be experienced as lived in the unseen presence of God.

Hick says that the focal point of the New Testament is the disciples' experience of Jesus as Christ, the Messiah. He interprets this experience, and the apostolic interpretation of Jesus as Christ, in the light of Wittgenstein's interpretation of religious experience. Hick says that the religious meaning can also be interpreted nonreligiously, that is, in secular or natural terms.

> [The] Jesus-phenomenon was importantly ambiguous, capable of being experienced in a number of different ways, as the Messiah, as a prophet, as a Rabbi and so on. This ambiguity is the characteristic of religious meaning. On a large scale we can say that the world, or indeed the universe, is religiously ambiguous—able to be experienced by different people, or indeed by the same person at different times, in both religious and naturalistic ways. This is not of course to say that one way of experiencing it may not be correct . . . and religious faith is that cognitive choice which distinguishes the religious from the secular way of experiencing our human situation.[44]

This ambiguity in the characteristics of religious meaning makes possible a plurality of religious experiences with their own superstructure of theological theories. In the light of the transcendental philosophy of Immanuel Kant and his concept of "noumenon" and "phenomenon," Hick considers that through different "divine phenomena" one "divine noumenon" is humanly experienced. Hick strives for a nonrealistic and naturalistic interpretation of religion. He considers nonnatural realities such as God, *Brahman*, *Dharmakāya,* and so on to be realities that should be described in psychological and sociological terms. Hick holds that religious experience is not always theistic.

Hick's conclusion is that there is a pluralism of religion and all religions are equal. In *The Metaphor of God Incarnate* he says:

> As a result of the twentieth-century explosion of information about the religions of the world, and an expanding movement of world travel since the Second World War, as well as large-scale immigration into the West from Muslim, Hindu, Sikh, Buddhist, and Taoist and Confucian areas, it has become evident to a growing proportion of educated Westerners that what the Christian faith is to the devout Christian, the Islamic faith is to the devout Muslim, the Buddhist faith is to the practising Buddhist, the Hindu faith is to dedicated Hindus, and so on.[45]

In *The Rainbow of Faiths* Hick repeats this idea: "this reality (which I have been referring to as the Real) is differently conceived, and therefore differently experienced, and therefore differently responded to from within the different world religions."[46] Thus Hick sees "experience as experiencing-as," applied to the idea of God which the subject already held, and this leads him to consider the variety of similar experiences as equal.

Thematic Similarity in Religions

Although Hick speaks of conflicting claims of truth in different religions, his comparative analysis of different religious concepts and themes points to religious pluralism. He quotes the Dalai Lama and Mahatma Gandhi, who say that all religions have similar ideas of love and that the followers of all religions are children of the same God. In *God Has Many Names* and *God and the Universe of Faiths* Hick gives his notion of religion, based on Karl Jaspers's concept of an *axial period.* He holds that a "demythologised Christianity" that is historically "honest" and "realistic" is "compatible with genuine religious pluralism."[47]

The Concept of Religion as a Human Response

Hick considers religions to be "distinguishable religio-cultural streams within man's history"[48] or distinctive socioreligious and historical entities or organisms,[49] each trying to show the "spiritual superiority of the creed" and the "moral superiority of the community"[50] and each creating human beings in its own image. Religion and civilization cannot be deemed true or false, but are to be accepted as developing realities, different individual and social responses to the divine. Hick observes this in Christianity and then says, "And of course just the same is true in their own ways of the other world religions. There is no time now to try to spell this out; but I think that if one has seen it in the case of Christianity one has no difficulty in seeing it in that of other religions also."[51] The Real is ineffable; it is difficult to say whether it is personal or impersonal. It is variously conceived and experienced through different religions and through religious and naturalistic interpretations of reality.[52]

The Concept of Religion as an Ethnic Reality

According to Hick, one's religious commitment is a matter of "religious ethnicity" rather than of deliberate comparative judgment and choice,[53] and therefore one's membership in a religious tradition depends mainly on "the accidents of birth."[54] The inherited religious tradition can be normative for the individual. Different cultures have constituted different ways of being human, and different ways of being human involve different ways of being religious. Even the major religious traditions are inherently pluralistic. Hick also says that while we can grade religious phenomena, we cannot grade religions as totalities.[55] Religion is an ethnic reality. All religions are equal.

The Global Theology and Equality of Religions

Hick fully agrees with contemporary attempts by historians of religions and many leaders of world religions to form a global ethics and theology based on "global philosophy." He says, "If God is the God of the whole world, we must presume that the whole religious life of mankind is part of a continuous and universal human relationship to him."[56] Hick holds that we must develop human theologies instead of Christian or Buddhist theologies. This conviction is a reaction to the history of Europeans forcing believers on other continents to accept Christian theology as global theology and the Christian God-experience as the only valid experience. Hick says:

> It is far from self-evident that the activity of God's love in the life of Christ is incompatible with divine activity in other forms, in other times, in other places. On the contrary, if the religious life of mankind is a continuous field of relationship to the divine Reality, the theologian must try to include all forms of religious experience among his data, and all forms of religious ideas among the hypotheses to be considered. His theology should take account of all genuine human experience of the divine transcendent. For the varied but continuous field of the religious life of mankind demands unified theories of commensurate scope.[57]

In constructing global and human theologies, Hick finds the Eastern concept of divine impersonality to be just as important as the Western experience of divine personality. "We must be prepared to respond to the new situation by beginning the long-term task of forming a global or human theology."[58] Hick's concept of global theology presupposes the equality of all religions; here Gandhi is the ideal religious thinker and his approach the model. Hick says,

> In this pluralistic understanding of Religions, Gandhi was far ahead of his time. Indeed he is still far ahead of our time, a generation after his death. Nevertheless, the kind of approach that Gandhi promulgated now finds favour with an increasing proportion of those thinkers, within all traditions, who are deeply concerned with the issue of religious pluralism. An increasing amount of literature now reflects attitudes which are basically in harmony with Gandhi's.[59]

In the context of this theological vision of a global theology, Hick openly refutes *The Logic of God Incarnate* by Thomas V. Morris (1986) and *The Absoluteness of Christianity* (1901) by Ernst Troeltsch, and affirms the nonabsoluteness of Christianity.[60] He radically criticizes the attitude of Christians who consider themselves superior and asks "to what extent this affluence and these ideals are gifts of the Christian religion and evidence of its moral and intellectual superiority."[61]

Jesus as One of the Mediators

According to Hick, Christianity is a way initiated by Jesus Christ whose conclusions will provide the starting point for our inquiry into the relation between Christianity and the other world religions. In *The Second Christianity,* Hick argues that Christianity is not the only world faith, but one among several. As a specific example, he points out the influence of Buddhism on Christianity and says that Buddhology and Christology developed in comparable ways.[62] He accepts the equality of Christ with other mediators: they are all "phenomenal manifestations of the noumenal Real-in-itself," not different names for the same.[63] "'Yahweh' and 'Siva' are not two rival Gods, but two different concrete historical 'personae' in terms of which the ultimate divine Reality is present and responded to by large historical communities within different strands of the human story."[64]

Hick's concept of Christianity as one religion among many and Christ as one mediator among many relativizes Christianity, as this has been understood by Christians. He claims that the Catholic theologians Hans Küng and Edward Schillebeeckx are close to his theological thinking.[65] As Hick himself says, this rethinking of Christianity is so radical that the product is no longer Christian.[66]

A Christology without Claims

The Deification of Jesus Christ

John Hick questions the Christian understanding of Jesus of Nazareth as God incarnate, saying "that Jesus himself did not teach that he was God incarnate and this momentous idea is a creation of the church."[67] He says that Jesus never claimed to be God or Son of God incarnate, although this was traditionally believed by Christians from the fifth century to the late nineteenth century. Hick argues that the essence of Christianity does not lie in the deification of Jesus, as has been believed. He denies the implicit claim of divinity in the act of Jesus' forgiving sins, citing the argument by E. P. Sanders that the forgiveness of sins pronounced by Jesus was a prerogative not of God but of the priesthood.[68] He questions the authenticity of the logia with regard to the deity of Jesus and argues that Jesus' use of *Abba* and his eschatological message mean that the church's belief in Jesus' deity rests on very shaky ground. The great christological sayings of Jesus in the Fourth Gospel and the content of the introduction to Mark's Gospel cannot be attributed to Jesus: this is a theological meditation in dramatic form, expressing a Christian interpretation of Jesus. "Jesus saw himself only as God's last messenger before the establishment of the Kingdom"[69] or as "the Greek *Christos* and the Hebrew *Messiah,* i.e. 'anointed,' a term used particularly of kings but carrying no connotation of divinity."[70]

The Denial of the Chalcedonian Formula

In *Problems of Religious Pluralism,* Hick proposes "degree Christologies" which "apply the term 'incarnation' to the activity of God's spirit or God's grace in human lives so that the divine will is done on earth," in place of "all-or-nothing Christologies" whose principle is expressed in the Chalcedonian definition of Christ.[71] In his essay "Jesus and the World Religions," Hick asserts that Jesus was a powerfully God-conscious man, intensely and overwhelmingly conscious of the reality of God, a man of God living in his unseen presence; but not literally God. In *The Rainbow of Faiths,* Hick clearly expresses the difficulty in giving a concrete meaning to the idea that any historical individual is both literally a human being and literally God; he presents Jesus as a man open to God's presence.[72] In *The Second Christianity,* he states: "Jesus was wholly and unambiguously a human being. . . . The original response was made by his disciples to Jesus as a man."[73] The center and starting point of Christianity are the impact of Jesus on mankind and the response of the disciples to Jesus of Nazareth; everything else came about as consequences of that response.[74] In *Disputed Questions in Theology and the Philosophy of Religion,* Hick presents many arguments in support of his rejection of traditional Christology, which he asserts is not authorized by Jesus but developed in the historical and cultural milieu of the first centuries to express the legitimate lordship of Jesus over "lords" and "gods." The historical development of the Chalcedonian formula was a solution to the problem of the divinity and the humanity of Jesus.[75]

The Uniqueness of Jesus

Hick openly rejects the central claim of Christianity, that is, the uniqueness of Christ and the unique role of the church in relation to his saving activity.[76] He is motivated by a global consciousness that has promoted a sensitive awareness of the variety of cultures and faiths within the human family,[77] and he regards Christianity not as the exclusively "true religion" but as one authentic spiritual path among others. He claims that "the conviction that [Jesus] had risen, or ascended, or is in glory, evidently arose prior to and independently of the later physical resurrection stories with which we are familiar from the Gospels."[78] The resurrection experiences of Peter and of the women are comparable to those of clinically dead patients, which occur in the realm of inner spiritual experience rather than that of outer sense experience. Hick says:

> The near death experiences which have been reported so abundantly in recent years by "clinically dead" patients, often include something rather like this in the form of a bright light, or a brightly shining figure, from which there emanates a profound accepting love and peace. Christians who have had this experience generally identify the 'being of light' with Christ; and the original resurrection "appearances" may quite possibly have been waking versions of this type of experience.[79]

He says that many of the New Testament narrations are later additions. Hick accepts the life, death, and resurrection of Christ as the permanent basis for Christianity and as a revelatory event (Christ-event), which is "a divine activity of communication and a human reception of that communication";[80] or in other words, "God's self-revealing activity and the answering human response which we call faith." Hick says:

> In his presence Jesus' disciples experience the presence of the transcendent God and his claim upon human life. . . . Thus to speak of the Christ-event is to speak of the language of faith. The Christ-event was not an event in public history, but an event experienced in faith. Jesus of Nazareth was of course a figure in public history, but Jesus, the Christ, Jesus as mediating presence of the transcendent God, is not known and therefore does not exist outside the religious field of vision.[81]

Hick distinguishes the language of faith from the facts of history. He considers the language of faith to be symbolic and metaphorical.

Hick refers to the resurrection experience of Paramahamsa Yogananda on June 19, 1936, of his *guru* (teacher) Yukteswar, who died on March 9, 1936, and the resurrection experience by Yukteswar in 1895 of Lahiri Mahasaya. Hick considers the resurrection experiences of these two Hindu leaders similar to the resurrection experience of the disciples of Jesus and concludes that the resurrection of Jesus is not a proof of his divinity.[82] Therefore it is clear that Hick does not accept Jesus as God incarnate, the second person of the Trinity, the *Logos* made flesh.[83]

At the same time, he argues that there is a plural revelation and that therefore the idea of the uniqueness of Christ should be reexamined. Non-Christian mediators are also God's revelations. Every revelation of God is unique. Jesus is only one among many human responses to the ultimate transcendent Reality we call God.

Another reason Hick adduces is Jesus' consciousness of God as Father.[84] If Jesus was aware of the presence of God as Father, how can he also be God? All we can say about the uniqueness of Jesus is that he sensed an eschatological uniqueness in his relationship with God. Jesus himself did not claim to be God.

Preexistence and the Universal Significance of Jesus

Hick rejects the concepts of "Immanuel" ("God with us"); that Jesus was personally preexistent as *Logos* and has universal significance; that "Jesus is fully God" and "fully man"; that Jesus is the only incarnation, the exclusive and final revelation as distinct from other manifestations; and the language of *physis, hypostasis,* and *ousia.*[85] Jesus never taught that he was preexistent,[86] nor that he was God, or God the Son, the Second Person of the Holy Trinity, incarnate.[87] The traditional language of Nicene and Chalcedonian two-natures Christology, which emerged as orthodox Christian doctrine, was originally meant to be understood as partly empirical and partly metaphysical; but this language has a mythological character and should be understood as symbolic, poetic, and more metaphorical than literal.[88] Hick understands the Chalcedonian dogma as a mystery, not as a "clear and distinct idea"; but "this is not a divine mystery, but one that was created by a group of human beings meeting at Chalcedon in present-day Turkey in the mid-fifth century."[89] Traditional belief constitutes not the permanent essence of Christianity but the mythical and superstitious character of Christianity.[90] The traditional doctrine of the incarnation was meant to assert the implicit superiority of Christianity over other religions.[91] In support of his rejection of the official teachings of the Catholic and Protestant churches, Hick says that many theologians think in this direction; he cites Karl Rahner's dictum that the Chalcedonian formulation is "not end, but beginning."[92] Rahner himself, however, was referring here to the developing nature of dogmatic formulations.[93]

The Idea of Incarnation as a Myth and a Metaphor

"Incarnation should be understood as a symbolic or metaphorical or mythic rather than as a literal truth."[94] New Testament and patristic studies in the English theological world come to the same conclusion and help Christians arrive at a genuine acceptance of religious pluralism. It is not necessary to accept Jesus as God in order to accept the teachings of Jesus.[95] Jesus incarnates the moral attributes of God, not the metaphysical attributes of God.[96] "If the dogma of Jesus' deity were to become understood, not as a literal claim with universal implications, but as an internal Christian metaphorical discourse, a barrier would be removed from the relationship between the Christian and other sections of humankind."[97] To call Jesus God, the Son of God, God incarnate, and so on is to use poetic, mythological, and metaphorical language that expresses loving devotion and commitment, but is not to be understood literally.[98] In the formulation of the idea of incarnation, Hick sees political influence at work, as well as the Christian attempt to establish claims of superiority vis-à-vis others.[99]

Hick agrees with the attempts of many contemporary theologians to express the religious concerns of Nicaea and Chalcedon by means of the biblical narratives of God's self-revelation in history, choosing the Hebrew alternatives of "purpose" and "action" rather than the Greek categories of "substance" and "essence."[100] The name God refers not to a nature but to an operation of *Agape,* and therefore it is meaningful to speak of "inhistorisation" rather than of divine "incarnation."[101] The action of God as *Agape* is manifested through Jesus of Nazareth, but this was not the whole of God's "agapéing."[102] Jesus had only "one nature" and "this nature was wholly and unqualifiedly human," but the *Agape* which directed this was God's. Jesus had "only one will, that of the man Jesus of Nazareth." This "inhistorisation" should be understood as "*homoagape*" and not as "*homoousia.*"[103]

Jesus' Self-consciousness

Jesus neither taught nor claimed to be God incarnate and the Second Person of the Trinity.[104] "We have the strange doctrine of a God incarnate who did not know that he was God."[105] Hick asks, "Have we really come to terms with the paradox of God incarnate who does not know that he is God incarnate? This provokes the question, How can the

Church claim to know who Jesus was better than he knew himself?"[106] Jesus would have probably regarded the idea of him as God incarnate as blasphemous; rather, he would have probably thought of himself as the final prophet.[107] Pauline theology does not reflect the original self-consciousness of Jesus. Jesus had an absolute sense of a divine Thou and taught the immanent presence of God.[108]

The Concept of Son of God

Hick cannot accept the concept *Son of God.* In the light of Geza Vermes's study of Jesus and the world of Judaism, Hick says that the title Son of God was understood in Jewish circles as metaphorical, not metaphysical.[109] Christ as Son of God is an image like other images within the church (e.g., Our Lady of Fatima, Our Lady of Lourdes) and operates within a particular culture; it follows that other images such as Krishna, Rama, and the like are also equally valid.[110] The Greek-dominated intellectual world of the Roman empire transformed the metaphorical Son of God into a metaphysical Son of God. "But in the ancient world the concept of divinity was much less clearly defined and the conditions for its use much less demanding." The title Son of God was applied to inspired holy men.[111] In *Disputed Questions in Theology and the Philosophy of Religion,* Hick argues that Son of God means servant of God and is applicable to pharaohs, kings, emperors, great philosophers, miracle workers, and the like. He also states that a parallel doctrine can be found in Buddhism,[112] which considers Buddha as *devādideva* (God of Gods). In Mahayana Buddhism, Buddhology developed parallel to Christology.[113] The concept of kenotic Christology is not revealed truth, but a defective human hypothesis. In his theocentric Christology, the concept of Jesus as Son of God or God incarnate should be understood in mythological, metaphorical, poetical, analogous, and symbolic senses, since it expresses the ideas of commitment and devotion. It should not be understood in a literal and metaphysical sense.[114]

John Hick articulates a theocentric model of Christology, accepting the equality of all religions and denying any special claim on behalf of Jesus. Christianity is one among many religions, and Jesus of Nazareth is one among many religious leaders, an inspired human being. Hick holds that the establishment of the church and the formulation of its doctrines have political, imperialistic, and capitalistic backgrounds.

Theology is a human response, and religious experience is a "phenomenon," an "experiencing-as" through which the "noumenon," the "real," is revealed and experienced. Hick wishes to understand Jesus Christ in secular terms in order to safeguard an "honest" and "realistic" Christianity. Contemporary philosophical thinking is very important for current theology, just as the ancient and the mediaeval philosophies were important for the church fathers and great theologians such as Thomas Aquinas. But Hick, unlike Rahner, uses the contemporary pragmatic, analytical and linguistic philosophies and scholarly studies more to substantiate his "secular theological thinking" than to do theology in the light of contemporary philosophy and scholarship.

The Revised Christology of S. J. Samartha as an Indian Response to Religious Pluralism

The Christology of Stanley J. Samartha is the result of his personal experience of the religious pluralism of his homeland and of his deep knowledge and awareness of the Hindu and the Christian historical and religious traditions.[115] This prompted him to change his early attitude of "inclusivism" and adopt the current attitude of "pluralism."

The theologies of many Indian Christian theologians, both Catholic and Protestant, missionaries from Europe and theologians of India, were not responses to pluralistic religious reality,[116] but rather attempts to interpret Christ and the Christian faith in the light of Indian culture and philosophy. They did not face the challenge of a pluralistic theology; in their day, they were accused of a Hinduization of Christianity. Most paid little attention to the independence of non-Christian religions and to religious traditions other than Hinduism. An exception to this general trend was the approach of K. T. Paul, perhaps the first Indian Christian theologian to offer a serious response to the multireligious context of India.

Stanley J. Samartha tries to present Jesus Christ and interpret the Christian faith in the context of the cultural and religious pluralism of India by means of a theological articulation of liberation and inculturation, the two main themes of contemporary Christian theology in Asia. Because of his early theological writings Samartha was considered to be an "inclusivist," but his subsequent theological standpoint means that he is looked on today as a "pluralist." However, one finds traces of both inclusivism and pluralism in his early writings.

Christology in the Context of "Dialogical Theology"

In Samartha's thinking, we find a development from a theology of dialogue, which embraces Jews, Muslims, Hindus, and Buddhists, to "dialogical theology," which promotes what Carl Raschke has called "dialogy" instead of theology. We find a gradual development in his theological idea from his *Hindu View of History* to his present-day writings—a development of revised Christology in the context of interreligious dialogue and a theology of dialogue. Samartha himself does not directly use the term "dialogy."

Interreligious Dialogue and Its Purpose Evoke a New Theological Vision

Samartha considers dialogue to be a spirit, a mood, and an attitude toward neighbors of other faiths[117] and a mode of relationship between people of different faiths.[118] Through dialogue between people of different faiths, we maintain relationship and co-operation "in pursuing common purposes like justice, peace and human rights."[119] Samartha says that dialogue helps us to confess Christ as fellow pilgrims,[120] to receive a fuller understanding of our faith and a deeper understanding of our neighbors.[121] All these aspects of dialogue constitute in general a new and revised vision of one's own religion and a new and revised attitude toward the faith of one's neighbors. This in turn helps believers to accept others as they accept themselves. But the politicization of religion in India is a threat to interreligious dialogue.[122]

Samartha identifies two types of dialogue. The first aims at a common investigation of "questions with the intent of reaching agreement whatever it is possible"; and the second aims to "bring about an encounter of commitments."[123] He recommends that we listen to our neighbors before beginning to share with them the "riches of God in Christ." "If we do not *listen,* how shall they *hear*?" asks Samartha.[124] The background of his discussion of religious pluralism is the experience of living together with people of other faiths, particularly with Hindus in India.

Revision of Theological Understanding

Samartha says that an assumption of "openness and dialogue" is not enough to maintain the Christian relationship with Jews, Muslims, Hindus, Buddhists, and others; "a serious revision of theological understanding" is necessary.[125] This leads him to suggest a revised Christology. A revised theological understanding is the necessary consequence both of Samartha's concept of social existence, which emphasizes the *interreligious* and *multiscriptural* context and the idea of *relational* hermeneutics, seeking a relationship between people "who use their particular scripture as inspiration and authority to guide their attitudes toward neighbors of other faiths," and of his change in emphasis from "mono-religious and mono-scriptural to multi-religious and multi-scriptural."[126] "My approach to the question of scripture is that we must recognise the plurality of scriptures. People of different faiths have their own scriptures as their authority."[127] "The Church needs to be redefined in a dialogical context."[128] Since Christology is central to Christian theology, dialogue leads to a new theological understanding which focuses on a revised Christology.

The Relationship between Dialogue and Salvation

Because religions offer answers about basic questions concerning human nature and destiny, "the quest for salvation and dialogue between religions are closely related."[129] The concept of salvation includes both social and soteriological dimensions.[130] To achieve greater substance in dialogue between religions, "the definition of salvation should be more inclusive."[131] Christianity offers salvation in Jesus Christ. To make this concept firm and clear, a "theological search for the essentials of the gospels" is needed.[132] The concepts of dialogue and salvation lead Samartha to the question of the Savior: If the church's message is salvation, is the "person of a Saviour necessary? If so why only Jesus Christ? . . . Moreover in a religiously pluralistic society, why is salvation possible in no other name except that of Jesus Christ?"[133]

The Philosophical and Theological Foundations of a Revised Christology

Pluralistic Nature of Reality

"Can it be that plurality belongs to the very structure of reality? Or can it be that it is the will of God that many religions should continue in the world?"[134] asks Samartha. He consults the *Vedas* to find an answer to the reality of pluralism, in the *vedic* sages' experience (ca. 1500 B.C.E.) of one reality with manifold names, recognizing a mysterious center, the Truth of the truth (*Satyasya Satyam).* If this is not accepted, genuine plurality is impossible.[135] Samartha says,

> Pluralism is part of the larger plurality of races, peoples, and cultures, of social structures, economic systems, and political patterns, of languages and symbols, all of which are part of the total human heritage. Religious pluralism—that is, the fact that the different religions respond to the Mystery of the ultimate reality or Sat or Theos in different ways—is important because it touches ultimate questions about human life and destiny.[136]

Human responses to the mystery of the infinite are culturally, philosophically, and theologically pluralistic. If salvation comes from God, we should accept the possibility of recognizing the validity of other experiences of salvation.[137] Therefore, the plurality of scriptures is a fact to be accepted, not a notion to be discussed. The normativeness of Christ, based on the authority of the Bible, cannot be generalized, since other scriptures supply other norms.[138] The hermeneutics of the West in response to science, philosophy, historiography, and other secular movements inevitably had to be a monoscriptural hermeneutics; but Christologies developed in the monoscriptural situation cannot be normative for Asia and Africa, where we need to develop a new hermeneutics in a multiscriptural society. Not only do other faiths, for example, Hinduism, Buddhism, and Islam, have their own hermeneutics; each land where these religions flourished developed a hermeneutic of its own in keeping with the local situation.[139] The experience of mystery, responses to mystery, and the experience of salvation are plural.[140]

The Existence of Pluralistic Christologies

In the New Testament, salvation through Jesus Christ was experienced and interpreted differently by Aramaic-speaking Jewish Christians and Hellenistic Diaspora Jews (who were much more open to the other peoples among whom they lived), and non-Jewish Christians such as Greeks, Syrians, and Romans who had no part in the Jewish "history of salvation." Yet there was no doubt about the root of this experience of salvation in Jesus Christ.[141] This is why we find in the New Testament "one Christ but many Christologies," and this in turn means that "any exclusive or normative claim on behalf of one particular Christology does not seem to have the support of the New Testament."[142]

> Jesus Christ is "the same yesterday, today and tomorrow" (Hebrews 13:8), but Christologies need to change, redefine, and revise themselves constantly to make sense to the church and the world at different times and in different cultural situations. Such revisions have gone on at different times in the history of the church. . . . Christian commitment however is not to particular Christologies, but to God in and through Jesus Christ.[143]

Pluralistic Christology as a Spiritual Source for the Struggle against Injustice

Samartha declares it impossible to think that only the Jewish, Christian, and Western traditions offer spiritual resources for the struggle against injustice, and that the ascetic spirituality of the Asian religions ignores the issues of social justice. Christianity, a religion that bears the culture, values, and ideologies of the north, seems to be a religion of the powerful, whereas the people of the south, who follow other religious traditions, are poor and weak at least in political and economic terms.[144] Northern study of the southern religions does not adequately express the content of these religions. Moreover, the concept of *dharma yuddha* (war to establish righteousness) of the *Bhagavadgita*[145] or *Shanti Mantra* (chanting of peace), the central Hindu experience, or the *mahā karuna citta* (consciousness of great compassion) of Buddhism[146] have given a more concrete foundation for a just struggle against the oppressive structures.

The Respect of Non-Christians for Jesus Christ

Samartha points out that there are many neighbors of other faiths such as Gandhi and Vivekananda who not only have great respect for Jesus Christ but try to follow him in various ways. They experience disappointment because of the "arrogant exclusive claims" of Christians, which are a barrier to greater recognition of Jesus Christ and of the universal dimension of his message. The teachings of the Sermon on the Mount and the death of Jesus on the cross made a profound impression on Gandhi, who accepted the person and the message of Jesus but not the exclusive claims of Christians. A pluralistic historical consciousness "within a global consciousness where different peoples and cultures are drawn together into one community"[147] means that we need a pluralistic approach in Christology.

Characteristics of Revised Christology

Revised Christology as an Ecumenical Theology

Samartha uses the term ecumenical to include believers of other faiths in the *oikoumenē* of God. He recognizes that this involves a "jump from intra-Christian to intra-religious." In order to achieve a "valid theological bridge," one must reject "open or hidden exclusive claims." He points out that "conservative evangelicals are in the forefront of a strident and aggressive rejection of other religions and have a powerful hold on their followers in Asia and Africa."[148] Samartha wants to work out a "wider Christology" "to support a 'larger ecumenism' but one that is sensitive to the work of the Holy Spirit in the whole world, not just of religions but also of secular faiths and ideologies."[149] Universality can be viewed as the extension of one particularity; but one can also recognize God alone as Absolute, considering all religions as relative, in order to develop new relationships in the *oikoumenē* of God.[150] Samartha opts for the second possibility, and it is against this background that he develops his revised Christology as an ecumenical theology.

Revised Christology as a Response to Religious Pluralism

Samartha attempts a revised Christology that does not overlook "the presence of other 'lords' and other 'saviours' in a multi-religious context,"[151] a Christology from below (in contrast to a Christology from above). This is not an attempt "to work out an Asian or Indian Christian Christology *against* the Christologies of the west," but "to respond to and articulate the mystery of Jesus Christ in an ecumenical setting."[152] His intention is not "to attack the truth of the classical christological doctrines";[153] however, historical pressures and theological imperatives demand a reexamination of all exclusive claims.

The acceptance of religious pluralism and the endeavor to present a Christian faith in terms acceptable to believers of other faiths are basic to the theology of Samartha. The term "non-Christian religions" as a designation of believers in other faiths is a negative term that reveals the theological oppression of the South by the North.[154] He recommends a *relational* hermeneutics of the word of God and a faith through which other creeds, scriptures, and experiences become acceptable to us. He tries to provide a basis for this hermeneutics by means of many examples of social life in India.[155] The perspective of the existing cooperation of different religious communities in India in various areas of social life and in interreligious marriages is an indirect argument for the equality of all religions.[156]

Sense of Mystery

Samartha's revised Christology is mystery-centered. God is Mystery, and religions are human responses to the Mystery. The description of the Mystery as *sat-cit-ānanda* is the Hindu response to Mystery, and the concept of the Trinity "is an attempt to make sense of this Mystery through the meaning disclosed in Jesus of Nazareth, identified with Christ, and using categories from Greek thought alien to the Indian context."[157] This confession of faith does indeed remain normative for Christians everywhere, but to make it "absolutely singular" and to maintain that the meaning of the Mystery is disclosed only in one particular person at one particular point, and nowhere else, is to ignore one's neighbors of other faiths who have other points of reference. The biblical understanding of God includes a suprapersonal element, a certain "mystery" and "unknowability," alongside the covenant relationship that provides a personal dimension.[158]

Rejection of Absolute and Exclusive Claims

An open and critical examination of all exclusive claims is a necessary first step toward a revised Christology:[159]

> A Christology which claims that God has been revealed in order to redeem humanity *only* in Jesus of Nazareth, and that this revealing and redeeming activity of God took place *once-for-all* in the first century, runs the risk of contradicting another strand of Jewish and Christian theology which affirms that God is God of love and justice as creator, sustainer, and redeemer of all creation.[160]

Samartha examines the development of the trinitarian framework of the faith and says: "The presence and the work of the Spirit of God cannot be limited to Jesus Christ and the Christian Church."[161] He argues against the absolute claim of Christianity on the basis of the incarnation itself: God has relativized his own self in history by incarnation in Jesus Christ, and Christian theologians are not justified in absolutizing in doctrine him whom God has relativized in history.[162] He asks,

> Does God reveal himself as truth only in Jesus Christ? . . . If God is free how can his freedom to act at all times in history be limited by an arbitrary "once-for-allness". To say that this is God's "self-limitation" does not solve the problem because the question still remains: why a limitation in this one particular instance?[163]

The second argument is based on the nature of mystery. This precludes any claim on the part of one religious community to have exclusive or unique or final knowledge.[164] A third argument is based on the ontological structure and symbolic significance of language.

For these reasons, diverse responses to the Mystery of the Infinite are possible. Samartha's concept of the distinction between faith and religion rejects at least indirectly any exclusive claim made by one single religion. While each individual response has a normative claim on the adherents of that particular religion, no one response can serve as the norm for judging the responses of other traditions. The imposition of exclusivism on Asia and Africa is a disaster and a tragedy.

A Christology Recognizing the Equality of All Religions

Samartha observes that although Christians have always lived with people of other religious traditions, the recognition of the fact of religious pluralism and its implication for Christian life and witness are something recent.[165] The implications of religious pluralism are "far wider and much more complex than just the Christian–Jewish or sometimes the Christian–Jewish–Muslim relationships."[166] Religious pluralism is possible: we need not become "intolerant fanatics or uncritical relativists"; relativism is born of a lack of "theological backbone."[167] The reality of religious pluralism "carries the possibilities of fresh discoveries and mutual enrichment."[168]

The attempt to create a world faith either by advancing one particular religion or by mixing selected elements of different religions is a "fruit-salad" approach that will fail.[169] Samartha argues that the colonialist mentality of affirming the superiority of one culture and ideology over another as an instrument of subjugation and exploitation extended to a spiritual exploitation and domination that proclaimed the superiority of one religion over another. The rejection of religious pluralism is a more serious form of injustice than mere economic colonialism.[170] Samartha argues in the context of the orthodox Hindu arguments that "the plurality of religions is 'intrinsic and purposeful' because of *dharma*": "there is the principle of *adhikāra* (which may be translated aptitude, competence, eligibility), which makes plurality necessary," and

> *adhikāra-bheda* (difference in aptitude or competence) is not a matter of choice, but a "given" element, even the will of God, and it allows persons to choose different *margas* (paths or ways). God defines one's *adhikāra* by the attraction (*ruci*) one feels towards a certain *mārga.* Hindus are Hindus rather than Christians because they have aptitude and eligibility only for their *dharma* and not for Christianity. Therefore the question of superiority or uniqueness of any one *dharma* over others does not arise.[171]

He points out that there is no equivalent word in European languages for the Sanskrit word *dharma* and in Indian languages for the European word "religion."[172] He compares one's commitment to a religion to the commitment to one's family or nation; the nation can accept a plurality of such commitments. "When these religions continue to offer alternative ways of salvation, how can any *world* conference on mission so blindly ignore them?"[173] Samartha distinguishes divine revelation from absolute truth, and various human experiences and responses to revelation from revelation itself. He quotes Harward R. Burkle, "To say that Christian revelation is relative, is not to deny the absoluteness of the divine truth which is revealed therein."[174] "Relativism" does not undermine religious life; rather, it "strengthens and mutually enhances the quality of the quest."[175]

Theocentric Nature of Christology

In order to avoid the danger of an impoverished "Jesusology" and a narrow "Christomonism" and to help to establish new relationships with neighbors of other faiths, Samartha suggests, on the basis of his conclusion that Jesus himself was "theo-centric" and that the priority of God is taken for granted in the Bible, a theocentric (Mystery-centered) Christology in the context of the "christologico-ecumenical issues that are taking shape in the Catholic Church and in the churches affiliated with the World Council of Churches."[176] Samartha finds support in the identification of Christology and theology by the International Theological Commission appointed by the pope in 1969, and the Catholic and Orthodox observation that the affirmation by the World Council of Churches that "the Lord Jesus Christ is God and Savior," is "christomonistic" and should be corrected by a trinitarian emphasis.[177] "To give the impression that Jesus of Nazareth is God is confusing," says Samartha.[178] "Theocentric circle includes Christocentric circle"; "Christocentrism without theocentrism leads to idolatry"; "Christianity belongs to Christ, Christ does not belong to Christianity."[179] The great christological councils help us understand how "God is in Jesus Christ and how Jesus Christ is related to God."[180] In the New Testament, the humanity of Jesus is emphasized; Jesus not only prayed to God, but he taught his disciples to pray to God as Our Father—thus Jesus himself is presented as theocentric.[181] The New Testament points beyond Jesus to God by emphasizing the activity of God, who raised Jesus from the dead.[182]

The Incarnation and the Concept of the Son of God

The Concept of Multiple Incarnations

Samartha tries to defend the Christian doctrine of incarnation in the framework of the Hindu concept of *avatārs,* that is, incarnation of God, so as to confirm the harmony of nature which Jesus realized through his Christ-event. He emphasizes the importance of the historicity of Jesus, relating it to the mystical consciousness of India, which neither Indian philosophy nor Indian religions oppose.[183] In his analysis of the "Significance of the Historical in Contemporary Hinduism," Samartha emphasizes the social consequences of the incarnation and the power of Christ to renew human beings and remake society, without denying the Christian doctrine of incarnation.[184] But Jesus Christ is one among many incarnations (*avatār*);[185] Samartha recalls Radhakrishnan's reasons for denying the Christian concept of unique incarnation, for example: "the perfect revelation of God in a relative world is not possible, the appearance of the infinite God cannot be limited to a particular place or time, and that there are the similarities between the revelation through

Christ, Krishna and Buddha."[186] In his later work, *One Christ—Many Religions,* Samartha says,

> The theory of multiple *avatars* seems to be theologically the most accommodating attitude in a pluralistic setting, one that permits recognizing both the mystery of God and the freedom of people to respond to divine initiatives in different ways at different times.[187]

As well as promoting the idea of multiple incarnations, Samartha sees some of the present attitudes and theories of Christianity toward non-Christian religions reflected in the Hindu scriptures, suggesting that Hindus could have the same attitude toward Christians. Samartha says,

> Bhagavad-Gita, faced with the possibility of many *margas* (paths of God), suggested that those who worship other gods, in reality worship Krishna alone, but not properly (IXX.23) or worship him unknowingly (IX.23). Does not this remind one of certain Christian attitudes today? The Gita goes even further. Krishna says, "Whatever form any devotee wishes to worship, I make that faith of his steady." (VII.21) Also, "in whatever way persons approach Me, in the same way do I accept them" (IV.11). If Christians can speak of the "unknown Christ of Hinduism," the Hindus can speak of the "unknown Krishna of Christianity."[188]

Samartha asks, "Would Christians accept Krishna or Rama or *nirvāna* or the Quran as meeting points? Would not Christians feel uneasy if our Hindu friends discover *Saccidānanda* or *Trimūrthi* in the Trinity."[189]

Incarnation in Terms of Divinity and the Christian Concept of Incarnation as a Later Development

Samartha suggests that we understand incarnation in terms of "divinity," not in terms of "deity": it is "one thing to say Jesus of Nazareth is divine and another thing to say that Jesus of Nazareth is God."[190] Incarnation understood in terms of "deity" leads to "Christomonism" and to an impoverished "Jesusology."[191] He quotes Vengal Chakkarai, "To believe that God is best defined by Christ is not to believe that God is confined to Christ."[192] Samartha asserts that there is a gulf between the New Testament teaching and the confession of the creed. In the early community's understanding of Jesus, there is "no hint of the doctrine of the incarnation" and Jesus is not regarded in the New Testament as a preexistent being.[193]

The Idea of Divine Sonship as a Later Development

The titles Son of God and Messiah in the Gospels of Matthew, Mark, and Luke do not imply divinity.[194] The infancy narratives do not convey the idea of incarnation, and the genealogy of Jesus in Matthew makes it clear that Jesus is "descended from David through his human father." The title Immanuel does not imply that "Jesus is God," and the confession of Peter at Caesarea Philippi (Matt. 16:13–20) means that Jesus is "Messiah and no more." Samartha likewise says: "it would . . . be a mistake to assume that Paul formally makes Christ co-equal with God."[195] Jesus did not consider himself identical with God.[196] In short, according to the teachings of the New Testament, Jesus of Nazareth is not God, and the idea of Jesus as God is the invention of the Councils of Nicaea, Constantinople, and Chalcedon, which also had political purposes. Samartha doubts the validity of the Nicene Council, since its president was the emperor Constantine, unbaptized at that time.[197] Belief in Jesus as the incarnation of God and the concept of the uniqueness of Jesus Christ are later developments, which gradually became exclusive claims.[198]

Samartha proposes a revised Christology as the answer to the quest of the religiously plural world, without any absolute claim on behalf of Jesus Christ and without negative judgments on the faiths of our neighbors: a Christology that is "biblically sound, spiritually satisfying, theologically credible, ethically responsible, and pastorally helpful,"[199] relevant not only in the context of religious pluralism but also when confronted by the poverty, underdevelopment, oppression, and suffering of Third World humanity—in concrete terms, of Indians. He calls this a "bullock-cart Christology." He tackles two basic issues simultaneously, viz., religious pluralism and liberation, whereas many theologians concentrate on only one of these problems. But we must verify whether a Christology without claims is biblically and historically correct and can do justice to the metaphysical truth of the reality of Jesus Christ.

Conclusion

In this chapter we have presented the modern global phenomenon of religious pluralism and the responses of a European and an Indian theologian. The relationship between culture and religion is obvious. The spread of religion beyond the barriers of culture and language, the implantation of culture together with religious faith, and later attempts to adapt culture and revive the cultural inheritance of the communities constitute the religious and the social predicament today. In a country such as India, this problem of religious pluralism is evident. Our analysis of this problem in the context of the cultural and religious history of the country bears witness to a unity and continuity in the development of religious ideas and practices. The theological approaches of John Hick and Stanley J. Samartha suggest a pluralistic theology that considers all religions equal and independent responses to experiences of the ultimate mystery. But the unity and continuity in the development of religious experiences and of the religious idea challenge the claims of Hick and Samartha. In a period that witnesses the tremendous influence of a pluralistic theology, where all religions are considered equal and mutually independent, it is important to attempt an alternative solution. This will be done by means of an evaluation of Karl Rahner's approach.

2

Karl Rahner's Transcendental Christology and His Concept of the Transcendental Christ

THE PHILOSOPHICAL AND THEOLOGICAL ROOTS of Rahner's idea of the "transcendental" and "categorical" are to be found in the philosophy and theology of Thomas Aquinas, Duns Scotus, Immanuel Kant, Johann Gottlieb Fichte, Georg Wilhelm Friedrich Hegel, Pierre Rousselot, Joseph Maréchal and Martin Heidegger. Rahner made the concepts "transcendental" and "categorical" the key to an all-embracing vision of Christian theology, by positing them as the starting point for the elaboration of his transcendental philosophy and theology. Through his "theology of the spirit" and "theology of the intellect,"[1] along with his "theoretical, scientific and theological reflection,"[2] Rahner lays down the path to a "theology of the heart." *Geist in Welt* (Spirit in the World) and *Hörer des Wortes* (Hearer of the Word) lay the foundation for his concept of the "transcendental";[3] his best-known book, *Grundkurs des Glaubens* (Foundations of Christian Faith), and many articles in *Schriften zur Theologie* (Theological Investigations) develop his transcendental philosophy, transcendental theology, and transcendental Christology. Rahner takes into serious consideration the inner unity of theology and philosophy and maintains this unity in view of the "human self-realisation of a Christian."[4] In this attempt at uniting philosophy and theology through theoretical, practical, and didactic legitimization, theology is philosophized[5] in today's social and historical context, where theology, Christian faith, and the religious atmosphere are not taken for granted. Rahner consciously reflects on faith with the help of the philosophical terminology, methodologies, and categories of the rational world, in order to present it as something reasonable to twentieth-century humanity, including believers of non-Christian religions and even atheists; all these persons are undeniably influenced by the rationalism of European society.[6] He does this in an attitude of respect and of readiness to accept others, since they too belong to the self-transcending process of the cosmos, which will achieve its self-realization in God, as it moves toward the climax in Christ.

Clarifications of the Word "Transcendental" and Related Terms

Transcendental, metaphysical, ontological, existential, supernatural, trans-categorical, anthropological, *a priori*—these are some of the mutually related expressions and concepts frequently used by Rahner in his discussion of almost all the themes of theology and philosophy. He employs them in his various methodological approaches to one and the same reality and in the various levels and aspects of his understanding of the question of being. Sometimes these different terms also express a kind of similarity and "interdependence" in meaning; Rahner often uses expressions such as "*a priori*, metaphysical, anthropological" to mean "transcendental"—if we understand the word "transcendental" as signifying the being of the human subject, which is the sole object of the present analysis. Here too we shall not neglect the variety of methodological approaches that Rahner employs. The thematic difference between the methodological significance and thematic content of these terminologies is very subtle, because his philosophy frequently fails to give serious consideration to the distinction, and also because Rahner sometimes employs these various terminologies in a rather broad sense. I hope that this terminological analysis will facilitate a clearer grasp of transcendental Christology, with its potential connotations and nuances.

Since the subject of this discussion is the attribute "transcendental" as applied to Christology, I have not analyzed other forms of this word, for example, transcendence (*Transzendenz*), transcendentality (*Transzendentalität*), and transcendentalism *(Transzendentalismus*). Some other concepts to which the term "transcendental" is applied are highlighted here, because these find their culmination in Rahner's "science of transcendental Christology." The term "transcendence" is discussed in the light of Rahner's application of this noun to God and the human being. In this context, transcendence unifies the entire being of the world with God, the entire creation with Christ, all the natural sciences with theology, the whole attempt of the knowing subject to know with God's free communication, and "humanity" with "divinity."

The Word "Transcendental"

The word *transcendental* is central to Karl Rahner's theological reflections; he uses this word in its multidimensional meaning throughout his entire oeuvre.[7] According to Thomas Aquinas, "transcendental" means that which goes beyond space and time and the possibility of the knowing subject to know. Thomas Aquinas understands "transcendence" in the relation of the world to God in the sense of the radical immanence of the world in God.[8] Joseph Maréchal also uses the concept "transcendental" with regard to the relation of the world and of the knowing subject to God. He presents it as the basic capacity of the subject, including a vertical dimension of "transcendence." In this he differs from Kant's ideas of the "transcendental" as the possibility of the subject with only a horizontal dimension.[9] Rahner uses the word "transcendental" in *Geist in Welt* in the contexts of the *intellectus agens* and metaphysics.[10] In *Hörer des Wortes,* the foundations for a philosophy of religion, Rahner develops and clarifies his concept of "transcendental,"[11] which becomes his key philosophical and theological concept in his attempt to make theology a science comparable to any other natural science. In Rahner's philosophical reflection "transcendental" is the *a priori* condition of the possibility for knowing the material object in subject and in being, which is in fact the capacity to hear God's revelation, which is inherent in the essence of the human being.[12] The "transcendental condition of the possibility" is the knowing subject's awareness of its unlimited possibility of knowledge and abstraction. The term "transcendental" in Rahner is related to many other concepts he employs. Since these are used in an analogous and sometimes identical manner, this particular term can be replaced by other terms.

According to Rahner, anticipation (*Vorgriff*) is the unlimited movement of the spirit, the condition of the possibility of conceptual knowledge on the part of the finite being. The finite being moves toward God, who is thus the goal of *Vorgriff.* Rahner's consideration of this concept must be seen in the framework of his general consideration of theology and philosophy, centered on the concept "transcendental." In speaking of the "transcendental consciousness" of human beings,[13] and "transcendence towards being as the basic composition" of human beings,[14] Rahner understands the concept "transcendental" in the Thomistic sense. In *Grundkurs des Glaubens,* Rahner presents the concept "transcendental" as the "simple, obvious and necessary condition of the possibility of all understandings and concepts."[15] The multidimensional and wide-ranging connotations make it rather difficult to define what Rahner means by the term "transcendental." This is why we shall examine it in specific contexts in his writings.

Transcendental and Anthropological

Rahner sometimes uses the term "transcendental" and the concepts related to this and denoted by it as an explanation or interpretation of the term "anthropological." Rahner's transcendental philosophy or theology is a philosophical or theological anthropology.

In the first chapter of *Hörer des Wortes*, Rahner discusses the relation between philosophy of religion and theology. The philosophy of religion is the ontology of the obediential potency. The problem of the relation between philosophy of religion and theology is a problem of metaphysical anthropology.[16] In the context of the metaphysics of Aristotle and of Thomas Aquinas, Rahner concludes that metaphysics is the first science offering a common metaphysical ground for the epistemological foundation of all sciences.[17] The epistemological problem of the relation between philosophy of religion and theology is an existential inquiry into the nature of the human being, because the epistemological question is a human activity.[18] In *Hörer des Wortes,* Rahner establishes that the intellect in the dynamism of its very operation implicitly affirms the existence of God in every judgment it makes, and in its freedom. He concludes (with Thomas in the *Summa*) that metaphysics is the foundation of the philosophy of religion, of theology, and of all other human sciences. Rahner identifies a mutual relationship and similarity among concepts and terminology such as general ontology, general metaphysics, philosophy of religion, theology, metaphysical anthropology, transcendental theology, and so on.[19]

In laying down the foundations of a metaphysical anthropology for the purposes of discussing the relationship between philosophy of religion and theology, Rahner approaches the essence of the human person in a double manner. First, the human person is understood as a spirit over against God; since a relationship to God is only a gift from God, never something that can be achieved from below, it is not possible to deduce the meaning of the human person from the meaning of the world. The human being should always be ready to receive a revelation from this God. Second, the human being is a historical entity and spirit, not in his biological existence but in his spiritual existence, one who can hear not only God's revelation but also God's silence.[20] These two ways of understanding the essence of a human being as spirit standing before God and as historical entity and spirit are the foundations of a metaphysical anthropology. They show that a transcendentality given by God is a basic datum in Rahner's anthropological concept, and that this is innate to the human being because he is spirit. The first sentence of a general ontology is that the "essence of being is knowing and being known in an original unity." This we call self-presence (*Bei-sich-sein*) or luminosity (*Gelichtetheit*). The first sentence of a metaphysical anthropology is that the "essence of human being is its absolute openness to being or in a word, the human person is spirit."[21] The anthropological nature of the human subject consists in the fact of the human person as spirit, which is the transcendentality of human being. This clearly demonstrates the mutual relationship between the terms transcendental and anthropological.

In dealing with the theme of the human being as spirit in *Hörer des Wortes,* Rahner says that in order for revelation to be possible "man should have an openness to the self-expression of the absolute possession of being through the light of the Word. And this openness is the *a priori* condition for the possibility of hearing such a Word."[22] This general understanding of being indicates something about a metaphysical anthropology of the human being as one who exists and is open to a potential revelation. This is not merely a question about the inherent substance of being as such, but something directly predicated of the human being who raises the question. In the light of metaphysical anthropology, this means that the human being is absolute openness; the human being is spirit; and transcendence to Being is the basic composition of the human being. Thus the first sentence of a metaphysical anthropology is the general question of the meaning of Being in its inherent substance, and of the reality of the human being and the reality of the pure Being who is God. Rahner calls the pure Being ultimate Being. Rahner interprets ultimate Being as transcendence, openness, the essence of human being, or as spirit.[23] In his metaphysical anthropology, the transcendental is also anthropological and vice versa. Hence this metaphysical anthropology can be called transcendental anthropology.

In Rahner's first philosophical work, *Geist in Welt,* which is an interpretation of Aquinas's metaphysics of knowledge in the light of the transcendental philosophy of Immanuel Kant and Joseph Maréchal, the anthropological perspectives of the philosophy of religion and theology are not fully developed, although the foundations are laid. His concepts of human knowledge, human intelligibility,[24] sensibility of the human intellect,[25] the necessary, *a priori,* metaphysics of human existence and human nature as "questionableness" (*Fragwürdigkeit*)[26] are evident in Rahner's idea of the "human"; thus, anthropological transcendentality is already implied here. When Rahner affirms that the human question is transcendental and the transcendental question metaphysical, he makes clear the relationship between the concepts of "transcendental," "anthropological," or "metaphysical."[27] When Rahner says that the world is the goal of the metaphysical question, where revelation takes place, and that the human being is "self-presence" (*Bei-sich-sein*) and "being-with-the-other" (*Beim-Anderen-sein*), he affirms the anthropological dimension of the transcendental nature of human existence.[28]

According to Rahner, the human being stands before God and is oriented toward God. God is absolute mystery,[29] the ground and substance of the essence of the human being. This standing before the absolute God and orientation toward God occur in the transcendental experience of the human subject as the essence of transcendence, responsibility, and freedom. At this point, theology and anthropology necessarily become one.[30] This is why the "theological" is also "anthropological." Because theology is the articulation of the transcendental experience of the human subject accompanied by the grace of God (expressed in other terms as "the supernatural existential of self-presence"), the "anthropological" is also "transcendental." Thus there is an interrelationship and a mutual dependence between transcendental theology and anthropology, while the concepts "transcendental" and "anthropological" are interrelated. The usage of the concept "transcendental" also implies the idea "anthropological."

Transcendental and Metaphysical

Metaphysical means beyond the physical; according to Thomas Aquinas, this is synonymous with transcendental.[31] In the theological language of Rahner also, the idea conveyed by the term *metaphysical* is closely related to what is meant by the term *transcendental.* In *Geist in Welt,* Rahner's statement that the "transcendental question," as a "metaphysical question," concerns Being[32] and that the "question about Being in metaphysics" is the "transcendental question"[33] refers to his understanding of the transcendental in relation to the metaphysical. The openness of "being to the Being of the human being" is "self-presence." In other words, this openness is the unity of being (*Sein*), knowing (*Erkennen*), that which is known (*das Erkannte*), to be known (*Erkanntsein*) and "being known" (*Erkanntheit*). It is openness toward pure or ultimate Being, openness to revelation, or to the word of God, which is "transcendence" of being to "Being." In Rahner's philosophical theology, this openness and transcendence of being toward Being is the first sentence of a metaphysical anthropology. Here the capacity to transcend is the capacity to be metaphysical.[34]

In his discussion of the analogy of being in *Hörer des Wortes*, Rahner draws on the analogous concept of the meaning of being as "self-presence" in Thomas Aquinas, the analogous identity of "existent (*Seiend*) with Being (*Sein*)" as "self-presence," pure Being and "knowing and known." Human beings are not "absolute consciousness" to their own selves, but "finite spirit." Their need to ask questions about the meaning of Being shows the finite character of the human spirit as "self-presence," "luminosity," "being-with-the-other" (*Beim-Anderen-sein*), the unity of "knowing" and "known." In this passage, Rahner interprets "metaphysics" by means of the term "transcendental consciousness," using these expressions interchangeably. However, one cannot deny the presence of a deeper and more comprehensive meaning of "transcendental consciousness." Thus, in his philosophical theology, the terms "transcendental" and metaphysical" refer to the same reality, though they imply different methodological approaches.[35]

In discussing the "hiddenness of Being," Rahner establishes that philosophy of religion, ontology of the human subject, general ontology or metaphysical anthropology, and so on are also elements of transcendental anthropology.[36] Metaphysical anthropology is always a general ontology.[37] In these sciences the metaphysical analysis of the essence of human beings is realized through transcendental analysis of the general question of Being in view of its transcendentality toward the Absolute, which is ontological openness to the transcendence of the pure Spirit, free Being, absolute Being. Therefore the philosophy of religion, or general ontology, can also become a "transcendental anthropology." Since Rahner uses the term "transcendental anthropology" in dealing with the concept of the transcendentality of being toward the Absolute, "transcendental" can also be considered "metaphysical," and "metaphysical knowledge" can be considered "transcendental knowledge."[38]

In *Geist in Welt,* Rahner discusses the basic nature of human beings as questioning beings[39] and presents "human existence as the question about being."[40] Thus, Being is both declared and concealed in its own questionableness (*Fragwürdigkeit*). The human being affirms the questionability (*Fragbarkeit*).[41] Being is the ability to be known (*Sein ist Erkanntseinkönnen*).[42] This question about being is a "metaphysical question pervading the ground of human existence."[43] The metaphysical question is a questionable question.[44] It is a question about being; but this is also a transcendental question. "The metaphysical question as the transcendental question is a conceptually raised form of this pervading question about being itself."[45] This "questionableness" of human existence in this context is in fact the transcendentality of human existence. Consideration of the metaphysical question as the transcendental question shows that Rahner understands the concept of transcendental as expressing that aspect of reality which is the precondition for being "metaphysical."

Transcendental and Ontological

Since Rahner speaks of the human being as absolute openness to being, he also says that the human being is spirit or transcendence. This is the *a priori* condition for hearing the word of God.[46] The human being, as transcendence, is a question about Being. This necessity of questioning shows the finality of the human spirit: it means that being is self-presence, luminosity, the unity of knowing, and that which is known. This is the starting point of our questions about an ontology of the human subject, which entail asking about the possibility of a revelation by the absolute God.[47] When the human subject is considered as spirit or transcendence, the phrases "ontology of human subject" and "metaphysical anthropology" mean the same.[48] Thus the term "ontological" is related to the "metaphysical" or "transcendental" or *a priori* character of the human subject.

Rahner considers the human being to be "existent-in-itself" (*An-sich-Seiendes*), which is "self-presence"; this in turn is "self-subsistence" (*In-sich-selber-Ständigkeit*).[49] The "ontological difference" in the understanding of Being (*Seinsverständnis*) is the permanent basis of each single judgment involving the question about Being.[50] As regards the ultimate ground of the capacity of the human being, as knowing and acting subject, to act in freedom and judgment, Rahner asks, "What is the *a priori* transcendental condition of the possibility of this subjectivity?"[51] The answer to this question is the first sentence of a metaphysical anthropology; Rahner answers by defining the human being as spirit, "a potential subject of a possible revelation of the divine depth of the absolute spirit who is God."[52] Discussing a "metaphysical anthropology" of the human capacity to hear the word of God (i.e., revelation), Rahner says that metaphysical anthropology becomes the "ontology of *potentia oboedientialis*" with respect to a possible free revelation.[53] Rahner calls this a metaphysical anthropology of the philosophy of religion.[54] In this context, the concept of the human subject as spirit open to the absolute Spirit, and the nature of the human subject, can be defined interchangeably as ontological, metaphysical, or transcendental. The different expressions and terms are employed to reveal different facets of the same supernatural openness of the human subject.

Such expressions as "*a priori* unity of being and knowledge"[55] or "ontological unity of knowing and the object,"[56] and reflections on the "unifying unity of being as ontological" as the "raising of that transcendental synthesis,"[57] help us become more aware of this problem of specifying the ideas conveyed by the terms ontological, transcendental, and *a priori*. In substantiating "being and knowing as the original unity in self-presence," Rahner says,

> Knowing is understood as the subjectivity of being itself, as self-presence of being. Being itself is already the original unifying unity of being and knowing, is onto-logical; and each actual unity of being and knowing in the actualisation of the knowledge is only the raising of that transcendental synthesis to a higher power which is being "in-itself."[58]

This means that the self-presence of being is ontological, while at the same time the unity of being and knowing is a transcendental synthesis of being. Here the transcendental synthesis is ontological, because it is the process of actualization of the self-presence of being. The various perspectives help to elucidate the relationship between the terms "transcendental" and "ontological."

TRANSCENDENTAL AND *A PRIORI*

Rahner sometimes employs the phrase *a priori* in *Hörer des Wortes* as an explanation, an interpretation, or even a synonym of "transcendental." The "openness of the human being to the self-declaration of the absolute possession of Being through the light of the Word" is the "*a priori* pre-requisite for the possibility of hearing such a Word." The "metaphysical anthropology of the human being as existent and open to revelation is constructed" on this basis.[59] In this formulation, the *a priori* prerequisite is the innate ability and existential characteristic of openness toward pure Being, the Ultimate. This *a priori* character is the "transcendental character" of the human being as an existent. Here, *a priori* denotes the transcendental character of the human subject.

In discussing the constitution of the essence of the human subject as *Dasein* in thinking (judgment) and acting (freedom), as "self-subsistence" or "self-subsistent subject" or as "coming to itself" (*Zu sich selber Kommen*), Rahner asks two questions. First, how must human beings grasp things in such a way that this grasping is freedom and judgment; second, what is the *a priori* transcendental condition that makes possible this subjectivity? Rahner finds the answer in the starting point of metaphysical anthropology. This answer clarifies the first tenet, viz., the "absolute openness of human being as transcendence and spirit towards God."[60] Rahner's understanding of the human subject in its possession of Being (*Seinshabe*) as "self-presence," "the unity of knowing and being known" as the starting point of an ontology of the human subject,[61] is comparable to the discussion of the starting point of a metaphysical anthropology, that is, the constitution of the essence of the human subject as "self-subsistence." Here we note a similarity between the terms "self-subsistence" and "self-presence," metaphysical anthropology and ontology of the human subject, metaphysics and transcendence, and so on. The two adjectives in the phrase "*a priori* transcendental condition of the possibility of this subjectivity"[62] do not apply two different attributes to the word "condition," since "transcendental" is an interpretation of "*a priori.*"

The chapter in *Hörer des Wortes* entitled "The Human Person as Spirit" explains the concept of abstraction according to Thomas Aquinas.[63] The technical term in Thomistic metaphysics for the problem of finding the universal in the singular is "abstraction."[64] This means (in Rahner's terms) that Thomism calls the endeavor to understand the condition of the possibility of self-subsistence "abstraction." Abstraction is the "knowledge of whatness" (*Washeit*), or the "knowledge of the unlimitedness of the 'whatness' of the individual." This condition is the "capability to abstract," the "transcendental condition of the possibility to abstract." This transcendental condition to abstract is the capability "to know the unlimitedness of the whatness of the knowing subject." Rahner explains it also as the "*a priori* condition of the knowing subject for abstraction and knowledge as the prior condition of the possibility." Thomas's terminology calls this the *intellectus agens.*[65] In this context Rahner uses two terms to denote and interpret the Thomistic concept of *intellectus agens:* "the transcendental condition of the possibility to abstract" and "*a priori*" condition of the knowing subject for individual knowledge and abstraction. Here, "transcendental condition" means the *a priori* condition.

In every judgment and action, the particular is affirmed and the universal is grasped in the singular. This may be called self-subsistence in the knowledge of the knowing subject.[66] An inquiry into the ultimate ground of the possibility of this self-subsistence is identical to the question concerning the basis for finding the universal in the single object,[67] the answer to which in Thomistic terminology is abstraction. Abstraction means "detaching," which is the condition for the possibility of judging,[68] says Rahner. In Thomistic terminology, the transcendental condition of this possibility is the *intellectus agens.*[69] "Abstraction" or "knowledge of the unlimitedness of the whatness of one's individuality of self-subsistence" or of "self-presence" is grasped in an "anticipation." This has an *a priori* character to grasp "more." This "more" is the horizon and ground of the possible object and its meaning. This horizon is "openness to the absolute," through which "the consciousness of this individual object's relation to the absolute" is grasped. Rahner clarifies the meaning of "anticipation" by saying that it is "an *a priori* possession of the dynamic self movement of the spirit towards the absolute," which belongs to the essence of what it is to be human. This anticipation is the conscious opening of the horizon of knowledge. The anticipation is to be understood as "knowledge" itself, and "knowing as the act of knowledge itself." Here Rahner asks what is the goal of human transcendence, as the human being anticipates knowledge in grasping its individual object. The answer is transcendental experience.[70] Here, anticipation, an *a priori* possession, the opening of the spirit, etc., denotes the act of the human being vis-à-vis the Other, the Ultimate. The nature of the human subject as "self-subsistence" and "self-presence" shows the basically transcending or "anticipatory" nature of the human subject.

In discussing the transcendental openness of the human subject to knowledge, to the *visio beatifica,* Rahner speaks of the "absolute transcendence of the spirit as the *a priori* opening of a space for revelation." It is not easy to discern any difference here between the terms "transcendental" and "*a priori*" in the discussion of the *status* of the spirit and character (openness) of the spirit.[71] In his analysis of the relationship between the transcendence of the human spirit and the historicity of the human being,[72] Rahner says,

> Since access to God exists only in the *a priori* structure of the human being as spirit, only in his own transcendence, and thus in an entry into the self, we may affirm that it is possible for the human being to enter into his own self, and therein to enter into God, only by stepping out into the world we share with others around us.[73]

Here the "*a priori* structure of the human being as spirit" is understood as the "transcendence of human being." In *Geist in Welt,* Rahner interprets the ontological space of sensibility as an *a priori* space of sensibility; here the term *a priori* conveys the idea of "transcendental."[74] In keeping with his own understanding of transcendental reflection, transcendental metaphysics, and categorical metaphysics, Rahner interprets "categorical metaphysics" as an *a posteriori* metaphysics, *a priori* as transcendental and *a posteriori* as "categorical."[75] In *Grundkurs des Glaubens,* Rahner identifies the transcendental knowledge of God with the transcendental experience of God, which is both *a priori* knowledge of God and *a priori* experience of God.[76]

"Transcendental" in Rahner means "beyond time and space," and is in many contexts synonymous with *a priori*. It is possible to interpret "transcendental" as the *a priori* character of the subject's possibility of knowledge.

Transcendental and Transcategorical, Existential and Supernatural

According to Rahner, the transcendental question is an existential question; the existential question is a metaphysical question; the metaphysical question is an anthropological question and an ontological question. This is both an *a priori* and a supernatural question. Thus, metaphysical analysis is also existential analysis, and existential analysis is also transcendental analysis. The essence of being is to know and to be known in an original unity which we call "self-presence." At the same time, "being" is the "possible object of knowledge," because "the being of Being is being known." The capacity to know is the transcendental destination of each existent. "Transcendentality" is used here in the scholastic sense of transcategorical. This knowability does not come to the being *ab extra,* nor is this knowledge acquired by means of an external relationship; it comes from within the being itself and belongs to the essence of being.[77]

In Rahner's theology, this transcendental, transcategorical, and ontological character and metaphysical content of the human being as "self-presence" or "self-subsistence" denote the supernatural "existential" of the human subject. In *Hörer des Wortes,* Rahner understands the "supernatural existential" as the capacity of the human being to hear the word of God, that is, revelation.[78] The terms "supernatural" and "existential" as attributes of human existence mean that grace is free and at the same time intrinsic to human nature and human existence.[79] William V. Dych says, "An existential is a transcendental determination in the sense that it permeates and pervades all of human existence."[80] Nikolaus Schwerdtfeger concludes that the supernatural existential is the transcendental self-communication of God.[81] Thus, a hermeneutical analysis of the terms "existential" and "transcendental" leads to the conclusion that these convey the idea of the human capacity and intrinsic orientation of the human being vis-à-vis the Ultimate.

In *Würde und Freiheit des Menschen,* Rahner outlines the essence of the human being, who possesses *a priori* transcendental and metaphysical elements and *a priori* reason. The dignity of the human being consists in the capacity to enter into direct personal communion with the infinite God, who has communicated himself in the love with which Jesus Christ communicated his own self.[82] The "supernatural existential" of a human person means that the human being as person is called to direct personal communion with God in Jesus Christ.[83] Thus, the transcendentality or "supernatural existential" of the human subject is the capacity to enter into personal communion with Jesus Christ. The basic nature of the human person is the orientation toward Christ in the transcategorical dimension of the human subject. Thus, Rahner's analysis and interpretation of human nature ultimately lead him to God's self-communication, which culminates in Jesus Christ.

Human Subject as Transcendence toward the Absolute

In *Hörer des Wortes,* Rahner affirms that the human being is basically constituted as transcendence toward the absolute Good, toward absolute Being, God.[84] The absolute transcendence of the human spirit is the *visio beatifica.*[85] This *visio beatifica* can also be called revelation.

Rahner understands the human subject as "spiritual transcendentality" with a "spiritual subjectivity," a "transcendentality," which is the capacity to hear the word of God (revelation). This is the basic constitution of the human subject, *a priori* to the human being.[86]

In the context of the critique of the "new theology" and discussion of the encyclical *Humani Generis,* Rahner takes up the question of the essence of the human person.[87] After pointing out the supernatural aspect of the nature of the human being, and grace as constitutive of the nature of the human being, Rahner says that the human being is the essence of transcendence, the overcoming of limitation.[88] He concludes in another essay that the metaphysical essence of the human person is transcendence and freedom.[89] Self-awareness and freedom make human existence spiritual and transcendental. This brings us to the experience of the unattainable, the experience of the mystery.[90]

In "Würde und Freiheit des Menschen," Rahner affirms that the human person is an individual, not merely an instance of the universal nor a spatiotemporal application of the universal idea. He has a valid and a real existence. He is immortal and the subject of an eternal destiny.[91] The essence of the human being comes from God and is directed to God, who is mysterious, nameless, infinite, self-communicating love.[92] The supernatural existential is related to the personal nature of the human being. It is received as a gratuitous gift of God, as grace. In this way both nature and supernature exist in the human being.[93]

Sometimes Rahner emphasizes the aspect of individuality and personality of the human being. The concept of the human being as spirit depends on the total unity of reality, that is, God. Reflection on the essence of the human being is a "process which exists in history" and is "essentially unfinished." The understanding of that which is essential is en route, in spite of its *a priori* and transcendental metaphysical element. Rahner develops the idea of the human person as partner of God:

> This personal dignity of the human being in the actual order takes on an even greater quality in respect to its absoluteness, in virtue of the fact that he is called to be the direct partner of God, the Absolute, the Infinite.[94]

In discussing the experience of the saints and persons of the Spirit, Rahner says,

> But they know that the human being as spirit—in real existence, not merely in theory—should really live on the border between God and the world, time and eternity. They try always to ensure that they really do

> this, so that the spirit in them is not only the medium of the human style of life.[95]

In *Grundkurs des Glaubens,* Rahner develops the concept of the human being as person and subject[96] who experiences himself as unlimited possibility.[97] In his transcendence he experiences himself as a questioning being,[98] and as the essence of transcendence.[99] The human being with his transcendental freedom and responsibility[100] experiences this responsibility and freedom as the reality of transcendental experience.[101] Rahner analyzes elsewhere the meaning of God's becoming a human being and the meaning of human nature, and affirms that the human being is essentially a mystery that is transcendence, and that God is mystery, transcendence.[102] He portrays the human being as the one who is consciously the essence of absolute and unlimited transcendence. This means that transcendence can be described in the context of categorical experience.[103] As spirit, the human being is transcendence and the essence of sacred mystery. His consciousness is based on the inconceivability of this sacred mystery.[104] This "entails that God is present to the human being essentially as a holy mystery."[105]

God as Transcendence

In *Hörer des Wortes*, dealing with the theme of the hiddenness of being, Rahner speaks of God as absolute transcendence.[106] The opening of the transcendental horizon of being makes us stand before God as the transcendence of the spirit and as love toward God and *vice versa;* this takes place in knowledge and love.[107] Rahner deals with the concept of God as absolute transcendence of the human being in his discussion of the absolute goal of the human person, which he defines as knowledge, or the *visio beatifica*. The human vocation is directed to the vision of God, who is transcendence.[108] There is no *a priori* rule governing the search for the place of transcendence of the human subject, where the human being stands before God in a "wordless tête-à-tête of spirit to spirit."[109] Rahner concludes that the answer to this question becomes a general question about Being. The revelation of God occurs in the transcendence of the human being.[110]

God remains absolutely transcendent in the world.[111] When Rahner reflects on the "human being as essence of transcendence" in *Grundkurs des Glaubens*[112] and in "Wissenschaft als Konfession,"[113] we find the ideas of God as transcendence, the essence of transcendence as spirit, the essence of transcendence as God, and so on. In dealing with the theme of "transcendental experience of God as the experience of mystery," Rahner says that the knowledge of God through transcendental experience constitutes the essence of transcendence itself.[114]

Transcendence is the experience of mystery by the human subject. In the experience of transcendence and in the experience of mystery, the experience of God is already present.

> One can call this goal and source of transcendence God. One can speak of Being, of the ground, of the ultimate reason, the illuminating and revealing *logos;* one can use a thousand other names to designate what is meant here.[115]

What we call transcendence is the holy mystery, or God.[116] Rahner concludes that God's self-transcendence takes place in history.[117] There is a transcendental and a categorical revelation, and there is a unity between these revelations. The climax of the unity of the transcendental and the categorical revelation is the person of Jesus Christ.[118]

In his discussion of the relationship between the different concepts of anthropology, theological anthropology, fundamental theology, fundamental theological anthropology, metaphysical anthropology, philosophy of religion, metaphysics, natural theology, general ontology, and so on, Rahner maintains that theological anthropology exists because the human subject has the innate capacity to hear revelation. We can call this fundamental theological anthropology and consider it a metaphysical science. "Fundamental theological anthropology" and the "philosophy of religion" are mutually related,[119] so that "philosophy of religion" and "metaphysical anthropology" denote two dimensions of the same reality. *Theologia naturalis* is general metaphysics, and general ontology is also metaphysical anthropology.[120] General ontology is *theologia naturalis* and is treated as anthropology. Philosophy of religion is *theologia naturalis,* an identification made possible through its unity with metaphysical anthropology.[121]

Thus Rahner employs the term "transcendental" in connection with many other terms and concepts. He speaks not only of transcendental Christology but also of *a priori,* metaphysical, ontological, transcategorical, descending,[122] cosmological Christology.[123] These are mutually related concepts, different perspectives on one and the same subject. Rahner's Christology can be studied from the perspective of anthropology,[124] ontology,[125] transcendental philosophy, transcendental theology,[126] the supernatural existential of the human person,[127] the metaphysics of knowledge, and the transcendental and categorical experiences of the human subject. These different perspectives do not create different theologies: they offer a variety of interpretations of the Christology of Rahner.

Some Important Concepts Related to the Transcendental Christology of Karl Rahner

TRANSCENDENTAL EXPERIENCE

Definition of Transcendental Experience

This is the experience of transcendence,[128] the *a priori* openness of the human subject toward Being.[129] Transcendental experience is an experience not only of pure knowledge but of the will and freedom, which share the same character of transcendentality.[130] The "unthematic," "anonymous," and "nameless" knowledge of God is present in the transcendental experience.[131] The "experience of the transcendence of love," the "experience of the holy mystery," and "the original knowledge of God"[132] are synonymous with "the supernatural existential." Rahner discusses this in his treatment of "salvation history and revelation history as co-extensive with world history as a whole."[133] Thus, transcendental experience constitutes the very being of the human being.[134] In "Naturwissenschaft und vernünftiger Glaube,"[135] Rahner says that faith in creation by God is actually a transcendental experience of the fact that all being has its origin in absolute Being.[136]

Transcendental Experience of Nothing

Rahner's concept of the "transcendental experience of nothing" is important for his transcendental Christology. He explains this in *Hörer des Wortes,* where he analyzes the essence of being as spirit with *a priori* transcendental knowledge that there is no limit to the "whatness" of that which exists.[137] This *a priori* condition is the power of abstracting, which every human being possesses; and the power of abstracting is the power of knowing. Thus, every human being has an *a priori* capacity to know. In abstraction, the individual experiences his limitation. Rahner applies the term *Vorgriff* to this reaching out for "more." The anticipation is an *a priori* power given to human nature. As long as "the knowledge of the finality of the immediate given object of knowledge can be interpreted" from an affirmative knowledge and thus from an "anticipation," this affirmation is of being and not of nothing. This anticipation of something "more" is the sufficient condition for the possibility of negation, the transcendental experience of nothing of the object, and therefore "for knowledge of the direct, experiencing objective individual." The positive unlimitedness of the transcendental horizon of human knowledge shows per se the finality of that which lies beyond this horizon. *Vorgriff* is the transcendental condition of the self-subsistence of the human being. Here the "transcendental experience of the nothing of the objects" is the sufficient condition of the possibility of negation, the anticipation of something more. This anticipation of something more is an anticipation of God.[138] Thus, the human being experiences God through the transcendental experience of nothing, which is the human subject's anticipation of something more.

Transcendental Experience of the Spirit

Rahner asks whether we experience the spiritual in ourselves:

> Have we ever experienced the spiritual quality in the human being? (What is meant here by spirit is in itself a difficult question which can not be answered in one word.) We may perhaps answer: Of course I have had this experience and always have it every day. I think, I study, I decide, I act, I maintain relationships with other people, I live in a community, which is not based merely on biological, but on spiritual factors. I love, I am happy, I enjoy poetry. I possess cultural, scientific and artistic values. Thus I know what is spirit. But it is not so simple. All that is indeed true, but in all these things the spirit may be as it were nothing more than an ingredient which is used to make earthly life human, beautiful and somehow meaningful. The spirit in its actual transcendence needs to be experienced in all these. This does not mean that the spirit as such is present only when one speaks philosophically about its transcendence. The opposite is true! This may be only a derived, secondary experience of the spirit which is not the governing inner element in human life. Where then is the real experience? At this point we would like to affirm: we seek the spirit in our experience.[139]

In various human experiences, we seek the experience of the spirit, of eternity, of God.[140] Rahner interprets this as the experience of the supernatural, of the Holy Spirit, and of grace,[141] which is substantially identical to the experience of the transcendental in day-to-day experience.

Transcendental Experience as the Original Experience of Creatureliness

The original locus of the experience of creatureliness is the transcendental experience, in which the subject is experienced as sustained by the inconceivable ground of being. This is the Catholic understanding of God as absolute mystery[142] In discussing transcendental and *a priori* knowledge of God, Rahner points out that the transcendental experience is transmitted through the categorical experience of the concrete, worldly, temporal, special, and particular.[143] The concept of transcendental experience as the experience of creatureliness can be better understood in the context of Rahner's theology of creation as the self-communication of absolute mystery and transcendence: the experience of creatureliness is the experience of self-communicating transcendence in categorical mediation.[144]

Transcendental Experience as Experience of the Unlimited

The *a priori* structure of the human being is the essence of transcendental experience: experience of the unlimited, nameless, mystery which eludes all human control. This experience is the unlimited openness of the subject. God is the goal of transcendence and of transcendental experience.[145] Thus transcendental experience is ultimately the experience of God.

TRANSCENDENTAL REVELATION

Transcendental Revelation as Transcendental Experience

Rahner identifies the transcendental dimension of revelation with the supernatural "existential": it is revelation in the inner depth of human existence, viz., in its "self-subsistence" as self-presence, distinct from categorical revelation in history.[146] Transcendental revelation makes it possible for the human subject to know God in freedom. It is at the same time the openness of God to the person, thanks to God's universal salvific will,[147] which is the supernatural existential of the human being, constitutive of human existence; it is also the existential dimension and openness of the human being toward God.

The human being possesses a nonspecific, transcendental consciousness and an *a priori* capacity to know.[148] God's self-communication takes the form of an offer. The metaphysical knowledge of God, on the basis of the transcendentality of the human subject, is the finalization of the immediacy of God realized in the *a priori* consciousness. The awareness of the supernatural self-communication of God in the innermost depths of the human being, thanks to grace which is bestowed as the *a priori* transcendental consciousness, is the supernatural faith of transcendental revelation.[149]

In an essay on "the experience of the self and the experience of God,"[150] Rahner says that these are not identical; nevertheless, they are essentially linked by the fact that the God-experience takes place in the transcendental subject and makes self-experience possible; this is why no self-experience is possible without God-experience. Furthermore, the history of God-experience is the history of self-experience. One can also go in the other direction: that is, the history of self-experience is the history of God-experience. The transcendentality of the human being in knowledge and freedom, oriented toward absolute Being, aims at the ultimate basis of absolute love and responsibility[151] (which is at the same time the love of neighbor). Thus the history of the self-experience of the human being is important for the history of human experience of God.[152] This transcendental experience of the human being is the ground of transcendental revelation, to which the human person is open, and which God freely offers to everyone.[153]

Transcendental experience, as revelation, is called transcendental revelation, while historical revelation is categorical revelation.[154] The transcendental radicalization of the human being for the immediacy of God should be understood as revelation. This revelation is personal because it is given through the personal self-communication of God; it should be understood basically as a historical revelation because the transcendental experience of the human being is given in communication and unity with historical experience. The transcendental essence of God comes to the human being in the intercommunication and experience of the world in which the revelation takes place. This is why the history of revelation is the history of the transcendental experience of the human subject.[155]

Transcendental Revelation as the Capacity of Natural Mystics to Receive Revelation

In the context of his discussion of the transcendental openness of the human subject, existence, self-presence and self-presence to oneself alone as the metaphysical and ontological openness of the spirit toward the absolute Spirit who is God, Rahner affirms that this openness is a basic quality of the non-Christian natural mystics. The transcendental openness of the human subject is the divine transcendentality of the human being to receive revelation, and this must be distinguished from the categorical revelation of the Word, of the incarnated *Logos,* of the prophetic religions.[156]

In the first part of *Hörer des Wortes*, where Rahner poses the question of the human being as spirit and discusses "the openness of Being and the human being," this idea of transcendental revelation as the capacity of natural mystics to receive revelation is developed.[157] In the metaphysical sense, revelation is simply the free dealing of God, the speech of God, the silence of God, human transcendence toward the Absolute, and the opening of the hidden essence of God.[158] This is "a transcendental question because it concerns the *a priori* property of the essence of the questioning subject" which one should find in oneself and in history.[159] In this sense "history is the event of transcendence."[160] Categorical revelation is spoken revelation, the historical sign or expressed revelation of God. But transcendental revelation is the revelation of God in human experience itself, permitting categorical revelations to be understood. Transcendental revelation is revelation in human hearts.[161]

Transcendental Revelation as the Universal Salvific Will of God

Transcendental revelation is the universal salvific will of God, while categorical revelation is the concrete salvific will of God, corresponding to the salvific path taken by the individual.[162] Transcendental revelation is natural revelation, the real self-revelation and self-communication of God.[163] The transcendence of the human person is the space for the self-communication of God.

In his reflections on theological method,[164] Rahner states that the self-communication of God in grace is the transcendental existential of the human being. Thanks to the universal salvific will of God, this self-communication is available to every human being at least in the mode of offer. Salvation history and revelation history take place in the transcendental existential of the human being, that is, in the metaphysical essence of the human subject. Transcendental theology tries to understand, elaborate, and articulate this aspect of the self-communication of God in the human subject, in the individual, and in the community.[165] In his imaginary speech of St. Ignatius to a modern-day Jesuit,[166] Rahner deals with the theme of intrinsic experience: the intrinsic experience of the human subject and the experience of God in and through the world are a revelation and communication of God. The fullness of revelation occurs when the revelation of God becomes human in the incarnation.[167]

Transcendental Idea of Christ

The transcendental idea of Christ is a very important concept of Rahner's transcendental Christology. Those who experience the person of Jesus Christ as God can attain an idea of God coming into history; this descending Christology has its own meaning and power. It follows that an ascending and a descending Christology should be developed in tandem.[168] Catholic dogmatic statements about Jesus Christ are not the end but the beginning of this transcendental Christology. The idea of God-man is a universal and intrinsic way of understanding and expressing Christian doctrine about the person of Jesus Christ, God incarnate.[169]

Rahner speaks of an absolute savior in the context of human history as a single history, against the background of the philosophy of final cause.[170] God and the divine self-communication are the goal of the world and of humanity.[171] The self-transcendence of the world and of the cosmos is directed to this self-communication and its acceptance by the world. This self-communication is addressed to all spiritual creatures and subjects in the cosmos.[172] Rahner concludes that the "history of the cosmos" becoming self-conscious and the history of "cosmos" becoming itself are necessarily a history of the inner-communication of spiritual subjects.[173] God's revelation is a self-communication which can take place "only in a free acceptance by free subjects and indeed in a common history."[174] The notion of the historicity of God's self-communication in the general history of the intercommunication of human subjects leads to the idea of an absolute savior,[175] an idea coexistent with the entire spiritual history of the human race. Thus, the absolute savior is the climax of God's self-communication in the totality of human history.[176] This means not that this self-communication is concluded but that the fullness of time for God's self-communication is inaugurated, and the previous history of salvation is concluded.[177] God's self-communication is addressed to the cosmos, and the movement of the cosmos and the self-communication of God culminate in the absolute savior. The acceptance of the absolute savior by the world makes the idea of the absolute savior real.[178] In this context Rahner defends the Catholic dogma of hypostatic union and incarnation.[179]

One can deduce the existence of God from the fact that every human being (not only the mystic) has the experience of God.[180] Everyone experiences the unspeakable, the mystery; this also has a public social meaning.[181] The conceptual reflection and institutionalization of this experience are called religion.[182] In faithfulness, love, responsibility, and hope the human being lives this experience of God in his transcendentality.[183] It is not necessary to be a Christian in order to have such a deep God-experience.[184] In Christianity, the deep experience of God culminates in Jesus Christ.[185]

Human experience of the highest stage of self-transcendence can be understood as the self-communication of God.[186] "An *a priori* draft of the 'idea of Christ' as the objective correlative of the transcendental structure of the human being and his knowledge, even if it happens purely *a priori*, would leave the question undecided, where and in whom concretely this idea is a reality (and without the realization, this idea is of less existential meaning than all other ideas)."[187] This *a priori* idea of Christ necessarily implies the fact of incarnation: the human being, as the essence of transcendence and the essence of the earth, expects an absolute fulfillment in history and can therefore expect a free epiphany of God in history. Jesus Christ is this epiphany. Thus, the *a posteriori* dogma of Christ is correlative with the *a priori* idea of Christ.[188] Since the *a priori* idea of Christ is realized in Jesus Christ, there cannot be other realizations of this idea.[189]

Transcendental Openness

Transcendental Openness of the Human Being

The transcendental openness of the human subject is existential openness to the absolute spirit, *potentia oboedientialis,* "the capacity to hear" the word of God.[190] This transcendental openness is the prerequisite for hearing the revelation of God, which in turn is the basic principle of a metaphysical anthropology. The nature of the human subject is self-presence, luminosity of being. This is the original unity of knowing and being known. The human being is self-subsistence. The *Vorgriff* belongs to the essential nature of the human subject as spirit. This absolute openness of the human being to the absolute God, pure spirit, is transcendental openness. Since the transcendental openness of the human subject is constitutive of the *a priori* structure of the person, it leads to transcendental experience, to the conception of the transcendental idea of Christ and to the acceptance of the incarnated *Logos.* The transcendental openness of the human person toward God is the basic existential structure of the human person, something brought to consciousness by the experience of grace.

Transcendental Method

Rahner begins from human experience, so that his transcendental methodology is anthropological, with the question about being as its starting point.[191] Rahner begins with the affirmation that the human being exists as *Seinsfrage,* a question about Being.[192] This becomes a transcendental question and thus ontological, metaphysical, and anthropological.[193] Rahner's transcendental method answers the question by searching for the "transcendental" *a priori*, the transhistorical, the supernatural, the transcategorical or "existential" in the human subject. He calls his theological method "theological hermeneutics."[194]

Transcendental Reduction and Deduction

In the philosophy of Rahner, *a priori* is based not on empirical experience but on ontological experience. Rahner speaks of an *a priori* metaphysical knowledge. The ontological or anthropological *a priori* is based on metaphysical knowledge. This *a priori* is the *a priori* of the formal object. Rahner discerns the unity of the multiplicity of experiences in the *a priori* of the formal object;[195] this unity makes the transcendental reduction possible. Rahner hopes for a reduction of many dogmatic statements (without reducing their content) to basic mysteries of revelation in which the Christian substance of revelation could be made more clear, showing the transcendental foundation of this substance.[196]

In his considerations of the relation between nature and grace, the *a priori* nature of the human subject, the *a priori* understanding of Christ, transcendental experience of God, and so on,[197] Rahner refers to the method of transcendental deduction through which the human subject grasps these matters which are constitutive of human existence. This can be explained as the inference of the concealment of Being from each individual existent.[198] This transcendental deduction is not a factual objective deduction, but a deduction of the subjectivity of Being as self-presence,[199] from which Rahner ultimately deduces faith in Jesus Christ.[200] Rahner moves from the *a priori* to the corresponding *a posteriori.*[201] Is it possible to experience grace philosophically, without revelation? Rahner argues that if one infers transcendentality in order to establish the essence of the human being, this must be drawn from the existential experience of the human being. This in turn means that grace is constitutive of the existential nature of the human being.[202]

Is it then possible to attain faith in Jesus Christ through transcendental deduction? Rahner's answer is positive. One can believe in the Christ of Christian dogma through the transcendental deduction made by the capacity of knowing; this is possible through an obedient hearing of the message communicated in history, and this implies the necessity of the fact of Christ.[203] The *a priori* idea of Christ is correlative to the transcendental structure of the human being. This *a priori* Christology is realized in the person of Jesus Christ through the light of grace. Through the realization in history of this *a priori* idea of the person of Jesus Christ, the *a priori* becomes *a posteriori,* and thus hypostatic union and incarnation. The human being is the epiphany of God, and Jesus Christ is the epiphany of God in the perfect sense.[204]

Systematization of Concepts in Terms of Theology and Philosophy

After this analysis of the term "transcendental" and related terms and concepts, we move on to a systematization of these concepts. In order to understand Rahner's transcendental Christology, we must grasp the term "transcendental" and the concepts of transcendental nature and their systematization.

Rahner's philosophy is transcendental philosophy. Since he begins with human experience and an anthropological development of theological themes, there is a transcendental anthropology in his thought.

His primary concern is to experience and to articulate the Being of being beyond physical and categorical reality; this is why his theology is called transcendental theology. It is impossible to study Rahner's philosophy without studying his theology, his theology without his anthropology, his anthropology without his soteriology. The entire thought of Rahner must be interpreted in the light of his philosophy, theology, anthropology, soteriology, and Christology.

Transcendental Philosophy

Rahner's central theme in *Geist in Welt*, *Hörer des Wortes*, *Grundkurs des Glaubens,* and many of his writings in *Schriften zur Theologie* is the transcendental question of the human subject vis-à-vis God. The human being possesses transcendental experience and transcendental reflection, and has the capacity to know the *a priori* of the human subject. This transcendental philosophical question is a metaphysical and therefore a theological question. In the strict sense of the term, Rahner wrote only one philosophical work, viz., his dissertation, *Geist in Welt;* his next book, *Hörer des Wortes,* is a theological treatment of the philosophy of the first book.

Rahner's transcendental philosophy is a metaphysics of knowledge, the capacity of the intellect for the natural knowledge of God. Transcendental philosophy is metaphysics in the strict sense of the word, the conceptualization of transcendental experience.[205] In support of this, he points out that the transcendental philosophy of the human being takes place only in historical experience as an element in human history.[206] Rahner's transcendental philosophy is an interpretation of the human quest for transcendence: it embraces both the realization of this quest and the theoretical and the practical conditions that make this possible.

Rahner's transcendental philosophy presupposes Kant's critical question about human knowledge,[207] Maréchal's interpretation of Aquinas in the light of the transcendental philosophy of Kant, and Heidegger's ontological and transcendental interpretation of Kant's transcendental idealism. Rahner's transcendental philosophy can be called a transcendental, anthropological and metaphysical existentialism.[208]

Heidegger considers any discussion about God to be the work of a theologian and holds that his task as a philosopher is to remain within the boundary of "existential" empirical reality. Rahner employs Heidegger's own terminology to go beyond him, locating the transcendental in the categorical, the unlimited in the limited, the eternal in the peripheral, the nameless in the names, the universal in the particular, and God-experience in self-experience. The implicit acknowledgment of the absolute through Heidegger's language of "being" becomes in Rahner an explicit profession and proclamation which brings philosophy to fulfillment in the climactic experience of the Absolute in the phenomenological, anthropological, and categorical status of the human being as "self-present." This makes Rahner's transcendentalism theological, in contrast to the idealism of Kant, and existentialist in contrast to the theological transcendentalism of Maréchal. It is anthropological and realistic in contrast to the phenomenological, existential, anthropological transcendentalism of Heidegger.

Transcendental Theology

Transcendental revelation, the transcendental self-communication of God in grace, the transcendental moment of revelation, the transcendental experience of the human subject as the essence of transcendence, transcendental faith, transcendental reflection, the supernatural existential of the human person as the transcendentality of the human nature, the transcendental idea of an absolute savior, the transcendental presence of God, transcendental consciousness: these are some of the foundational concepts of a transcendental theology[209] which is the extension of transcendental philosophy.[210]

Transcendental theology deals with particular themes of theology (for example, the concept of God, Christ, grace) under a particular aspect. It is systematic theology using the method of transcendental philosophy, which is not determined by one specific historical background. It draws on transcendental philosophy to conceptualize the "*a priori* conditions in a believing subject" for knowledge of the important truths of faith.[211] This is why Rahner does not see transcendental philosophy and transcendental theology as separate entities, but views them as a single entity and an analogous concept. Transcendental philosophy is the "inner moment," "instrument," and original essence of transcendental theology. Transcendental philosophy is metaphysics. Transcendental theology should be understood as "transcendental philosophical theology."

The transcendental philosophy of human existence takes place within historical experience.[212] Transcendental theology can make comprehensible the historical events of salvation and revelation,[213] because the transcendental knowledge of God and the transcendental method make clear the relationship between God and the world. Transcendental philosophy "conceptualizes the genuine theological questions of the *a priori* conditions in the believing subject for the knowledge of the truths of faith."[214] The nature of the human being, as the condition for the possibility for grace, belongs to theology.[215] The transcendental is implied in every analysis of faith and in the concept of the capacity to hear revelation and to receive grace.[216]

Transcendental theology makes trinitarian doctrine meaningful because transcendental reduction shows that the revealed self-communication of God is present to the human being as history and transcendence. Rahner defends the identity of immanent Trinity and economical Trinity.[217] A transcendental Christology from below presupposes a transcendental theology. Transcendental deduction of the idea of the absolute savior leads us to the historical person of Jesus Christ.[218] Transcendental Christology develops the transcendental idea of an absolute savior as the culmination of God's self-communication, realized historically in the person of Jesus Christ. Without transcendental Christology, the concept of Christ as absolute savior would be a mythological idea.[219]

Transcendental Anthropology

Dogmatic theology today must be theological anthropology: this change in perspective is both necessary and fruitful.[220]

> As soon as the human being is conceived as the essence of absolute transcendence towards God, the anthropocentrism and theocentrism of theology are no contradictory perspectives, but one and the same in the strict sense (expressed from two sides respectively). None of these two aspects can be understood without the other. The anthropocentrism of theology is no contradiction to the theocentrism[221] of theology.[222]

Anthropology and Christology serve each other, if both are correctly understood.

Dogmatic theology must be developed as a transcendental anthropology[223] which begins with the transcendental question of the condition of the possibility of knowledge or action in the human subject.[224] Theological statements must be based in the *a priori* structure of the human subject. The objective basis of the *a posteriori* known historical object is the theological *a priori* of the subject.[225] In order to liberate Christology from monophysitism and mythology, dogmatic theology and Christology should be carried out as theological anthropology.[226]

The "supernatural existential" of human beings allows us to do theology by engaging in anthropology—but we can do anthropology only by engaging in theology, speaking about God on the basis of God.[227]

Rahner is disturbed by a tendency in the natural sciences and biological anthropology to lower human beings to the status of animals; his response is to defend human dignity by means of his theological anthropology. We do not find in animals this transcendentality of the human subject.[228] The human being is spirit, the absolute openness which is called the transcendentality of the human being.[229]

Transcendental Hermeneutics

In *Geist in Welt* and *Hörer des Wortes,* Rahner interprets Christian faith and dogma with the help of a transcendental hermeneutics reminiscent of Kant, Dilthey, and Heidegger. Since he identifies theological hermeneutics with theological method, this means that transcendental hermeneutics is the transcendental method of Rahner. But theological method as such never plays a prominent role in Rahner.[230] Theological hermeneutics is a necessary theme within theology.[231]

Transcendental Christology

Christology in keeping with transcendental revelation is "transcendental Christology," which is "essentially" and "existentially" "ontological" or "existentially onto-anthropological"[232] and makes Christ and Christian revelation meaningful for the whole of humanity. Rahner considers the traditional classical Christology with its history of two thousand years as important, and a basis for any contemporary Christology.[233] Classical Christology uses a model of descent, an "incarnation Christology" whereby the *Logos* takes on human nature. But this incarnation Christology and Christology of descent do not satisfactorily explain the context of the incarnated *Logos* and his saving function, since they speak of an abstract human nature. There is very little fundamental theological Christology in traditional incarnational theology and Christology.[234]

The words "transcendental" and "anthropological" signify related concepts; it is on this basis that Rahner speaks of a "transcendental theological anthropology" and a "transcendental anthropological dimension of theology."[235] Transcendental Christology can also be called metaphysical Christology, *a priori,* anthropological, ontological, existential, supernatural, transcategorical Christology, and so on. But the most comprehensive term is "transcendental" Christian theology, which is essential, existential, ontological, transcendental theology. It should outline an *a priori* doctrine of "God-man" within a general ontology and anthropology. This is an attempt to define what makes possible a genuine capacity to hear the historical message of Jesus the Christ and the necessity of hearing this message.[236] To call transcendental Christology an *a priori* doctrine of the "God-man" does not mean that it is constructed *prior* to the historical encounter with Jesus Christ.[237] Transcendental Christology, as an *a priori* human potential for understanding the dogma of Christ, depends on the historical event of Jesus as Christ.[238]

Transcendental Christology is necessary in order to give a foundation to an *a posteriori* Christology and save traditional Christology from being considered mythology.[239] It is developed on the basis of a transcendental anthropology and the transcendental experience of the human subject.[240]

Transcendental philosophy, theology, anthropology, and hermeneutics encounter the person of Jesus Christ transcendentally and categorically as the culmination of their endeavor. From Rahner's philosophical perspective, the question of the philosophy of religion as a science is a question about metaphysics and its constituents. The question is therefore why we cannot refrain from turning to metaphysics.[241] General ontology, transcendental anthropology, religious philosophical anthropology, metaphysical anthropology, transcendental ontology of the human subject, and so on are other approaches to the same goal. In short, the different discussions in Rahner under different terminologies and under different branches of sciences refer to a single thought pattern which displays coherence and unity in development. The discussion centers on the supernatural existential of the human individual transcending and reaching out toward the Absolute, whose ultimate revelation is the fullness of transcendence, the incarnated *Logos*. "Christology is the end and the beginning of anthropology, and this anthropology, in its radical realization, viz. christology, is theology."[242]

The Transcendental Christology of Rahner in Relation to Other Christological Disciplines

According to Rahner, the philosophy of religion and theology are based on and united to each other in metaphysical anthropology or general ontology, so that ultimately, philosophy of religion and theology are metaphysics. Fundamental theology is understood as the *potentia oboedientialis* for hearing God's free revelation through natural revelation, historical experience, and human concepts and words. It is in this context that we must understand Rahner's transcendental Christology. Thanks to its christocentrism, transcendental Christology includes the trinitarian and eschatological dimensions of theology.

Transcendental Christology and Consciousness Christology

If there is an "ontic Christology," there can be also an "existential Christology" in the categories of consciousness, in which we ask whether the radical understanding of the statements of the Lord about his spiritual relationship with God the Father as "existential statements" could be equivalent to an ontic Christology.[243]

Biblical theology is and should be the source of dogmatic theology and Christology, which otherwise will be "sterile."[244] In the light of *Humani Generis,* Rahner asks whether the Chalcedonian dogma and scholastic Christology, although "obviously true and important to the extent that they are dogma," are the exhaustive "condensation" and "summary" of everything we have heard and could hear about Jesus Christ.[245] One who answered this question in the affirmative would in effect be denying that scripture is the inexhaustible source of truth about Christ. Rahner asks whether "scriptural assertions" about Jesus as Messiah and Lord are formulations devised to defend the uniqueness of Jesus against possible criticisms from the Jews, and whether the Christology from below of the Acts of the Apostles, which begins from human experience of Jesus, is primitive and may have something to tell us that classical Christology does not express with the same clarity. The Letter to the Philippians does not express the idea of incarnation in the Chalcedonian sense; a Christology that failed to see this would become mythology. In this sense, biblical theology has something to contribute to classical theology.[246] Whereas scholastic Christology was content merely to present a few biblical texts in defense of the dogma of Ephesus and Chalcedon, the question now is whether it is possible to construct a Christology in terms of Christ's consciousness.[247] Rahner's consciousness Christology is his transcendental Christology: he believes that the dogmatic affirmations of transcendental Christology, consciousness Christology, categorical Christology, and biblical Christology agree with one other.

Transcendental Christology and Anthropological Christology

The central theme of Christian theology is the final and definitive self-communication of God in Jesus of Nazareth, who reveals both who God is for us, and who we are before God. Anthropological theology and its transcendental concerns deal with the starting point of this incarnation in human existence. Such a question is absolutely necessary for Rahner, if he is to salvage the Christian message from merely mythological concepts of a god disguised in human form. This is why his transcendental hermeneutics lays the foundation for his transcendental Christology, a systematic Christology in the pure sense.[248] Systematic theology must be a transcendental anthropology which deals with the transcendental anthropological question.[249] Theological anthropology understands the human being as person and subject.[250] As person and subject, the human being experiences the essence of transcendence and an *a priori* openness toward absolute Being, with responsibility and a freedom that may be called transcendental freedom.[251] "Spiritual creatures" enter into relationship with God in a special way "as *persona* of transcendence and freedom." This means that Christology "can be studied as self-transcending anthropology" and anthropology as "deficient Christology." Christology is the "primordial conception" of anthropology and the "doctrine of creation."[252] The evolution of the world is an evolution into Christ, a gradual ascent with Christ as the summit and the point at which God "becomes all in all." This evolution of the world into Christ as summit is essentially christological, not abstractly metaphysical, "because God became in Christ really world and so all in all."[253] Rahner sees the essence of the human being in its transcendentality as spirit.[254] The self-experience of the human being is a transcendental religious experience.[255] Thus, in order to understand the meaning of concepts such as God, Christ, and prayer, one should be aware of transcendental self-experience.[256] The self-communication of God is ultimately constitutive of the essence of the human being.[257] The supernatural dimension of the human being belongs to the very essence of its existence.[258] Thus, the starting point of Christology is theological or metaphysical anthropology. The human being's subjectivity as spirit and freedom enable him to become God's partner in a pure dialogical relationship and by participation in the divine nature.[259]

There is an individual and a collective history of the transcendental revelation and the self-communication of God; both histories culminate in the person of Jesus Christ.[260] Through this concept Rahner overcomes the opposition between ontic Christology and consciousness Christology. These are one and the same, viz., an onto-logical Christology. At the same time, Christology is theological anthropology and transcendental Christology is transcendental anthropology. In the incarnation, the humanity of Christ is not merely an "instrument" through which the unseen God becomes visible; rather, in the incarnation God really becomes a human being, God becomes the other.[261] This is why Christology is the criterion of anthropology; Christology and anthropology constitute a single discipline.[262]

The essential and descending Christology is developed in the framework of transcendental anthropology. The predicate of the proposition "God became a human being" shows us what the subject, viz., "God," means. God is the incomprehensible abyss. This God is a historical possibility of "being for us." God himself became a human being and he remains so in eternity. Therefore theology remains anthropology. The human being is the eternal mystery of God. "Because it is the unity of the real essence of God and of the human being in the personal self-expression of God in his eternal Logos, christology is the beginning and end of anthropology and this anthropology in its most radical realization is in eternity theology."[263]

Transcendental Christology and Existential Christology

Christianity is no abstract theory, but rather an objective reality that understands itself in an existential process which we call a personal relationship with Jesus Christ. This is why an existential Christology is necessary.[264]

We must first note that there is an "anonymous Christianity." Individuals without a concrete experience of the Word and the sacraments can have an anonymous but genuine relationship to salvation history and thus also to Jesus Christ. This relationship is implicit and existential, thanks to the obedience they display to the absolute God in the self-communication realized in history, in which a human person accepts his own being. There is a parallel between what is achieved in an individual through baptism, membership in the church, sacraments, personal relationship with Christ, and "faith, hope, and love," and what is achieved through God's free offer of his self-communication (thanks to the "supernatural existential" of the human subject) through individual religious experience in openness, faithfulness, and patience: both these evolve into an experience of the fullness of God's self-communication.[265] The latter is anonymous existential Christology.[266] But this term is not limited only to this anonymous religious experience. Existential Christology takes into consideration the anonymous implicit existential religious experience on which dogmatic Christology is based and which is verified by dogmatic Christology.

The apostles had the original experience of Jesus as Christ, the living encounter between God and the world. What they handed on is the reflection, articulation, and explication of the original experience in language. In the later apostolic period, theological reflection on the "implicit" and "explicit" meanings of their words made further development of dogma possible.[267] This understanding of the apostolic tradition lets us grasp the necessity of an existential Christology. Life shared with the Lord was the original revelation on which the apostles reflected; this is why an existential Christology should coexist with a traditional and biblical Christology.[268]

Thus, the existential Christology of Rahner is his transcendental Christology, which supports and defends the validity of both dogmatic and biblical Christology. It is a searching (*suchende*) Christology, because it deals with the implicit act of faith searching for its object of faith (Jesus Christ) and is oriented toward this object of faith.

Transcendental Christology and Official Church Christology

Rahner never intended to posit his transcendental Christology as a parallel to official church Christology. On the contrary, he wanted to pursue his theological investigations within the context of the official teachings of the church, in order to support and defend these. At the same time, his theology displays a philosophical, theological, and natural openness to the world and to the natural sciences. Rahner asks, "Why do Christians who are conscious of the contradiction between their conceptions and the official teachings of the Church remain in the Church?"[269] His work on the publication of all church dogmas and the most important church declarations (Neuner-Roos) shows his commitment to the official teachings of the magisterium.

Although Rahner says that the christological formula of Chalcedon is not the end but the beginning of Christology, he does not mean that dogmatic theology should have its beginning in this formula; rather, as the Second Vatican Council says, Christology should remain biblical theology.[270] The theological formulations of the magisterium are the outcome of centuries of work, praying, thinking, and struggling about God's mysteries. They are the beginning, not the end; a means, not the goal; a truth that makes free for the greater truth. If we do consider this clear formulation to be as an end, viz., in order to preserve the truth from error, this end can also be a beginning.[271] Every formula transcends itself precisely as it becomes a formula.

Official church Christology is basically a descending or incarnation Christology which affirms that "God became a human being" and employs the concept of substantial unity and hypostatic union between the *Logos* and human nature.[272] Transcendental Christology as metaphysical, anthropological, and existential Christology provides a theoretical basis for a descending Christology based on faith in Jesus Christ as God and savior. An ascending Christology based on the experience of the life, work, death, and resurrection of Jesus can also find support in a transcendental Christology based on human experience, intelligibility, existence as a knowing subject, and transcendence. Thanks to his understanding of the unity of transcendental and categorical Christology, Rahner's concept of incarnation—God becoming a human being, God becoming world, the self-utterance of God, self-transcendence and self-communication—in no way contradicts the magisterium, provided that these concepts are understood in the framework of Rahner's own theology; it is equally true that we have to understand the dogmas in their own context, without denying their universal significance. Therefore the statement that "the confession of the Council of Chalcedon (451 C.E.) of the hypostatic union of the two natures in the person of Jesus Christ is the reference point for every christology"[273] does justice both to the official position of the Catholic Church and to the need of Rahner's own time for new interpretations of the dogma.

The Chalcedonian formula was made according to the needs of the time. It was formulated to overcome the problems raised by the heresies of the *Logos-sarx* schema, Apollinaris, and Sergius of Constantinople. Rahner suggests a transcendental Christology as a bulwark against considering the theory of the incarnation as mythology. This will also present the Christian faith as something reasonable to natural scientists, agnostics and atheists, and to believers of non-Christian religions.

Rahner's "christocentric" or transcendental christological understanding eliminates any contradiction between his transcendental Christology and that of the magisterium. The church is the "irrevocable victory of the self-communication of God,"[274] his eschatological self-communication to the world in Jesus Christ.[275] It is a community of believers. Therefore, the church as community and society has (and needs) an authority and an institution.[276] This understanding in Rahner's transcendental theology of the existential relationship between the experience of the self-communication of God in Jesus Christ and the teaching authority of the church makes possible the complementarity of his Christology and that of the magisterium. In reply to Cardinal Ottaviani, who objected that new thought patterns in Christology employed concepts alien to Christian dogma, leading to a Christian humanism,[277] Rahner says that the use of such terminology never underestimates the teaching authority of the church and never communicates relativism. Rather, it interprets the existing truth anew, since modern concepts are necessary for a new christological confession.[278]

Transcendental Christology and Categorical Christology

Categorical Christology is the historical interpretation, display, or realization of transcendental Christology, which is neither an ideology nor an idealistic presentation of the Christian faith, but a theoretical foundation and philosophical validation of it. The categorical history of revelation is the historical mediation of the transcendental supernatural experience of God which occurs in human history.[279] Rahner argues that God intends an explicit religious categorical revelation as the history of transcendental revelation.[280] This categorical revelation in history need not be only the history of salvation in Old and New Testaments. The historical display of the transcendental and supernatural experience of God is categorical revelation.[281] Transcendental revelation is always mediated in history, because the transcendentality of human beings has a history.[282] There is a historical realization and mediation of God's self-communication in transcendental revelation,[283] with Jesus Christ as the climax.[284] Thus transcendentality and historicity require each other.[285]

Rahner's transcendental Christology is not totally independent of other approaches to Christology, which it complements and qualifies: it legitimates, defends, theoretically validates, and necessarily promotes Christology in all its forms. It comprehends all other natural and supernatural sciences within the science of transcendental Christology itself and presents itself as the culmination and fulfillment of all such sciences. Transcendental Christology is the climax of all "evolution" and "involution." Jesus Christ is *alpha, omega,* and *pleroma.*[286]

Transcendental Christology of Karl Rahner with Special Reference to His Concept of Incarnation: Relevance to Current Christological Discussion

THE INCARNATION AS THE CLIMAX OF GOD'S SELF-COMMUNICATION AND AS HYPOSTATIC UNION

The incarnation is the self-communication of God in Christ. It is valid for all human beings, expressing the fact that all human reality belongs absolutely to God.[287] Jesus Christ is the decisive "existential" of human beings; in other words, he is the Christian answer to the question of human meaning.[288] The self-communication of God is to be understood not in the sense of "Word revelation" but in the sense of the communication of Being, the communication of the life of God. The final revelation of God is a "unique becoming" to which there corresponds a very precise *a priori,* viz., revelation and grace.[289] The revelation of the word of God in history has its climax in Jesus Christ, the Father's Word made flesh.[290] Rahner's theology of God's self-communication is his greatest achievement.[291]

The incarnation is the hypostatic union, that is, the union of the divine and human natures in one person:[292] Jesus is truly God and truly a human being. Rahner summarizes this doctrine of the incarnation, as it has been declared by the magisterium, in "Grundlinien einer systematischen Christologie."[293]

Descending Christology teaches the cosmic and the transcendental meaning of the incarnation:[294] the *Logos* which created the world becomes a human being. This means that incarnation is the climax of the relation of the *Logos* of God to the world. Creation is the moment of the self-revelation, self-expression, and self-communication of God.[295] The incarnation is the historical climax of the transcendental free relation of God to that which is not God, a relationship which is cosmological, existential-ontological, and eschatological.[296] This self-communication of God is his self-offer, self-expression, and self-utterance to the human person.[297] The incarnation is the self-expression of God in and to a historical reality capable of grasping it.[298] In the incarnation, the power of the mercy of God and his self-expression were realized in the freedom of the human being.[299] In the self-expression of God, the Word of God is addressed with love to that empty nothingness which is devoid of God. Thus, the *Logos* who became a human being is the abbreviated Word of God and the human being is the abbreviated cipher of God.[300]

The Incarnation as an Actualization of Human Reality

In his discussion of the analogy of being in *Hörer des Wortes,* where he treats of the ontology of the human subject and the possibility of revelation of the absolute God, Rahner tries to establish philosophically the innate possibility of the human subject to be open to the absolute and to absolute revelation in the self-presence of the existent. In the light of the Thomistic ontology of being and knowledge, Rahner concludes that being is the "self-presence" of the existent. In his interpretation[301] the formulation of the concept has an analogous character: since the concept of being is analogous, the meaning of being as "self-presence" is also analogous. "All deeds and dealings from the merely material to the inner life of the trinitarian God are only modifications of the one metaphysical theme of the meaning of being."[302] Aquinas understands in an analogous manner the essence of being as "self-presence" and of being as knowing. Each existent is not "knowing" or "true" in the same sense or measure; nor is every existent in the mode of absolute identity, so that it is not the inner element of the knowledge of absolute consciousness. Only pure being is absolute identity and knowing, in which we realize what is meant by the concept of being. In this case of the absolute identity of "being" and "knowing" in a pure being, in absolute being, there are no more questions to be asked.[303] The transcendental consciousness of the human being is a need to ask questions about being. It shows the finality of its spirit and the "basic comprehension" of its being as self-presence, the original unity of knowing and being known. This concept of the human being as "self-presence" is the starting point of all the questions about the ontology of the human subject in relation to a potential revelation by God.[304] "The ultimate unity of being and knowing is the ultimate presupposition of the communication of God in his 'divinity' to the human being through speech and through the Word. Only if the being of the existent is *a priori logos* can the Word made flesh give utterance in the word to that which remains hidden in the depths of the Godhead."[305] Jesus is the absolute presence of God in the world.

Rahner explains incarnation as the fullness of the mystery which is the human being, and as the highest enactment or actualization of the essence of human reality.[306] The *potentia oboedientialis* for the hypostatic union is the acceptance of human nature through the Person of the Word of God. In this concept the *potentia* is identical with the essence of the human being. Since this is based on ontology, there is no room here for the mythological impression made by traditional Christology.[307] God accepted that human nature which is essentially open to God.[308] The eternal *Logos* himself accepted human nature through incarnation. Seen from this perspective, the incarnation is the highest single instance of the actualization of the essence of human reality.[309] Human nature is the "common element" in us and in the incarnated logos; the difference is that the incarnated logos is the self-expression of God. The incarnated logos liberates the content of our essence and our history and opens it up to the freedom of God.[310] This is not a consciousness Christology in opposition to an ontological Christology of the substantial unity of the *Logos* with human nature, but an ontology constructed on the metaphysical vision in order to understand incarnation better, and to avoid any mythological impression that God merely assumed a human form but did not genuinely become a human being.[311] The "becoming of God" is real; it is the self-expression of God, a primordial possibility, not a necessity.[312] Theology is anthropology because God became a human being. "Christology is the end and the beginning of anthropology and this anthropology, in its radical realisation, viz. in christology, is theology."[313]

The Incarnation as the Climax of Creation

Rahner believes in a single incarnation as the climax of creation and as a descending historical event that happened for the sake of the entire future with its cosmic, moral, religious, and eschatological dimensions.[314] The christocentrism of creation and the development of the world toward Christ are basic concepts in Rahner. God is not only the efficient cause of creation. The Word of God who became human is the one who begins (and who can begin) a human history. This world is not only a work distinct from him: it becomes his own reality.[315] As infinite fullness, he creates by emptying himself, and therefore he himself is there in this emptying.

Interpreting Col. 1:15, Rahner says that it is wonderful to see the development of the world toward Christ.[316] Statements about Jesus Christ as general statements about a theological ontology can be made with the help of a general ontological theory of creation. Christology will help to maintain parallel ontological and anthropological statements, by which we attain a philosophical knowledge of God and of the world.[317] God can be known on the basis of the world, and we can say what the world is on the basis of God.[318]

Rahner understands incarnation to mean that the logos who created the world becomes a human being. Thus creation makes possible the self-revelation, self-expression, and self-communication of God. Human beings are to be understood existentially, ontologically, and cosmologically as God's self-expression, which reaches its climax in the person of Jesus Christ.[319]

The Incarnation as the Climax of Human Possibility

The incarnation is the climax and fulfillment of the human reality of being.[320] There exists a natural absolute openness of the human being to God.[321] God expresses himself in the emptiness of the nondivine: God engages in theology outside his own self, and the result is an anthropology that finds its self-expression in the incarnation. For this theology, anthropology is the pre-established vocabulary. God makes this grammar of his self-expression out of nothing and this nothing is God himself.[322] Rahner does not derive Christology from anthropology, but he asks what anthropological correspondence is there to this theological profession of faith. If God communicated himself to humanity in a unique way in Jesus of Nazareth, then there must be some connecting point in humanity through which God can communicate himself completely in a human being. This connecting point in each human being is bestowed by God and awaits fulfillment through God.

Rahner gives the following definition of the concept of incarnation: "If a human being now receives his essence from God in absolute purity and radicality and actualizes it, such that God genuinely allows this human being to become the self-expression of God and of God's irrevocable self-expression to the world, then that which we call 'incarnation' exists in a believable sense."[323] In Jesus Christ, God has made the human face his own, opening himself definitively and directly to the reality of a human being and establishing the real possibility for all human beings to have immediate communion with God.[324] Human existence is an unlimited and undetermined openness, to which meaning must be imparted by the specific realities of history; the history of Jesus can be understood as the fullest actualization of that meaning and the fulfillment of the human potential for self-transcendence.[325]

In order to understand Rahner's concept of the fullness of humanity as the fullness of divinity which only Jesus Christ has realized, we should examine his idea of humanity, i.e. the concept of human dignity. Rahner refers to the metaphysical understanding of the nature of the human being, that is, a knowledge of that which is essential.[326] Rahner expresses this in two ways, viz., through the transcendental methodology and through reflection on the human being's historical self-experience. The transcendental method is in the strict sense "the metaphysical aspect of the knowledge of the human being about himself," and belongs to the necessary metaphysical nature of the human being. Reflection on the human person's historical self-experience permits one to know the metaphysical possibilities of the human person as a free being.[327] Human beings are created in such a way that they are open to a total fulfillment by God, as happened in the case of Jesus of Nazareth. Second, God creates human beings in such a way that God can reveal himself fully and totally in a human being; God can become a human being, and a human being can realize and acknowledge this in his history. God could have created the world without the incarnation, since the self-transcendence of the world toward God could be possible without incarnation.[328]

"In Christ, the *Logos* did not merely become (statically) a human being, he accepted a human history. But this is a part of an entire history of the world and of humanity before and after it and indeed the fullness of that history and its end."[329] Rahner reaches this conclusion not via the Chalcedonian formula but theologically, historically, and philosophically. To be human means to be open to the absolute. The reality of the highest stage of being human comes when the *Logos* of God enters the world and becomes a human being.[330] The existence of the human being with his unlimitedness shows that to be human means to have the existence of God in the world.[331] Because God himself became a human being,[332] "Christian anthropology reaches its original meaning only when the human being is understood as the *potentia oboedientialis* for hypostatic union."[333] If we wish to elaborate a Christology that will establish the hypostatic union free of any suspicion of mythology, the only basis is this kind of transcendental anthropology.[334]

The Incarnation as Self-Transcendence

Christmas reveals the mysterious and holy meaning of the transcendence of the Spirit of God.[335] The incarnation of the divine *Logos* is not to be understood as the attaching of a foreign element to the spirit of the human being[336] or as an accidental foreign element in the world. Such misunderstandings are possible if spirit is not considered as the goal of matter.[337] Rahner defends the relation between matter and spirit, the unity of the world, natural history, and human history.[338] The unity of matter and spirit is evident for Christian philosophy and theology.[339] We should try to understand the human being as the existent in whom "the basic tendency of self-realization of matter into spirit comes to its definitive break-through in self-transcendence, so that the essence of the human being itself can be seen inside the entire conception of the world."[340] Thanks to his free, God-given, full self-transcendence in God, and thanks to God's self-communication, the human person can look to the fulfillment of his own self and of the world.

> The first step, the permanent beginning and the absolute guarantee, that this ultimate self-transcendence, which is fundamentally unsurpassable, has happened and already begun, is what we call the hypostatic union. It is not to be seen primarily as something which makes a distinction between us and Jesus as the Lord, but rather as something that must occur once and only once, when the world begins its last phase, in which it is called and realizes its final concentration, its final climax and its radical nearness to the absolute mystery, God. From this perspective, incarnation seems to be the necessary, permanent beginning of the divinization of the world as a whole.[341]

Both the status of the human being as the self-transcendence of matter[342] and the mutuality of matter and spirit show the unity of the human being,[343] in whom we experience matter and spirit. To be a Christian is the fulfillment of the entire reality of the human person and of the cosmos.[344] At the same time, this self-transcendence is "a transcendence into something substantially new,"[345] just as procreation is not only a biological happening but also a co-activity with God. There is a unity of the history of the world and the history of humanity, natural history, and human history, and the history of the spirit (revelation).[346]

The self-transcendence of the cosmos in the human being has its own history of the self-communication of God,[347] which is the goal of the world. The history of the self-communication of the cosmos is necessarily the history of the intercommunication of these spiritual subjects, and God's self-communication imparts freedom and intercommunication in the plural cosmic subjectivity.[348] In the incarnation, the *Logos* becomes matter, the Word becomes flesh. This is the climax of the unity of the spirit and matter, the full self-communication of the cosmos and of the history of the cosmos. In the incarnation, spirit is fully realized in matter. The incarnation is the special realization of the spirit in time, through the free self-communication of God and through the free acceptance on the part of the cosmos in natural human and spiritual history. It is the climax of the self-transcendence of the world, when God becomes concretely part of the history of the cosmos, part of the cosmos as its climax.[349]

> Jesus is truly a human being, truly a piece of the earth, truly an element of the biological becoming of the world and of human natural history, for he is born from a woman; he is a human being, who in his spiritual, human and final subjectivity is (like ourselves) one who receives the graced self-communication of God, which we predicate applies to all people and therefore to the cosmos. He is the climax of that development in which the world comes to itself absolutely, and comes absolutely to the immediacy of God.[350]

The concept of the savior fulfills the history of the cosmos. The idea of the hypostatic union of God and human beings is implicit when world history is understood as the history of self-transcendence into the life of God.[351] The savior is a historical personality in time and space; he is the absolute self-communication of God and is coexistent with the entire history of humanity and the world, a spiritual subjectivity, the highest point of human history, in the temporal and special plurality of human history.[352]

> That this event of the final self-transcendence of the human being towards God has taken place in the most radical self-communication of God precisely in Jesus of Nazareth, cannot be deduced in a transcendental christology, which understands the idea of God-man as the climax and intersection of the final self-transcendence of the world towards God and of the radical self-communication of God to the world (both in history), does not point in any other direction: it is nothing other than the historical experience of the crucified and risen Jesus, an experience, that as such cannot be communicated any further. It does not alter the fact that an evolutionary world-view can think of the idea of incarnation as the asymptotic goal of the development of the world towards God, provided only that such a world vision understands the self-transcendence of the world in the power of God and the immanence of God in the world in such a radical manner that this self-transcendence comes to the end at the point where it receives the self-communication of God as the irrevocable climax of the dynamic immanence of God.[353]

With regard to the self-transcendence of the human subject in the incarnation, Jesus Christ is the perfect human being.[354]

Credibility of the Christ-Event

Rahner makes a transcendental deduction of the credibility of Christ's incarnation.[355] The fact that some persons cannot assimilate the dogma of incarnation does not minimize the importance of the formula.[356] Rahner argues from the perspective of the metaphysics of the knowledge of the subject. There exists a transcendental idea of Christ in the transcendental structure of the human being and in his knowledge. Without a concrete realization of this transcendental idea of Christ, this idea remains less existentially important than all other ideas. The *a priori* Christology takes place "in the illuminating light of the grace of the real Christ." This *a priori* schema actualizes itself *a posteriori*.[357] We must ask not only about the knowability of the object but also about the property of the subject and its specific openness to this object. The transcendental deduction of the capacity of the subject to know this object[358] makes the dogma of the incarnation credible.

The birth of Jesus was a human birth.[359] Jesus was a human being like us. To experience Jesus, we must experience human beings, we must experience ourselves.[360] Jesus had a human consciousness distinct from the consciousness of the *Logos* of God, prompting him to call God his father and to be obedient until death.[361]

God took on human nature without any change in his divine nature; thus no monophysitism is involved here. The incarnation is the descending of the eternal Son of the Father from the eternal preexistent glory into the world, into history.[362] At the same time, there is no duality in the person of Jesus Christ. The divine consciousness is present in the human consciousness, in the hypostatic union. According to Rahner, one person with two natures is a philosophical and logical possibility. His transcendental deduction of Christian faith (in the Kantian sense) makes it clear why human beings can believe in the Christ of Christian dogma.[363]

Only One Incarnation

It is only after the incarnation, death, and resurrection of Jesus Christ that the opening of the world to God is revealed explicitly and becomes an irrevocable, historically tangible date in the history of salvation. The love of God revealed in the incarnation also has a cosmic character, and is eschatological.[364]

> But unfortunately, not every dogmatic theology affirms that the religious act always and in every case, if it wants to reach God, has and must have exactly this incarnational structure, subjectively parallel to the objective condition; viz. that God has communicated himself to the world in the one who became a human being, and that this one therefore remains eternally the Christ. . . . Naturally, this does not mean that there must always have existed a thematic consciousness of this incarnational structure of the religious act, or that it would have been possible, practicable and necessary, within the confines of our earthly consciousness, to aspire to such explicit awareness.[365]

The Christ-event is the center of world history and salvation history, through the life, death, and resurrection of Jesus of Nazareth, the Word made flesh. The occurrence of salvation in world history and the idea of the coexistence of world history and salvation history lead Rahner to the conclusion that Christianity must see world history as christocentric.[366]

If we consider God to be the genuine mystery, ultimate ground, and inner dynamism of human beings, then Jesus Christ is the irrevocable, final self-expression of God in history, to human beings, and to the world.[367] The climax of all revelation is the logos of God, who becomes a human being, Jesus Christ.[368] The incarnation is a historical event, but at the same time a cosmic event which results in the transfiguration of the world.[369] Jesus is the unique, historical, irrevocable self-expression of God, the logos who becomes a human being, the hypostatic union of the preexistent Son of the Father with the full human reality of body and soul in time and space, in human freedom, in life and death.[370] For Rahner, the climax of God's love and revelation is in the incarnation, whereas Hans Urs von Balthasar locates this in the death of Christ and Wolfhart Pannenberg in the resurrection.[371]

The Meaning of the Transcendental Dogmatic Christology in the Context of the History of Religions and Human History

In opposition to interpretations of the Christ-event as a mythological conceptualization, Rahner proposes a transcendental reduction of a credibility of Christ or a possibility of faith in Christ through his theology of an *a priori* concept of the idea of Christ as the objective correlative of the transcendental structure and perception of the human being.[372] He excludes mythology from the concept of incarnation:[373] the human nature of Jesus Christ is not mere docetic clothing, since God really became a human being.[374] This affirmation defends the dogma of the church. But Rahner does not make this dogma a matter of faith alone, nor does he neglect other transcendental and categorical religious experiences. He presents this dogma as an ontological truth by establishing the possibility of such an incarnation on the basis of the metaphysical anthropology of the human subject, whose intellect has an innate capacity to know the truth, to know God. Rahner identifies the culmination of the self-communication of God in human history as a unique historical event and as the climax of human history and the history of religions, by analyzing it and the historical experience of it in the context of the history of religions and human history. Rahner logically, ontologically, and theoretically establishes the fact of the incarnation as an event in history which occurred in God's free revelation.

Possibility of a Central Point in Salvation History and in Human History

Rahner asks, "Could there not be a theology of the history of salvation, of the old covenant and (explicitly) of the way of salvation outside the history of Israel?"[375] Metaphysical anthropology indicates that the human being has a transcendental relationship to an absolute savior in history: it is in history that the human being actualizes its essence. Divine transcendentality has an individual and a collective history. The beginning and end of human history is the attainment of immediacy to God through God's own self-communication.[376] Christianity claims that this salvation, revelation, and self-communication are intended for all people.[377] From the point of view of metaphysical anthropology, the human being, "subject and person," is a historical essence. As subject of transcendence and historical essence, the human being realizes its transcendental subjectivity historically. Transcendence itself has a history, viz., the event of this transcendence.[378] The transcendental structure of the individual and of the human race is grounded in God's free self-communication,[379] which reached its climax in the person of Jesus Christ, the absolute savior of humanity. He is the criterion for distinguishing between human misunderstandings and legitimate interpretations of the transcendental experience of God.[380] Thus it is possible to have a central point in human history, salvation history, and revelation history, viz., Jesus Christ. He is the historical categoricalization of the transcendental experience of the absolute savior who is ontologically, anthropologically, and historically a reality and a necessity.

According to the Christian understanding, human history is the history of freedom.[381] The God who gives grace is the lord and the goal of history,[382] and Jesus Christ is the center of this history. Revelation history is a part of profane history.[383] Jesus Christ, the fullness of God's self-communication thanks to the hypostatic union, is the climax of all revelations.[384] The world religions find a place within revelation history because their history belongs to world history.[385]

Rahner argues that the human history of salvation has its place within the totality of the natural history of the cosmos.[386] Within general evolution and history, we find the living history of freedom of the human person, as the spiritual personal essence who provides the raison d'être of cosmic existence and motion. This does not represent a difficulty, provided that matter is understood as spiritual and as oriented toward spiritual consciousness.[387] The revelation of God is understood as an extension of world evolution.[388] Universal salvation history is the categorical communication of the supernatural transcendentality of the human being. It coexists with world history in such a way that this is at the same time revelation history.[389] Natural revelation, that is, the collective and individual philosophical knowledge of God, is general revelation history, which coexists with human history and salvation history. World history is therefore supernatural salvation history.[390] There is a salvation history outside the Old Testament and the New Testament history of revelation and salvation.[391] The God of the Old Testament and the New is at work there also. This in no way reduces the absolute claims of Christianity.[392] Rahner (as we shall see) accepts other religions without compromising the absolute claims of Christianity.

Correspondence of Transcendental Christology with Categorical Christology

In *Grundkurs des Glaubens,* Rahner states that his transcendental theology should not give the impression that he deals only with an abstract transcendentality, rather than with the historicity and history of the subject of faith and religion. Transcendentality in freedom is history.[393] Jesus Christ is a historical being, not someone who is present only in faith. The transcendental *a priori* ontological searching Christology and the categorical, empirical, *a posteriori*, historical Christology necessarily intersect in the person of Jesus of Nazareth.[394] Transcendental Christology is also a searching Christology, because it is necessary to discover the transcendental Christ in the person of Jesus of Nazareth.[395] Thus, transcendental and categorical Christology are one and the same. The transcendental revelation is present in every human acceptance of faith, hope, and charity.[396] Each religion tries to transmit transcendental revelation.[397] The history of religion is the history of revelation, and the irrevocable climax of all revelations is Jesus Christ.[398]

The *A Priori* Christ as the Historical Christ

The *a priori* idea of Christ is the correlative of the transcendental structure of human being and knowledge. Concrete realization of this idea is needed, if this idea is to be existentially meaningful.[399] The transcendental structure of the human being, the transcendental idea of Christ and the historical Christ-event correspond to each other; the supernatural transcendental experience, the *a priori* idea of Christ, and the *a posteriori* Christ-event correspond with each other.[400] The *a priori* Christ is the universal Christ because he is the absolute universal savior.[401] The historical Christ is both the transcendental Christ who is absolute savior, and the universal Christ who is absolute human possibility. Since transcendentality is thoroughly historical, and historicity is the categoricalization of the transcendence, the transcendental Christ is the historical Christ. The tension between transcendentality and historicity is overcome through the concept of the human subject as transcendence toward the absolute God, a God who has a history, and of God as self-communicating, historical transcendence.

The Historical Christ as the Universal Christ

In his analysis of the development of Protestant theology, Rahner argues that its initial confessional character developed into a liberal, dialectical, and subjective theology. The relativism of the nineteenth-century school of the history of religions understood Christianity as a "relative phase of a relative history of religions."[402] Rahner refutes this position ontologically and historically and defends the Chalcedonian dogma. Transcendental and categorical revelation and the history of revelation coexist with the spiritual history of humanity and thus with Christian truth.[403] The relationship with Jesus is a relationship with the absolute savior who is experienced historically.[404] The transcendental, *a priori*, absolute savior is the experience of this idea in human transcendental subjectivity, which is both universally significant and historical. Therefore the historical Christ is the universal Christ and the transcendental and *a priori* Christ. Thus transcendental and categorical Christology intersect and are actualized in the historical person of Jesus of Nazareth.

Conclusion

In this chapter, we have investigated the universal significance of Jesus Christ in Karl Rahner's Christology. Jesus Christ, the Word made flesh, is the absolute and universal savior for all humanity and the central point in human history. Rahner reaches this conclusion through his transcendental philosophy, transcendental theology, transcendental anthropology, and transcendental Christology. An analysis of the term "transcendental" and related terms has established that Rahner's theological discussion consistently concentrates on the logical development of the idea of christocentrism by showing the similarity between various terms and explaining these. Rahner has been criticized for elaborating a transcendental philosophy as an *a priori* that does not examine in detail God, history, and the social situation during the time of Jesus, with the result that the social and political dimension is absent from his theology.[405] But this very criticism takes on a positive and relevant note in the context of Rahner's theological approach to the reality of religious pluralism. His transcendental Christology is the foundation of his concept of the presence of Christ in non-Christian religions. As William V. Dych has pointed out, Rahner's transcendental categories link the past with the present, the variety of cultures, and religions, the secular and the religious.[406] To be Christian is to be human. Jesus Christ is the perfect human being. God communicates himself in Jesus Christ completely and perfectly. Each human being has the potentiality to receive this total self-communication. No other religion is centered on such a concept. Rahner starts with the idea of the human being as mystery and concludes with the theology of God as mystery.

3

The Philosophical and Theological Foundations of the Idea of the Presence of Christ in Non-Christian Religions according to Karl Rahner

RAHNER ASKS: "WHAT DOES IT MEAN exactly and concretely when it is said that Jesus Christ is present in the non-Christian religions also? This is the question the following reflections will answer. The question may have been already dealt with more or less implicitly in previous considerations. But it is correct to raise this question explicitly at the end of this chapter."[1] But what does Rahner mean by the phrase "previous considerations"? Rahner wrote this article originally not as a chapter of *Grundkurs des Glaubens* but as a contribution to a symposium on the concept of revelation in India.[2] The phrase thus applies not only to preceding chapters of *Grundkurs des Glaubens* but also to his earlier writings. In the edition of this article in *Schriften zur Theologie*, Rahner points out in the footnotes that he makes these reflections on the presence of Christ in non-Christian religions in the context of his transcendental Christology and of the concept of "anonymous Christian."[3] Therefore it is possible to elaborate and interpret this article in the light of his previous writings. At the same time, we can shed some light on the implicit philosophical and theological foundations of Rahner's study of this question. He writes: "The profession of a universal salvific significance of Jesus for all times and for all people seems for non-Christians to be a scandal, in view of the fact that Jesus was limited in time and space."[4] He intends to affirm the significance of his Catholic faith to believers of non-Christian religions. This he does in a manner analogous to his explanation of how atheists indirectly believe in God and in Christ.[5] On the one hand, his transcendental Christology philosophically and logically developed the concept of Jesus Christ beyond time and space; on the other hand, he affirms his profession of faith in the historical Jesus of Nazareth as valid and correct on the basis of his faith, experience, and conviction in the intersection of transcendental and categorical Christology in the person of Jesus of Nazareth.

For Rahner, Christianity is the religion for all human beings, thanks to the historical mediation of the absolute savior in the person of Jesus Christ.[6] Dialogue is possible with the believers of other religions;[7] one must keep the door for dialogue open and accept believers of other faiths as equal.[8] Rahner defends non-Christian religions as legitimate religions.[9] H. Vorgrimler points out that Rahner does not find a dichotomy between nature and grace, and Rahner's concern about the church's attitude toward non-Christian religions shows his vision of future problems in the church.[10] Through his writings Rahner develops the concept of Christ and church in a wider perspective.[11] He affirms that Jesus is present in non-Christian religions and that it is the task of historians of religions to establish the manner of this presence.[12]

Rahner spent his life defending and interpreting official Catholic teachings in the context of existing social, philosophical, religious, and secular situations. The center of his entire theology is the concept of Christ, the church, and the Christian life, which he develops in presenting the significance of Christian faith for all humanity.

The Background of Karl Rahner's Concept of the Presence of Christ in Non-Christian Religions

Awareness of the Reality of the Other Religious Traditions

Karl Rahner never went to Asia. He had no direct experience of Asian religions, nor was he a specialist in the history of the great religious traditions of the world. He acknowledges that he is not competent enough to discuss the themes of Hindu philosophy.[13] He appreciates the religion of the Vedas and its success in leading people to God. Rahner calls the upanishadic sages mystics.[14] The vedic and upanishadic sages attempted to communicate their experience of God.

Rahner developed a philosophy of religion with an openness toward the world which consists intrinsically in an openness toward the other in faith, hope, and love in the realm of religious experience and in the expression of this experienced reality. This also implies openness toward other religious traditions and experiences. This understanding presupposes a knowledge of other religious traditions and an interest in the experiences of their believers. Cardinal Franz König has written:

> I can understand that the expression "anonymous Christian" is considered by many as confusing and unacceptable. But I believe that Rahner intends it to indicate the new significance of inter-religious dialogue. This concern derives from Rahner's pastoral attitude, his interest in the fate of people in other religions too.[15]

Rahner's concept of Christ's presence in non-Christian religions was influenced also by the process whereby the church becomes genuinely universal, assuming and assimilating world culture. Until the Second Vatican Council, the church was determined by European culture and exported bishops from Europe to other continents, but now it has become a world church manifested in the multiplicity of races, languages, and cultures.[16] Rahner repeatedly speaks of the need for the inculturation of Christianity in Asia, Africa, and Latin America, in order to make the Christian faith relevant and meaningful there.[17]

Rahner's Awareness of Pluralism

In his later writings, Rahner clarifies his response to pluralism in faith, theology, philosophy, culture, lifestyle, and social life.[18] In the introductory part of *Grundkurs des Glaubens,* he analyzes the fact of pluralism in present-day philosophy and theology.[19] His concept of pluralism in theology here does not go beyond the compartmentalization of theology into disciplines such as dogmatics or exegesis. Later in this book, Rahner deals with the topic from another perspective, highlighting ideological and cultural pluralism.[20] The church is not a part of these world visions or ideologies, but the community of the absolute freedom of human existence and the absolute reign of God, thanks to the full self-communication of the God of love in the person of Jesus Christ, to faith in the crucified God, the presence of the Holy Spirit, and the sacraments. A Christian has the opportunity and privilege to show non-Christians this fullness of mystery in faith, hope, and love; the absolute living and loving God becomes victorious in his self-giving love through the pluralism of his creation.[21]

Another aspect is the pluralism of human existence, viz., of life, of milieu, and of the society that a Christian encounters. It is in such a pluralism of profession, art, sciences, politics, and so on that the Christian vocation must be lived.[22] Christians have the right and the duty to convey the experience of the fullness of eternal mystery in the person of Jesus Christ, in the midst of this manifold pluralism.[23] Rahner also discusses pluralism in theological schools and the unity of faith in the context of this theological pluralism.[24]

In the ninth part of *Grundkurs des Glaubens,* Rahner considers a pluralism of eschatological expression,[25] for example, the deathlessness of the soul, the resurrection of the body, an intermediary status, the relation between individual eschatology and universal and collective eschatology, and the pluralism of anthropological expressions. He does not compromise faith in the absoluteness of Christ and Christianity: Jesus Christ is the unifying person in pluralism[26] and the fulfillment of different religious experiences.[27] Christians who live in a society of religious pluralism must come to terms with this.[28] This is an urgent question; religious pluralism offers Christianity a chance to understand its own essence.[29]

How can the unity of the world church be preserved in the context of local pluralism?[30] Rahner emphasizes the importance of the eastern churches, observing that the ancient churches of Jerusalem, Antioch, Rome, Alexandria, and so on were independent centers of Christian life; this makes the promotion of pluralism in theology all the more important. He refers to existential plurality.[31] As his entire theology is centered on his transcendental philosophy and transcendental theology, Rahner is the real inspiration for many modern theological developments such as the theology of religions, pluralistic theology both Catholic and Protestant, and liberation theology.[32]

Rahner's Attitude toward Non-Christian Religions

Rahner's attitude toward non-Christian religions can be better understood in the context of his understanding of transcendental experience, the experience of grace, the general history of salvation and revelation, the supernatural existential, transcendental Christology and anonymous Christianity. The transcendental experience of every human being is ultimately the experience of God. This means that it is possible for different religions to have a common root.

Rahner affirms that non-Christian religions are positive ways of salvation intended by God. The explicit and official history and institution of salvation in the Old Testament is not basically meant for all human beings. Each human being possesses the possibility of supernatural salvation. Because of their spiritual and social nature, persons are saved not through an inner religiosity, but through a religion that is necessarily concretized in society and institution. Because of the coexistence of human history with the supernatural history of salvation and revelation, religions outside Christianity and the Old Testament are not the results of human speculations, but are to be accepted as coming from God. The grace of God is at work in them.[33] It follows that non-Christian religions have a positive salvific function.[34] Rahner accepts non-Christian religions without any compromise to his faith in Christ and to the claims of Christianity. He says,

> Each religion which exists in the world is, like all the cultural possibilities and realities of other people, a question and a possibility offered to each human being. Just as one experiences the cultures of others as something that relativizes one's own, making a concrete and existential challenge, so it is necessarily with foreign religions. These have become an element in one's own existential situation, no longer in a merely theoretical sense, but in a concrete manner. This is why they are experienced as posing a question to our own Christian claim to absoluteness.[35]

Rahner's attitude toward non-Christian religions is summarized in the following four theses. (1) Christianity is the absolute religion meant for all human beings. It cannot recognize other religions as of equal right.[36] (2) The non-Christian religions contain not only elements of the natural knowledge of God, but also the supernatural grace bestowed on human beings as a gift due to Christ; thus, they can be recognized as legitimate religions. (3) Believers of non-Christian religions can or should be considered in this respect as anonymous Christians.[37] (4) It is too much to hope that pluralism will disappear in the foreseeable future; it is permissible to interpret non-Christian Christianity as anonymous Christianity. The church cannot be an exclusive community claiming salvation; rather, it is an explicit expression of a hidden reality that is present even outside the church.[38] Therefore the attitude of the church should be that of Paul who said, "What therefore you do not know and yet worship, that I proclaim to you" (Acts 17:13). Accordingly, one must be tolerant, humble, and firm toward non-Christian religions.[39] "People of good will who cannot yet call Him by his earthly name search for Him in a nameless manner."[40] Rahner clearly says that he can accept Buddha as a saint or as a prophet but not as an irrevocable expression of God, since God has in fact become a human being.[41]

Rahner's Theology of Grace

The foundation of the whole theology of Rahner is his theology of grace, understood as a christological reality. Creation itself is grace. The self-communication of God to his creatures is made in freedom.[42] Rahner identifies the grace of God with his self-communication, which is the supernatural "existential"[43] in which grace is present.[44] The historical realization of the grace of God is Jesus Christ.[45] Therefore, grace is the self-communication of God, the communication of the Trinity, which reached its climax in history in the person of Jesus Christ, the absolute savior. Each individual possesses supernatural sanctifying grace.[46] This experience of grace is an experience of God. The "mystics prove through their life" the "truth of their saying" that they have "experienced God and grace." But the experience of God in mysticism is a dark and mysterious thing about which we cannot speak when we do not have it; and even when we do possess the experience of the mystical, we are unable to speak of it.[47] Sanctifying grace is the liberating freedom which is God's presence in us.[48] Each human being has a supernatural vocation to grace.[49]

In order to maintain the mysterious character of the grace of God, Rahner speaks of a quasi-formal causality. Rahner considers the relationship between nature and grace not from an ontological point of view but from that of his theology of grace, which accords more with Thomas than with the traditions of the Jesuits.[50] He sees anthropology and the theology of grace as mutually related.

The possibility of experiencing revelation as free grace belongs to the very essence of the human being, who is potentially a receptive subject of revelation.[51] Grace is the unity of being and knowing in the human subject, and this is the condition for the communication of God.[52] Rahner analyzes modern projects to create one's own world through technology and the manipulation of nature, and says that in such attempts nature is no longer "mother-nature" and death no longer acceptable. As a result, human beings isolate themselves from God. In this context, Rahner presents his idea of grace: grace is what makes the world divine, and this divinization culminated in Jesus Christ, whose death became a victory for the human person because God himself accepted death.[53]

Rahner's Knowledge of Patristic Traditions and Mysticism

Rahner's repeated emphasis in his later writings and talks on themes such as the universal salvific will of God, free supernatural grace, the salvation of non-Christians, pluralism, the anonymous Christian, anonymous Christianity, the openness of being toward the other, the openness of the spirit, and so on shows that Karl Heinz Neufeld was correct to affirm, in the foreword to the new edition of Rahner's *Aszese und Mystik in der Väterzeit*, that ascetics and mystics from the patristic age play a larger role in Rahner's thought than has often been noted.[54] The study of mysticism and the mystical experience in patristic theology, together with Ignatian spirituality's experience of finding God in the world and in all things,[55] shaped Rahner's openness in his approach to non-Christian religions and nonbelievers. After publishing his first article in 1924 on prayer,[56] Rahner turned to a number of patristic themes.[57] In *Die geistliche Lehre des Evagrius Ponticus,* Rahner points out that the concept of grace and of the human being as spirit are the central themes of Evagrius.[58] Later these two themes became very important for Rahner's own theology. In his study of the concept of ecstasy in Bonaventure, Rahner elaborated Bonaventure's concepts of God as spirit and of the experience of God;[59] these concepts also became very important in the theology of Rahner. *E latere Christi,* Rahner's dissertation for the doctoral degree in theology, is mainly a study in patrology,[60] analyzing the concept of Christ as the second Adam and the church as the second Eve in the writings of Cyprian, Origen, Clement of Alexandria, Justin, Irenaeus, Tertullian, Polycarp, Hippolytus, Ambrose, Jerome, Augustine, Chrysostom, Ephraem, and the later Greek and Latin fathers.

Aszese und Mystik in der Väterzeit is an elaboration of *La spiritualité des premiers siècles chrétiens* by the French Jesuit Marcel Viller, as Rahner himself acknowledges in his foreword.[61] Nevertheless, as Hans

Urs von Balthasar comments, this work of Rahner is basically an original work.[62] The idea of union with Christ and becoming one with him in the innermost soul; the concept of grace; the supernatural life; glory, mystical experience, and revelation; the conviction that martyrdom is the highest perfection; martyrdom as baptism by blood—these ideas, as developed by Polycarp of Smyrna, Origen, Tertullian, Cyprian, Clement of Alexandria, Gregory of Nazianzus, and John Chrystosom, influenced Rahner's theology in various ways. Rahner shows the gradual development from the concept of martyrdom as an instrument of perfection and as union with God into asceticism. The Ignatian understanding of the world on the basis of the experience of God[63] and the Ignatian mysticism of finding God in everything[64] became Rahner's own experience. This mystical experience of God in daily life influenced Rahner as he reflected on non-Christian religions.[65] Contact with his brother Hugo, professor of patrology at Innsbruck, kept alive Karl Rahner's interest in the fathers. Many themes of his theology, especially the question of the salvation of non-Christians, reflect his deep knowledge of patristic writings.[66]

Rahner's Involvement in the Second Vatican Council

Karl Rahner was invited to take part in the council as the adviser of Cardinal Franz König of Vienna. He was named a council theologian in October 1962 by Pope John XXIII.[67] Cardinal König confirms the influence of Rahner in the Second Vatican Council by comparing Rahner's theology with different texts of the document *Lumen Gentium*.[68] Not only did Rahner influence the theology of its documents: the council in turn influenced Rahner. He was a member of the theological commission for *Lumen Gentium* and *Dei Verbum,* and he contributed to *Gaudium et Spes.*[69] On Rahner's influence on changes in church attitudes as a result of the council, Paul Knitter writes:

> In 1965 Rahner himself came to the Gregorianum as a guest professor. Listening to him, I realized clearly how, with his carefully crafted doctrinal arguments, he had laid the theological foundation for Vatican II's new positive view of other religions. Even more than the Council's terse but revolutionary recognition of truth and goodness in the world religions, Rahner's theologically honed case that Christians not only can but must look upon other religions as "legitimate" and as "ways of salvation" was a breath of fresh, liberating air for me. It enabled me both to make sense of what I had been seeing in the religious world beyond Christianity and

> to shake free of what I felt was the ungrounded hubris of the Christian claim to be the only authentic religion.[70]

Rahner points out that the Declaration on the Relationship of the Church to Non-Christian Religions offers a positive appreciation of these. *Lumen Gentium* and *Gaudium et Spes* proclaim a universal and active salvific will of God. Thus there is the possibility of a salvific revelation of faith outside the Christian revelation.[71] Rahner himself evaluates the attitude of the church toward non-Christian religions before and after the Second Vatican Council:

> According to the old concept the non-Christian religions symbolize only a frightening darkness of paganism. . . . But today, with the Council, one can acknowledge even in the institutional dimensions of the non-Christian religions a positive salvific function for humanity, without thereby necessarily denying the truth of the claim to absoluteness on the part of Christianity and the Church.[72]

Cardinal König says that the theology of the council with regard to the relationship of the church to non-Christian religions took the direction intended by Rahner.[73] Hans Waldenfels points out that the themes of the declaration on this subject (*Nostra Aetate*) express the theology of Rahner, though in different terms.[74] It was during and after the council that increased interest by Christian theologians in Asia in non-Christian religious traditions, scriptures, and ceremonies opened up new approaches and challenges to Christian theology. Rahner was fully aware of these theological developments.

Rahner's Philosophical and Theological Foundations of the Presence of Christ in Non-Christian Religions

NATURE OF THE INQUIRY

Rahner says that he studies the nature and limits of Christ's presence in non-Christian religions as a dogmatic theologian, not a student of the history or phenomenology of religion. A dogmatic theologian draws on sources that have no immediate contact with the great non-Christian religions (scripture, the magisterium, and the declaration of Vatican II about non-Christian religions), and therefore cannot do the work of a historian, whose task is to discover Christ *a posteriori* in non-Christian religions. The dogmatic theologian tries to find Christ *a priori.*[75]

Rahner develops his interpretations of classical Christology and soteriology on the basis of the experience of the disciples of Jesus in the New Testament, as these are recorded in the Gospels and Epistles. His theology of the foundation of the church by Jesus Christ and the concept of the church in the New Testament is based solely on the biblical documents and exegetical studies,[76] and Rahner displays a profound knowledge of the New Testament as he explores the development of the concepts of Christian perfection and discipleship in the Gospels and Paul and applies these insights to his own theological investigation.[77]

Rahner observes that official church statements of the patristic age were formulated without any direct contact with the majority of non-Christian religions; the situation is different with the documents of the Second Vatican Council on non-Christian religions. Materials drawn from the history of religions for consideration of this question have not been properly studied hitherto. Earlier church statements are based on dogmatic rather than on historical principles and understand non-Christian religions in a limited and external manner.[78] This provides sufficient reason for Rahner to begin a dogmatic inquiry.

Rahner says that Vatican II clearly indicates two prerequisites for the presence of Christ in non-Christian religions, viz., the supernatural universal salvific will of God[79] and the salvation of non-Christians through faith, hope, and love.[80] But the council is extraordinarily reserved about how such a saving faith leads to a real revelation of God outside the Old and New Testaments.[81] Rahner's dogmatic inquiry is based on dogmatic principles and reflections, antecedently to any inquiry from the point of view of the history of religions.[82]

Rahner begins *Grundkurs des Glaubens* by quoting *Optatam totius* 14; an introduction such as this is demanded by the Second Vatican Council in order to safeguard the coherence of the theological and philosophical formation of seminarians, a discipline he calls the unity of theology and philosophy in explaining the mysteries of Christ.[83] This dogmatic foundation for Rahner's transcendental Christology, based on conciliar documents and papal encyclicals, is very evident,[84] and Rahner tries to establish the relevance of dogmatic inquiry in his various theological discussions. This dogmatic nature of the theological treatise is evident also in the study of the presence of Christ in non-Christian religions.

Foundations in the Philosophical Traditions

Philosophical Basis in Thomistic Philosophy for the Concept of the Presence of Christ in Non-Christian Religions

Rahner is interested in this question from the perspective of dogmatic theology,[85] not from that of the history of religions. The idea of the presence of Christ in non-Christian religions must be seen in the context of Rahner's entire theological and philosophical approach, as well as of his historical situation. Hubert Wolf holds that Rahner is opposed to making theological and philosophical consciousness a part of history:[86] Rahner's ideal is a direct interpretation of the philosophical and theological concepts learned in Heidegger's seminar.[87] But this must be modified. Rahner points out that one has to learn from the historical texts and from the history of the development of the theological concepts,[88] but he goes beyond a merely historical understanding. He considers a philosophical analysis and interpretation possible and fruitful, and these are based on the hermeneutics learned through his philosophical studies.

The dogmatic roots of the idea of Christ's presence in non-Christian religions can be found in Rahner's interpretation of Thomistic philosophy. Rahner's concept of the human being as spirit in the world, and God as Spirit and Jesus Christ as the fullness of the "spirit in the world" (perfect human being) who is the incarnation of the Spirit (God), provide sufficient basis for the affirmation that the same presence of the Spirit (God) in the world—Jesus Christ, God incarnate—is present and operative in every human being and every religion. The dogmatic question whether Jesus Christ is present in non-Christian religions can be answered if we ask, How is Christ present and operative in the faith of individual non-Christians?[89] From this viewpoint, Rahner's interpretation of Thomistic philosophy provides the philosophical basis for the later development of his idea of the presence of Jesus Christ in non-Christian religions.

The Presence of Christ in Non-Christian Religions Is an A Priori Approach to Theology and God

The Catholic approach to God and to theology was always *a posteriori,* since it began from the notion of God and belief in God. Rahner's approach is *a priori,* starting from human experience to arrive at God. He asks, "How can Jesus Christ be understood as present and operative in non-Christian religions from the perspectives of Christian dogmatic theology and thus *a priori* to a description that is drawn up *a posteriori?*" The answer will focus on another question: How is Jesus Christ present and active in the faith of individual non-Christians? Rahner does not explain what is *a priori* theology and how the presence of Christ in non-Christian religions can be established through such an approach. He also says that we cannot deal with the question of non-Christian religions as social and institutional realities, because this is the task of theologians who work *a posteriori* and from the point of view of the history of religions. All we can say about the presence of Christ in non-Christian religions concerns the presence of Christ in the salvific faith of non-Christians.[90] In this way Rahner limits his inquiry to the framework of the Christian dogmatic theology, an *a priori* approach. By leaving the question of the presence of Christ in non-Christian religions as social and institutional realities to those theologians who study the history of religions, Rahner both confesses his own limitations and invites theologians engaged in the history of religions to further research.

Rahner employs the transcendental method. Through phenomenological explication and transcendental reduction, he arrives at an *a priori* idea of Christ. The transcendental deduction provided the ground for his assertion of an *a priori* approach to theology. Such themes as the universal salvific will of God, the supernatural self-communication of God, the presence of God in creation and in the human individual, the idea of an absolute savior, the experience of this savior in Jesus Christ and the idea of the transcendental and *a priori* Christ, allow one to explain and understand the presence of Christ in the salvific faith of the non-Christian individual.

Theological Reasons for the Presence of Jesus Christ in Non-Christian Religions

Because of the Universal and Supernatural Salvific Will of God Operative in the World

One of the two presuppositions for the theory of the presence of Christ in non-Christian religions is the universal salvific will of God, which is genuinely operative in the world. "This means that the possibility of a supernatural faith in revelation exists everywhere, i.e. in the whole length and breath of human history."[91] This is explicitly taught by the Second Vatican Council;[92] but the council is unusually reserved about how this supernatural salvific faith in the revelation of God is present outside the Old Testament revelation of God.[93] Hebrews 11 presupposes this universal supernatural saving will of God, which is the cause of the incarnation, antecedent to the cross and to Christ.[94] Rahner writes against the background of his concept of human transcendentality, supernatural and transcendental revelation, and the faith that is received in freedom, antecedently to the historical and objective communication of this transcendental revelation that the salvific will of God is universal. This faith in salvific revelation has a christological character.[95] Jesus Christ is sent by God as the redeemer of the world, so that Christ and the cross are the cause of the communication of the Holy Spirit always and everywhere in the world.[96]

In his article "Jesus Christus in den nichtchristlichen Religionen," Rahner says that Jesus Christ is present in non-Christian religions because of God's universal salvific will, something explained in greater detail in the fifth chapter of *Grundkurs des Glaubens,* where he discusses the history of salvation and revelation in general and concludes that Jesus Christ, the Word made flesh, is the irrevocable climax of revelation history and salvation history.[97]

The divine transcendentality of the human being—God's free self-communication which bestows forgiveness—is actualized in human history as the foundation, the beginning, and the goal of this history.[98] Christianity believes in a single human history of revelation and of salvation for every human person, understanding itself as a religion that possesses absolute value.[99]

But God communicates himself in creation, in revelation history, and in salvation history as the innermost center of everything.[100] The human being, as historical essence and as subject of transcendence, is also historical. The transcendental subjectivity of the human being is not realized outside of history, nor does the human being grasp this transcendental subjectivity by means of an unhistorical reflection.[101] Transcendence has a history, and this history is the event of transcendence.[102] Human history, both individual and collective, transcends toward God. The "supernatural existential," that is, the orientation of the human being toward the Absolute, has also a history.[103]

World history and salvation history are neither contradictory nor parallel. The history of humanity is a history of salvation and revelation. God reveals himself to human beings, and human transcendentality is openness toward God's revelation and salvation. Therefore there is the possibility of revelation history outside the Old Testament history of revelation.[104]

God's universal salvific will implies the existence of supernatural revelation and faith throughout the history of the human race.[105] The church is the visible sign of the kingdom of God which unites everyone.[106] God denies his love to no one, because he wants the salvation of all.[107]

"According to the scripture and the teachings of the church, every human being has sufficient grace to work out his salvation."[108] Rahner argues in the light of *Mystici Corporis Christi* (Pius XII) that if anyone fails to attain salvation, it is due to his or her own fault. Those who are saved attain salvation in and through the church, even if they are not visible members of the church.[109] God calls all nations to salvation in his freedom and love. The confession of God as the creator of the world takes on specific vitality and clarity thanks to one's own experience of the free and personal activity of God in history.

Final salvation depends on Christ. Accordingly, if adherents of non-Christian religions are saved in their religion, and salvation comes in and through Christ, this means that Jesus is present in non-Christian religions.[110] Referring to *Singulari Quadam* of Pius IX (DZ 1647), Rahner says no one is guilty in the eyes of the Lord for not being a member of the church. "We are allowed to hope, indeed we must hope for the saving mercy of God for all others too."[111]

The Self-Communication of God

God's self-communication comes only as the result of the history of salvation and revelation with its climax in the God-man, Jesus Christ.[112] This immediacy of God in his self-communication is the revelation of God as the absolute mystery that exists in us.[113] Jesus Christ is the starting point in the discussion about the presence of Christ in other religions.[114]

Rahner understands this as an "ontological self-communication of God" in the innermost part of the human being:

> The word "self-communication" really means that God in his innermost reality makes himself the innermost constitutive of the human being. It is

> an ontological self-communication of God. However, to remove a possible misunderstanding, this word ontological should not be understood in a merely objectivistic, as it were objectively material sense.[115]

This is the communication of God to the human being as personal absolute mystery, as the essence of transcendence, as a spiritual and as a personal being. God is in the process of self-communication,[116] where he bestows himself as a gift.[117] The transcendental element in God's self-communication has the primacy, when it is considered in the light of the theory of revelation and of the theology of grace.

> Seen from the point of view of God, all these historical presuppositions are conditions of the possibility that the God of revelation himself creates and prefixes to his revelatory deed, so that secular history should be understood as a secular element of the divine revelation which communicates God himself.[118]

If God reveals himself to everyone without exception, it follows that Jesus Christ, the fulfillment and the climax of God's revelation and self-communication, is also revealed to everyone. But how does this occur? According to Rahner, this revelation takes place in the transcendental experience of human beings. He does not specify the external phenomena of this revelation, leaving that to philosophers of religion.

In the sacraments, in the church, in revelation, and in scriptures, we find the categorical referent of the transcendental presence of God.[119] The transcendental self-communication of God is present in concrete historicity and in the historical revelation of God.[120] The universal salvific self-communication of God is present whenever and wherever human freedom exists, without excluding any individuals or groups.[121] J. B. Metz says that Rahner was a universalist who never thought of God as the private property of the church, or of theology, or of faith.[122] God allows himself to be experienced by human beings of all times and places.[123] The difference between Jesus and other human beings lies not in the acceptance of God's self-communication but in the offer of this self-communication.[124]

The Presence of Christ in Non-Christian Religions Originates in the Concept of God

God is the absolute mystery which draws near to the human being. God is not an object of theology.[125] The Christian concept of God is of a free and transcendental personal existence, the Lord of nature and history.

This confirms natural and supernatural knowledge of a personal God even outside revelation history. Precisely from the point of view of revelation, it will allow what is supernatural in these truths of non-Christian religions and philosophy to appear as part of the human being's innate and inalienable nobility.[126] The Christian concept of God does not accept polytheistic and pantheistic notions: according to the Christian faith, the transcendental God has disclosed his innermost self to human beings in grace and brings his triune life to the world in the incarnation of his Son.

The history of revelation displays distinctions in the concept of God.[127] Rahner's view of the presence of Christ in non-Christian religions can be better understood against the background of his evaluation of these different concepts of God. The early Greek concept of God is polytheistic, not in the sense of many independent gods but in the sense of an ordered totality of gods. Plato, Aristotle, the Presocratic Xenophanes and Heraclitus argue against the Homeric polytheism, elaborating the idea of a monotheistic personal Absolute, a "thou" transcending many.[128] Old Testament monotheism was based not on a rational search for the ultimate unity of the world, but on the experience of Yahweh's saving action in the people's history: the Jews experienced Yahweh as the absolute sovereign Lord of the world and of nature.[129] But the New Testament knows with absolute assurance that everything lives and moves in him, and that God is everywhere, at work in nature too.[130] "The New Testament is indeed aware of a self-consistent possibility of the knowledge of God from the world." The true and only God and God's sanction of a natural moral law can be known through what is created, always and everywhere.[131] For a metaphysical knowledge of God in the world, where God is conceived in the understanding of Vatican II as the *principium et finis* of all reality, God is in a certain sense concealed. God is metaphysically everything. Each objectification is the activity of God. But God's activity remains absolutely transcendental.

> God himself, as the abiding and holy mystery, as the incomprehensible ground of the transcendental existence of human beings, is not only the God of infinite distance, but also wants to be the God of absolute closeness in a true self-communication, and he is present in this way in the spiritual depths of our existence as well as in the concreteness of our bodily history.[132]

If God, the absolute mystery, transcendent personal existence, the Lord of nature, of history, and of all human beings, is present always and everywhere and communicates himself to human beings in absolute proximity, then the incarnation of this absolute transcendent, personal existence, who is one with him, should also be present always and everywhere.

Central Truth of Faith

God, the central truth of our existence and of our faith, is mystery.[133] The central truth of our existence and of our faith is mystery. This idea is the basis of Christ's presence in non-Christian religions.[134] "There are absolute mysteries only in the self-communication of God in the depth of existence which is called grace, and which in the history is called Jesus Christ." We know mystery, that is, the Trinity, through Jesus Christ in the economy of salvation. If our starting point is the economy of salvation, we find that God (grace, mystery, or the Trinity) is present in human history in and through Jesus Christ; on the other hand, if we begin with the orientation toward God, this leads human beings to the mystery and grace, and therefore to the Trinity and to Jesus Christ, who "makes historical" grace or mystery. "Therefore there is now only one question, whether this God wants to remain merely in eternal distance, or whether he wants to be innermost center of our existence in free grace and in self-communication."[135] Rahner affirms the second possibility.

Everyone belongs to the church, because everyone belongs to the people of God,[136] and Jesus Christ is the center of the church and of our existence. This conclusion is also drawn in his interpretation of the encyclical *Mystici Corporis Christi,* where he sees the human race as united and universally redeemed by Jesus Christ.[137] He distinguishes two concepts of the church, viz., "church as an established organisation with sacramental laws, and as humanity consecrated by the incarnation."[138] The incarnation made Jesus Lord of the universe.[139] Reflection on what *Mystici Corporis Christi* says about the ecclesiological aspect of the sacraments leads to the conclusion that, while the sacramental visibility of Christ's salvific work belongs to the church, ecclesiality exists outside the church too.[140] The encyclical does not discuss the salvation of those who are not members of the church (in the full sense of this term); it indicates the necessity of belonging to the church for salvation but does not deny that those who are not members (because of personal ignorance) can be saved.[141] Thus Rahner presents Jesus Christ as the center of existence and the reference point for salvation. All are saved. The experience of Jesus Christ is available to everyone.

The Natural Knowledge of God

Rahner distinguishes three kinds[142] of knowledge of God: natural knowledge, acknowledged by the First Vatican Council; knowledge of God through the Christian revelation of the Word, that is, God's own revelation and self-communication to humanity, called incarnation,[143] and knowledge of God by "means of his self-revelatory salvific activity in the history of humanity and of the single human being." This third type originates in the individual and collective personal experience of existence.[144] The natural knowledge of God is *a posteriori* and is possible through the transcendental experience of the human person as a free subject in his encounter with the world. This knowledge is also transcendental because it is the human awareness of the absolute mystery realized through transcendental experience, the basic divine experience of the human being as subject.[145] This *a posteriori* experience of God is not a mystical, experiential aspect of personal spirituality, but evolves from the transcendental structure of the world. We may misunderstand the *a posteriori* nature of the knowledge of God if we neglect the transcendental element.[146] God is always a present reality to which one opens oneself to find the basis for one's existence.[147] Rahner asks whether we can call this natural knowledge of God revelation outside Christian revelation. He also asks how can we distinguish the revelatory experience of God of the adherents of other religions from the natural knowledge of God.[148] We can link the second and third ways of knowing God in the revelation of the Word. The object of our discussion is not pure metaphysics but the historically constituted transcendental experience of God.[149]

Although Rahner believes in the human capacity to know God naturally, he sees an element of revelation and grace in natural knowledge of God: "In the concrete actuality of existence there is no knowledge of God that would be purely natural, because the theological knowledge of God is once again our own activity, taking place in freedom."[150] The orientation of human existence toward the immediacy of God is called grace. Even the rejection of the knowledge of God is more than a merely natural knowledge of God. Any knowledge of God in the mode of acceptance or rejection is a natural knowledge and a knowledge in grace, and is both knowledge and revelation, present in the depth of existence.[151] Human reason can know God independently of revelation: this is knowledge of God as the cause and goal of the world, knowledge of God's transcendence and his existence as personal existence.[152] "The human being must of course stand in the presence of God as of the free Person who transcends the world."[153] Rahner asks what it means to say that faith is necessary for revelation, and whether the metaphysical and natural knowledge of God can be a substitute for this faith in revelation.[154] His answer is that natural knowledge is not a substitution for revelation; however, natural knowledge and revelation can complement each other. Natural knowledge of God leads to knowledge of Christ, who is present in the general history of revelation and salvation.

Finding God in the World

The foundation of Rahner's theology is the Ignatian spirituality that finds God in everything, and this reflects his transcendental anthropological theology.[155] Rahner believes in the experience of God in the world and through the world. The experience of Christmas is the experience of God in the world, his nearness and closeness and his presence in the human heart.[156] However, this idea of finding God and his actions in the world in concrete historical experience creates a difficulty, since God is understood as transcendence, the creative ground of everything, the ineffable mystery, the incomprehensible presupposition and Being beyond the world. "By definition God cannot be localized in time and space."[157] It is difficult for Christianity—as a religion which speaks of the definitive and exclusive objectification and manifestation of God in his salvific historical interventions—to have a transcendental starting point. Conversely, "our basic assertion seems to say that God is everywhere in so far as he grounds everything and he is nowhere in so far as everything grounded is created by Him and that what we see in our world of experience is different from God, and separated by an absolute chasm between God and that which is not God."[158]

Rahner's concept of the presence of God in the world is established in his first book, *Geist in Welt*. He begins with the affirmation that "the human being asks questions."[159] The metaphysical question is a transcendental question about being itself which pervades the ground of human existence, a question about being in its totality. "In actually asking the metaphysical question the human being becomes aware of what it is in the ground of its existence."[160] The starting point of metaphysics is the questioning human being.[161] "The human being finds itself already in the world when it ponders who and what it is." "The human being is in the presence of Being in its totality in so far as it finds itself in the world."[162]

Metaphysics, which is an inquiry into Being, is "ontology" in that it inquires into the universal ground of Being, and theology if we call this universal ground *theos,* or God.[163] Thus Rahner experiences God as the basis of the world and of human beings. This experience leads to the experience of Jesus Christ, the fullness of God's self-communication of God to the world.

Rahner refers to the statement of the Fourth Lateran Council that we can know God from the world, and points out that we forget this, although we speak of God, his existence, personality, Trinity, and so on in our theologizing.[164] According to the Christian world vision, the world is supernatural, since it is oriented to the personal trinitarian God who lies beyond the world. The whole of nature is always embedded in a supernatural context. "Therefore all religious history and all philosophy is encompassed by a conscious or unconscious theological *a priori.*"[165]

Rahner recalls the doctrine that the one God, as *principium et finis* of the world, can be known on the basis of the objective world through the light of natural reason. Human nature can know God independently of revelation.[166] Everything is the action of God, and this action is absorbed to a certain extent into the anonymity of "always and everywhere," as far as human knowledge is concerned. The New Testament experience of God is of the concrete salvific activity of God in the world, distinct from all other being.[167] The New Testament knows with absolute assurance that everything lives and moves in him (Acts 17:27–29; Eph. 4:6). God is everywhere and is at work also in nature.[168] After analyzing the New Testament concept of God,[169] Rahner says,

> This uniqueness of the divine essence in the world and in history is not meant just in the sense of a static fact that we can observe. The uniqueness of God must still be established in the world and in history. God has still to become the unique God for the human being.[170]

This is not merely a confession of a fact; it is also a challenge to experience God. God is the ultimate referent of the transcendental ground and abyss of the world, of devotion and respect of the human being vis-à-vis the world.[171] God is everywhere.[172] This God, and his historical presence in the person of Jesus of Nazareth in the world, is present also in non-Christian religions and religious experiences.

Argument from Different Theological Viewpoints

The Presence of Christ in Salvation History and the Concept of Human History as Salvation History

According to Rahner's philosophy and theology, human being is spirit. It is being. The other names given to the human being are self-presence, coming-to-oneself, and self-subsistence. The human being is such because of anticipation or, in other words, because of its *a priori* nature or transcendency. In its inner, personal, metaphysical, ontological, existential substance, the human being is the historicity of spirit. The human being as historical spirit is basically and ontologically open toward the Ultimate. This metaphysical openness, as self-presence, is called transcendental revelation. This revelation of the pure Spirit occurs in the space and time of human self-presence. The human being is a historical spirit with a historicity open to the ultimate. This encounter between *Dasein* and the absolute in its historical dimension is understood as epiphany, and this epiphany is revelation. This revelation also occurs in the individual.[173] Here the individual history of human beings and general human history constitute the same historicity, the locus of epiphany, the relation between transcendence and historicity, and the free activity of the transcendental openness of God vis-à-vis the open transcendental ontological existent, viz., the human being. This means revelation.[174] The historicity of a potential revelation in time and place is to be understood as specific events in general human history.[175] This historical character of revelation to the human being—as a historical being with a necessary openness to the absolute, an inherent capacity to receive revelation—means that each human being can receive revelation.[176] Metaphysical anthropology proves to be an ontology of the "obediential potential" for a free revelation.

> This makes philosophy of religion the analysis of the capacity of the human being to hear a possible revelation. But every natural religion that might be constructed with the help of such an anthropology and metaphysics, has understood its own essence only when it is itself the act of listening whereby it understands its own self and reckons with the possibility of a revelation of God in human history.[177]

Rahner understands the history of the world as the history of God's presence in the world, humanizing and socializing humanity. The history of religions is a part of the history of the presence of God in the world. Accordingly, religions are part of revelation and of the history of salvation, which leads to the total Christ.[178] Christ has a central role in human history, when this is understood as salvation history;[179] this is not limited to biblical history, but embraces the whole of human history, which is brought to fulfillment in Jesus Christ.[180] If God's history of salvation and revelation began only with Abraham in the Middle East, and if the history of salvation existed only for a few decades in a remote place, how can it be a saving history of the whole world? How can Christ be the center of the entire religious history of the world?[181]

According to Rahner, the prehistory of Christianity reaches back to the beginning of humanity. There is only one history of the world for both Christians and non-Christians.[182] The church does not encompass the revelation of God, which has its historical climax in Jesus Christ; but human history can encompass this.[183] The supernatural history of salvation and the supernatural history of revelation are coextensive.[184] According to the council, the possibility of supernatural salvation and faith in revelation is offered everywhere and to every human being.[185]

Rahner holds that the council is very reserved about the question of saving grace and a genuine revelation of God outside the realm of the Old and the New Testaments. At the same time, a theologian is not forbidden to ask this question.[186] Rahner says that Jesus Christ is the mediator between God the Father and human beings: "But if there necessarily is a presence of Christ throughout the whole history of salvation, this cannot be missing where the human being is concretely religious in its history, namely, in the history of religion."[187] The human being is the personal essence of transcendence and freedom in a temporal and historical existence. The question about salvation is posed to the human subject as a historical and free being. "Therefore the history of salvation and the human history should be finally coexistent."[188]

In *Weltgeschichte und Heilsgeschichte,* Rahner says that salvation history occurs in world history and is a part of world history.[189] God communicates himself and salvation is realized in the free acceptance of this self-communication, an acceptance called faith, hope, and love.[190] There is also a general salvation history, revelation history, and faith history involving those outside the old and new covenants,[191] coexistent with world history. Thus the general history of religions is coexistent with world history.[192]

Rahner affirms the unity of matter and spirit. Spirit is the goal toward which matter transcends. The human being is the unity of matter and spirit, or spirit in matter. In the self-transcendence of matter lies the fullness of the spirit. The history of the cosmos, natural history, human history, the history of the spirit and revelation history are all one.[193]

The Centrality and the Uniqueness of Jesus Christ as the Savior of All People

Jesus Christ himself is the starting point for any discussion of the presence of Christ in non-Christian religions, since the long process of development in the history of salvation and revelation reached its climax in his person.[194] Rahner argues that since non-Christians are saved by Christ, he is present in their religions:

> Such a presence of Jesus Christ in the whole of salvation history and in relation to all people cannot be denied or overlooked by the Christian if he believes in Jesus as the salvation of all and is not of the opinion that salvation of the non-Christians is worked out by God and his mercy independently of Jesus Christ.[195]

Rahner says that Christ is the savior of non-Christians of good will, even where this good will has nothing to do with Christ.[196] Thus, Christ must be present in the whole history of salvation, wherever human beings are concretely religious. The resurrection of Jesus confirms that he is the absolute savior.[197] Rahner says,

> Jesus is thus the historical presence of this ultimate, unsurpassable word of the self-revelation of God. This is his claim, and he is confirmed and experienced in an eternally valid manner as such, by means of the resurrection. In this sense, at least, he is the "absolute bringer of salvation."[198]

In his discussion of the content, validity and limitations of classical Christology and soteriology, Rahner defends the universal significance of Catholic teaching about the person of Jesus Christ by referring to the christological conclusions of the ecumenical councils and to the Christology of the church, which he defines as a descending Christology of the incarnation of the *Logos*, the Son of God, the hypostatic union of the divine nature with fully human reality.[199] Rahner concludes that the classical Christology is valid and precludes any attempt to consider Jesus merely as a prophet, a religious leader, or a source of inspiration in the history of religions; rather, Jesus is the unique full revelation and communication of God, the hypostatic union of God and human being.[200] Jesus Christ is the absolute savior,[201] in whom the history of revelation culminates.[202]

The Interval Separating Creation History from Old Testament Revelation through Moses

The distance separating creation and the Old Testament revelation of Moses is not to be considered empty of divine revelation. *Dei Verbum* passes over this interval rather quickly.[203] Rahner holds that this does not mean that this period is void of revelation, and also that the revelation in the Old Testament is not absolutely separate from the history of other religions; otherwise it would be impossible for the history of God's revelation and salvation to be found in the world.[204] This is why Rahner cannot neglect the pre-Christian religions.[205] If we consider these religions part of the primordial revelation, we must take into account at least two million years of the history of religions.[206] Belief in a universal salvific will means that we can affirm the positive salvific function of pre-Christian and non-Christian religions.[207]

For standard dogmatic theology, nothing happened between Adam and Moses. Rahner holds that the just would have had God's grace during the period before Christ.[208] He points out that the interval between Adam and Abraham is not a period in the history of revelation, but belongs to the history of God's salvific providence. Was there a genuine history of revelation in this period? Can we think of this period of many millennia as a further supply of primordial revelation? Or was there a supernatural history of revelation without any revelation?[209] How can we think of faith in this period in the strict sense? Rahner says that the dogmatic constitution on the church remains silent on this point[210] and that the Decree on Mission accepts the salvific faith of non-Christian religions. The Dogmatic Constitution on the Church and the Pastoral Constitution accept this faith as possible and as presupposed in every human being.[211] May not this long period of divine salvific providence be considered as the period of God's salvific revelation?[212] The history of salvation and revelation begun with Abraham and the patriarchs is presented in the Old Testament independently of the general history of revelation and salvation.[213] God spoke through the fathers in the past in different ways and finally through his own Son.[214]

The Historical and Social Character of the Salvation Event

Rahner argues for the presence of Christ in non-Christian religions on the basis of the historical and social character of the event of salvation:

> If a non-Christian religion is supposed a priori to have no positive influence whatever on the supernatural event of salvation of the non-Christian individual (or is not allowed to have such an influence), this would mean conceiving of the event of salvation in such a person in a completely a-historical and a-social way.[215]

This would fundamentally contradict the historical and social nature of Christianity and the basic nature of Christian revelation, since even the most personal decisions of the human being are mediated by the concrete reality of his social and historical life.[216] Discussing the theology of the death of Jesus from the perspective of the resurrection, Rahner points out that "later" New Testament soteriological Christology considers the death of Jesus to be the cause of universal salvation.[217] The concept of the suffering Servant of God in Second Isaiah and Jewish theological ideas about the suffering of the just support the salvific significance of the death of Jesus, which has been verified through his resurrection.[218] We must link the concepts of an "absolute savior" and the "event of absolute salvation" to form a unity that is historical, whereas the "transcendental" aspect of such an event cannot be final on its own. Such a unity is fulfilled in the "free acceptance of God's self-communication" as the fulfillment both of history and of humanity, namely, in Jesus Christ.

> We presuppose here, of course, first of all, that Jesus of Nazareth understood himself as this absolute savior and this understanding came to its fullness and epiphany in his resurrection. Naturally Jesus did not make use of this abstract formulation with which we have tried to outline and give some brief indication of the concept of an absolute savior.[219]

Rahner argues that Catholic doctrinal concepts such as "Son of God," "absolute savior," the incarnation of the *Logos,* or the hypostatic union should be understood not as mythological but as ontological and metaphysical.[220] Thus, there is unity and identity between classical Christology and "incarnational soteriological Christology."[221]

Do Non-Christian Religions as Concrete, Historical, and Social Phenomena Have a Positive Significance?

Rahner says that we must investigate the question of the presence of Christ in non-Christian religions after answering the question whether non-Christian religions as concrete, historical, and social phenomena have a positive significance.[222] If they do not have a positive influence on the supernatural salvation of a non-Christian, then the salvation of such individuals should be thought of in nonsocietal and nonhistorical terms.[223] But such an idea "fundamentally contradicts the sociological and historical character of Christianity itself."[224] The Council of Jerusalem acknowledged the positive value of other religious traditions by liberating non-Jews from the Jewish law (cf. Acts 15).

Rahner understands the concepts of God, faith, and the person of Jesus Christ in the context of the social, cultural, and political situation of the world. This dimension is clear even in his early writings. Rahner believes in a unity in the universality of religions.[225]

The Second Vatican Council says that salvation is possible for non-Christians; Rahner points out that according to *Nostra Aetate* there exist truth and holiness in different religions.[226] A positive coexistence with other religious communities should be promoted because of God's universal and supernatural salvific will.[227] The affirmations of *Mystici Corporis Christi* about membership in the Catholic Church as membership in a community organized under the bishop of Rome do not exclude the possibility of understanding "church" in a wider sense;[228] the statement of this encyclical that only the baptized belong to the church does not mean that Christianity ceases at the boundary of the church. It is a truth of faith that the baptism of heretics is valid and that there are sacraments outside the church. Outside the organized church, there is the Bible as the inspired word of God, and there is the church of the apostles. Truth and tradition exist outside the church, truth brought by Christ and handed on through his message and the work of the Holy Spirit. The truth of the Christian faith exists even outside the church, though not in its fullness and purity.[229]

Rahner analyzes the teachings of the magisterium and the conclusions, opinions, and teachings of the fathers of the church, the councils, and ancient and contemporary theologians. He comes to the conclusion that baptism is the prerequisite for membership in the Catholic Church.[230] But this does not rule out the possibility of a broader category of membership in the case of nonbaptized persons who are justified before God because of a virtuous life lived according to their conscience. The criterion of membership and nonmembership should be the inner personal state of being justified or nonjustified before God. To consider the nonbaptized as outside the church is to equate them with sinners. Baptism is the sacramental sign of the confession of the faith of the church.[231] According to Vorgrimler, Rahner proposed the concept of anonymous Christianity in order to concretize the attitude of the church toward non-Christian religions and to defend the salvation of their adherents.[232]

Although *Nostra Aetate* does not give any definite answer to the question whether the history of non-Christian religions can be considered to be part of salvation history, non-Christian religions—though in an incomplete manner—have a positive history of salvation and revelation.[233] If we find some substance and expression of Christian faith outside Christianity, we can accept this, provided we do not water down the Christian faith. "Such a fact only proves that the living God, who revealed himself in Jesus Christ, is also at work with his light and grace outside that zone which is salvation history in the narrower, theological sense of the term."[234]

Means of Salvation in Non-Christian Religions

"As far as the attainment of salvation of a non-Christian through faith, hope, and love is concerned, non-Christian religions cannot be thought of as playing no role in the attainment of justification and salvation, or only a negative role."[235] This proposition does not offer a definite Christian interpretation of any one specific non-Christian religion, nor does it attribute to non-Christian religions a soteriological significance equal to that of the Christian faith.[236] Rahner attempts to establish the salvific significance and validity of non-Christian religions:

> If the history of religions is a part of human history in general, in which the theological essence of the human being not only is lived de facto (just as in any history) but also becomes the object of conscious reflection, then the history of religions is at the same time the most explicit part of the history of revelation and the spiritual place where the historical false interpretations of the transcendental experience of God are made most explicitly and with the most fatal consequences, and superstition rears its head most unambiguously.[237]

This does not mean that Rahner accepts all the sects as a revelation of God, but he does argue for the salvific significance of non-Christian religions on the basis of the transcendentality of the human subject.

The Salvation of Non-Christians through Faith, Hope, and Love

Salvation through faith, hope, and love is one of Rahner's major themes, and the concept of the salvation of non-Christians through faith, hope, and love is one of the prerequisites of Rahner's idea of the presence of Christ in non-Christian religions. His aim here is not a Christian interpretation of non-Christian religions, nor does he aim to equate the "salvific relevance of the non-Christian religions with the Christian faith." He does not dispute whether a concrete religion negatively or positively influences the salvation of an individual non-Christian.[238] Categorical mediation of the transcendental relationship of the human being to God is realized in grace in faith, hope, and love.[239] Rahner develops this idea of an anonymous faith among non-Christians through faith and love toward God and neighbor independently of any relationship to the Old Testament and to the New Testament revelation of Jesus Christ.[240]

The Manner of the Presence of Christ in Non-Christian Religions

The Presence of Christ in Non-Christian Religions through His Spirit

"Jesus Christ is present and operative in non-Christian believers (and hence in non-Christian religions) . . . in and through his Spirit. Such a proposition is taken for granted in dogmatic theology," says Rahner.[241] Non-Christian religions have a redeeming faith, thanks to the supernatural grace of the Holy Spirit. This is deduced from *Dei Filius* of Vatican I, even though this document deals with the faith of Christians.[242] The Spirit is everywhere at all times *intuitu meritorum*.[243] "This is the Spirit who proceeds from the Father and from the Son; the Spirit of the eternal *Logos*, of the Word of God made flesh, and in this sense the

Spirit of Christ."[244] Rahner says that according to scholastic dogmatic theology the Spirit of God working in the nonbaptized can be called the Spirit of Christ. That means that revelation and salvation history and their communication and acceptance took place not in "abstract transcendentality, but in the historical mediation."[245] There is an intrinsic relation between the Spirit of God, operating everywhere and always in the world, and the Spirit of Christ,[246] who is present and operative in all faiths.[247] Since the climax of salvation and revelation is the historical Christ-event, the "communication of the Spirit in the world" is "the Spirit of Christ, the *logos* of God who became a human being."[248] The incarnation and the cross bring about the communication of the Holy Spirit to the entire world.[249]

In talking about the experience of the saints and persons of the Spirit, Rahner says,

> They know that the human being as spirit, in real existence and not merely in theory, should genuinely live on the border between God and the world, time and eternity. They always seek to ensure that they are really doing this and that the spirit in them is not only a medium of a human kind of life.[250]

The revelation of God in the human spirit develops until it reaches fulfillment in Christ, who is the ultimate revelation.[251] The human being is a spirit dependent on the unity of reality, that is, God.[252] The experience of the Spirit is the experience of the "supernatural." This may be anonymous; perhaps we have experienced the "supernatural" in such a way that we could not "dare to look at the supernatural straight in the face." But if we lose ourselves in the experience of the Spirit, when everything disappears as if in an inexpressible beatitude, then actually it is not only the "spirit," but the Holy Spirit who works in us.[253]

The Analogical Sayings about God and Finding God in Other Names and Forms

In his meditations on the word "God," Rahner analyzes the words used to signify God in different languages and cultures. He comes to the conclusion that what is meant by these words is more important than the words themselves.[254] In his discussion of God as person, Rahner analyzes the analogical sayings about God and says that it is only by analogy that we can say many things about God.[255] In *Hörer des Wortes,*

Rahner explains what analogy is and how a discussion about God is analogically possible.[256] It is possible to conclude from Rahner's theology that Christ is invoked and adored under many names and forms.

Rahner's Concept of the Presence of Christ in Non-Christian Religions and the Official Teaching Position of the Church

As we have seen, Rahner's intention as teacher and theological writer was to defend Catholic teaching and make it comprehensible and relevant not only to believers but to nonbelievers and adherents of non-Christian religions, thanks to his philosophical and scientific approach to theology, to Catholic doctrines, and to the Christian social situation. Rahner considers the presence of the historical Jesus in the pre-Easter period as "absolute savior" to be the climax of the history of salvation. "The historical abiding of Christ through the community which believes in him and considers him explicitly in the profession of faith as mediator of salvation—this is what we call the church."[257] Rahner criticizes the tendency from the eighteenth century to the first half of the twentieth century to consider religion a private affair. Religion is a social and a historical phenomenon. The history of salvation is the history of the transcendental self-communication of God to human history in time and space. Therefore religion in the Christian understanding is necessarily an ecclesial religion. Since we are aware of the unity in world history and of the human person as a social being, we must understand the Christian religion as a ecclesial religion.[258] The teachings of the church are the substance and the ultimate truth of Christianity.[259] Thus Rahner not only affirms the uniqueness and absoluteness of Christianity as a religion; he also establishes the validity and necessity of the church as the religion of the absolute savior.

Although Rahner admits that there are historical, biblical, and theological difficulties involved in discerning the true church, and the matter is complicated by the plurality of Christian confessions, he says that Catholic theology explains the dogmas of faith from the point of view of the Catholic Church, which expresses the essence of the church intended by Jesus Christ. He affirms that a Catholic Christian is convinced that he encounters Jesus Christ in his church. Rahner finds no reason to deny the theological position of this tradition.[260] He presents the church as founded on the historical and risen Jesus Christ.[261] Jesus was not a preacher of general religious ideas; he preached an eschatological message, a historical event that is fulfilled through his own person. The kingdom of God is fulfilled in the person of Jesus Christ in a totally new and radical way.[262] The church is founded through Jesus, whom believers experienced as the absolute savior, the fulfillment of the historical self-revelation of God.[263] The only full religion is Christianity; and for Christianity to be Christianity, the personal decision in faith, hope, and love is required.[264] The church's teaching authority is based on Christology, because the church is established through Jesus, the absolute savior, the climax of salvation history and of God's self-communication.[265] While the Catholic Church is the legitimate church of Christ,[266] the other churches too are significant.[267]

The article "Ist Christentum eine absolute Religion?"[268] which Rahner published about the same time as his lectures on foundations of Christian faith in Munich, which later became *Grundkurs des Glaubens*, presents his theological position with absolute clarity. He states that the Catholic Church should enter into a relationship with the pluralistic world. Rahner understands the church as a community of believers that can become the unifying element in a pluralistic world.[269] The most difficult element of this pluralism is the pluralism of religions, which remains a reality in spite of two thousand years of Christian missionary activity. The religions of other cultures and histories were foreign to us. But today, thanks to global communication, every other human being in any life situation anywhere in the world has become our neighbor. Therefore "each religion is a question and a possibility offered to each individual. Each religion is therefore experienced as questioning the absolute claim of our own Christianity."[270]

Rahner's approach is from the perspective of dogmatics, not that of the history of religions. In relation to other religions, Christianity understands itself as the absolute and legitimate religion, since it has its beginning in the historical person of Jesus of Nazareth who is the Word made flesh, the historical presence of God in the world, whose presence is continued through the church. "Christianity understands itself as the absolute religion meant for all the human beings, and cannot acknowledge any other religion as its equal."[271] The second thesis is that until the Gospels reach the historical situation of a specific human being, the non-Christian religions have not only the natural knowledge of God but also the supernatural elements of grace; for this reason, they should be acknowledged, although in different degrees, as legitimate religions.[272] It follows that the pre-Christian and post-Christian non-Christian religions should not be considered illegitimate. Christians should consider non-Christians as anonymous Christians.[273] Rahner not only defends the theological position of the magisterium, but also explains and interprets it. His contribution here is his acceptance of non-Christian religions as legitimate logically, philosophically, and theologically, without compromising the absolute claims of Christianity.

Conclusion

I have attempted in this chapter to present Rahner's idea of the presence of Christ in non-Christian religions. We have dealt with this theme from the perspectives of his transcendental, philosophical, anthropological Christology. We have not referred to the concepts of anonymous Christ, anonymous Christian, and anonymous Christianity, because these are consequences of the transcendental Christology; besides this, there are a number of works written on these topics. Now our question is how Rahner's transcendental Christology, with the idea of the presence of Christ in non-Christian religions, can offer a valid and satisfactory answer to the question of the "relativization" of Christ and the Christian faith through pluralistic theologies, and how the transcendental Christology presents Christ and the Christian faith in a manner that is comprehensible in a pluralistic, social, and religious situation.

4

The Importance of the Theological Position of Karl Rahner in the Context of Religious and Theological Pluralism

AFTER DISCUSSING IN DETAIL the transcendental Christology of Rahner, the challenges of the pluralistic theology of John Hick and Stanley J. Samartha, and the continuity and unity in the religious consciousness of the human being in the religious and cultural context of India, we must now discuss the importance of Rahner's theological position in the context of religious pluralism. I shall argue that the application of Rahner's theological position offers a valid solution to the problem of religious pluralism, indicating also the relevance of the Catholic faith in this context and defending Catholic teachings on the mystery of the God-man, Jesus Christ.

Various Approaches to Religious Pluralism and the Significance of Rahner's Approach

We have discussed in the first chapter two influential theologians whose theocentric approach to religious pluralism is the most discussed approach today, viz., the theocentric Christology of John Hick and the revised Christology of Stanley J. Samartha. Both reject the absolute claim of Christianity and profess a pluralistic theology. Another important theologian who professes theocentrism and supports religious pluralism is Paul F. Knitter.[1] A short note on different theological positions and approaches to religious pluralism will help us understand the development of the pluralistic theological position of many present-day theologians and appreciate the relevance of Rahner's theological approach and theological position. These approaches are generally grouped in three categories: exclusivism, inclusivism, and pluralism.[2]

Exclusivism, Inclusivism, and Pluralism

Exclusivism is the older attitude of Catholic and non-Catholic European churches to religious pluralism. This position considers Jesus Christ to be the only savior and Christianity to be the only true religion. The discontinuity between Jesus Christ and other religions means that all other religions are false and there is no salvation in any religion other than Christianity.[3] The traditional understanding of the dictum *extra ecclesiam nulla salus*, the declarations of the international missionary conferences in Edinburgh in 1910, in Jerusalem in 1928, in Thambaram in 1938, in Lausanne in 1974, in the Congress on World Mission in Chicago in 1960, and the "Frankfurt Declaration" of the Convention of Evangelicals in 1970 all express this exclusivist position. Paul Knitter points out that the "conservative evangelical model of the Christian attitude to religious pluralism" is an exclusivist position.[4] The theology of the Dutch missionary Hendrik Kraemer (1888–1965), the theology of the Protestant theologian Karl Barth (1886–1968), of the bishop of the Church of South India, Stephan Neil, of Bishop Lesslie Newbegin, Norman Anderson, and the theology of Emil Brunner (1889–1966) are examples of exclusivist theological positions.[5] The extreme exclusivist view of Christian revelation and Christian religion condemns other religions and denies salvation to all who are not explicitly members of the church. This is why exclusivism is characterized as "Christomonism."[6]

Inclusivism considers other ways and religious traditions as directly or indirectly included in Christianity. Paul Knitter distinguishes two models, viz., "the mainline Protestant model," which recognizes the possibility of salvation in Christ alone, and the "Catholic model" of "one norm and many ways."[7] Gavin D'Costa observes that inclusivists are in a way "inclusivist exclusivists" or "anonymous pluralists."[8] Mariasusai Dhavamony says, "The inclusive approach . . . holds that whatever is found to be true and good in other religions is claimed to be included and transcended in Christ and Christianity. This inclusivist position is certainly catholic."[9] Alan Race believes that the theology of the Acts of the Apostles is inclusivist and the genealogy of Jesus in Luke considers Jesus as the fulfillment of God's dealings with humanity since the beginning of history.[10] The fulfillment theology of the Anglican missionary J. N. Farquhar,[11] the transcendental Christology of Karl Rahner, who emphasizes the necessity of Christ and the church, the theology of Edward Schillebeeckx with the concept of "anonymous supernatural revelation and faith,"[12] and the theology of J. A. T. Robinson and Paul Tillich with the concept of Christ alone[13] represent the "liberal wing of inclusivism,"[14] while the "cosmotheandric" theology of Raimon Panikkar with his concept of Christ as mystery and mystery not totally identified with Christ, the theology of Jules Monchanin, Henry le Saux (Swamy Abhishiktananda), Bede Griffiths, Klaus Klostermeier, Heinz Robert Schlette, Yves Congar, Henri de Lubac, and John Cobb are generally considered as inclusivist theological positions.[15]

Relativism and pluralism are actually two different expressions of the same attitude toward religious pluralism. Knitter considers relativism to be the popular attitude to religious pluralism. "All religions are relative. Christianity is the best religion for Christians. Hinduism is the best religion for Hindus."[16] This is based on the concept of the radical relativity of all historical forms.[17] Ernst Troeltsch (1865–1923) arrives at the concept of religious relativism through his idea of cultural and historical relativism.[18] He started as an exclusivist and later became a relativist. In *The Absoluteness of Christianity* Troeltsch claimed with the help of Hegel's philosophy of religion that Christianity is the absolute religion and Christ the absolute revelation.[19] But in the *Oxford Lectures* he posited the irrelevance of the absoluteness of Christianity, and the need to be aware of its relativity and individuality:[20] Christianity as a religion has no special status, but is one among equals. No religion is absolute. All religions are relative. Similarly, pluralism maintains the independent validity of other ways: all religions are equal and valid for salvation. Theocentrism is the term used by pluralistic theologians like John Hick. Alan Race says that the knowledge of God is partial in all faiths.[21] Jürgen Moltmann speaks of the relativism of the church and Christianity and of the absolutization of Christ.[22] The Catholic pluralist Paul Knitter affirms the independent validity of other ways. In the theologies of Ernst Troeltsch, Stanley J. Samartha, Knitter and others we can observe a movement from inclusivism to pluralism.

The Catholic theology of religions is christocentric. The tendencies of some of the theologians who deal with the problem of religious pluralism to move from christocentrism to theocentrism has provoked suspicion on the part of the Vatican. Such topics were discussed at the Synod of the Bishops of Asia in 1998. The christocentric theologians can be exclusivist or inclusivist. Ignatius Puthiyidam says,

> The Christocentric theologians can be exclusivist or inclusivist. All Christocentric theologies proceed from the theologians' reflections on the fundamental trends of Christianity. The theocentric schools take into consideration the date offered by other religions too in some way or other. The exclusivist Christocentric schools certainly want to solve the problem of religious pluralism through conversion. The inclusivist Christocentric schools are ready to accept the provisional salvific value of other religions. They certainly want to promote dialogue in order to further better understanding and harmony. They accept the fact and the provisional right of religious pluralism.[23]

This acceptance of the provisional right of religious pluralism on the part of Catholic theology can be the starting point for a new theology of religions. Both the theocentric pluralistic schools and the christocentric inclusivistic schools agree on the need of dialogue between the followers of world religions. This can help evolve a new theology of world religions. It is in this context that Karl Rahner's approach and method interest us.

Is Rahner an Inclusivist?

Karl Rahner is generally considered an inclusivist, since he attempts a solution to the problem of religious pluralism that accepts the salvific validity of other religions.[24] Rahner is considered either an exclusivist inclusivist or a pluralist inclusivist, and his position is accepted as a Catholic answer to the question of religious pluralism, since it is based on official church documents. At the same time, it is generally accepted that Rahner influenced the teachings of the Second Vatican Council on the relation of the church to non-Christian religions. Theologians like Paul Knitter think that Catholic theology has gone today much further than the theological position of Karl Rahner. But up to this time no serious doubt has been raised by theologians about the position of Karl Rahner and about his significance.

It is not our aim to question the inclusivism present in Rahner's theology. Our goal is to evaluate the theological position of Rahner and his interpretation as an inclusivist. The concept "inclusivism" is better understood on the basis of the meaning of this word and its usage elsewhere than in Christian theology. This usage is much older than the classification of theological approaches as inclusivism, exclusivism, and pluralism. We can better evaluate the understanding and interpretation of Rahner's theological position and that of other theologians as "inclusivism" when we compare it with the Hindu concept of religion and its self-understanding.

Paul Hacker's analysis of Indian Hindu and Buddhist religious texts concludes that inclusivism is the concept of Indian religions and philosophy of religion.[25] Hacker discerns an inclusivist religious philosophy in the Brāhmanās, the Āranyakas, the Upanisads, in cosmogonies like Hiranyagarbha,[26] in concepts like *tat tvam asi,*[27] in *Bhagavad gīta*[28] Śaiva Purāna, Pancarātra literature, Vedānta literature, the literature of neo-Hinduism, the writings of Tulasidas, and in the Dighanikāya of the Pali canons of early Buddhism.[29] The concept of Hinduism as *sanātana dharma* (universal righteousness), which includes and manifests all other forms of righteousness and the Hindu concept of reality (God, self, and the world) as *advaita* (not dual) in which all reality subsists and consists in one single reality, expresses a perfect form of inclusivism. Vedantins believe that all religions must acknowledge that they find their unity in *Vedānta.*[30] Radhakrishnan affirms that all religions are equal in worth, or in their essence or aim. But all religions find their essence in *Vedānta*, which constitutes the spiritual unity of Hinduism: "Then all religions are in a way included in Hinduism."[31] The words of Vivekananda clearly express the inclusivistic character of Hinduism:

> ours is the universal religion. It is inclusive enough, it is broad enough to include all the ideals. All the ideals of religion that already exist in the world can be immediately included, and we can patiently wait for all the ideals that are to come in the future to be taken in the same fashion, embraced in the infinite arms of the religion of the Vedānta.[32]

Radhakrishnan says, "Vedanta is not a religion, but the religion itself in its most universal and deepest significance."[33] Thus, the Hindu scriptures and theologians understand Hinduism as an inclusivistic world vision and a religion that includes all religions and a way that is essentially identical to all other ways. Hindu tolerance originates from this vision of inclusivism.

Rahner himself never uses the term inclusivism to describe his theology. Is inclusivism the most suitable characterization of Rahner's theology?

RAHNER AS TRANSCENDENTALIST

Rahner himself calls his theology transcendental theology and his Christology transcendental Christology. According to Rahner, every human being has the capacity to hear the revelation of God.[34] He calls this capacity the transcendental nature of the human being. This transcendentality is at the same time the *a priori* condition of the possibility of knowing the material object in the subject. Rahner considers the human subject as transcendence. The absolute transcendence of the human subject toward God is called revelation.[35] Revelation is the self-communication of God. Transcendental revelation is the transcendental experience and the universal salvific will of God.[36] The self-communication of God is present to the human being as history and transcendence.[37] Rahner considers God as absolute transcendence. He develops his transcendental theology by means of transcendental reduction and deduction. Transcendental theology allows us to understand the historical events of revelation.[38] Rahner also calls transcendental theology transcendental hermeneutics.[39] The idea of an absolute savior is found in the context of God's self-communication, which is coterminous with the entire spiritual history of the human race.[40] "An *a priori* sketch of the idea of Christ is the objective correlative of the transcendental structure of the human being and his knowledge."[41] This is the transcendental idea of Christ. The transcendental Christ is the *a priori* Christ. Rahner arrives at this concept by means of an analysis of the transcendental nature of the human subject with the capacity to receive the self-communication of God; this is verified through the historical experience of Jesus of Nazareth as Christ and God incarnate.

As we have seen above, Rahner understands transcendental experience as transcendental revelation. The Christology corresponding to transcendental revelation is transcendental Christology.[42] Thus it is evident that Rahner considers Christology to be the central discipline in theology. He develops his transcendental Christology philosophically with the help of transcendental hermeneutics. His understanding of transcendental theology as an extension of transcendental philosophy and as transcendental hermeneutics makes his theses more acceptable to non-Christians. Through a philosophical understanding and interpretation of the human subject in terms of transcendental philosophy, Rahner arrives at the concept of an absolute savior as a philosophical and logical possibility; he calls this the transcendental Christ. This absolute savior is absolute transcendence, the most perfect human being, the incarnation of God. He is the fullness of humanity and fullness of divinity. Since he is fullness, there can be only one absolute savior who is the absolute self-communication and transcendence of God. The question now is: Where do we find this absolute savior? Rahner believes that the absolute self-communication of God is present to human beings as history and transcendence. He is Jesus, the Christ. Our task is to discern out this absolute self-transcendence of God in history, in our historical experience.

Like many other theologians, Hick repeatedly affirms that the theology of Rahner is inclusivist. Regarding Rahner's theology of religions and his concept of anonymous Christianity through which the followers of other religious faiths "can be saved by Christ within their existing religious traditions," Hick writes,

> The attraction (to those who hold it) of this inclusivist position is that it negates the old missionary compulsion and yet is still Christocentric and still leaves Christianity in a uniquely central and normative position. For the Christian inclusivist can continue to hold that Jesus was in a literal sense God the Son incarnate, adding (a) that the same divine Son or Logos who became incarnate as Jesus has also been at work in other ways within other religions as "the unknown Christ of Hinduism" and so on; and (b) that the redeeming work which required his incarnation as Jesus of Nazareth was for the benefit of all people, within all religions and even outside all religions. Muslims, Hindus, Sikhs, Buddhists and Jews are accordingly redeemed by Christ as Muslims, Hindus, Sikhs, Buddhists and Jews. But Christians are those who know this, whilst the people of other religions do not; and Christians consciously center their lives upon the Redeemer, whilst others, outside that personal relationship, are unknowingly benefiting from his saving work. Thus Christianity can continue to regard itself as uniquely superior to all other religions.[43]

Although this summary seems to be correct, is it inclusivist—a term Rahner never used and a concept that Hinduism professed from a very early time? Is it not better to call Rahner's theology transcendentalism, a term that does justice to his philosophical theology? It is evident that the foundation of the philosophical theology of Rahner is his concept of transcendence. The transcendentality of the human subject and the concept of God as absolute transcendence form the key concept of his thought. The innate capacity of the human subject to transcend toward the Absolute and the idea of the self-transcendence of God whose fullness is incarnation defend the philosophical validity of incarnation. In this context, the theology of Rahner could be better called transcendentalism. This transcendental concept of the human experience promotes tolerance and openness toward the other. "Inclusivism" gives the impression of including all other religions in one's own religion, as does Hinduism. Our task is to inquire whether the transcendentalist Rahner offers a theological position that goes beyond inclusivism, while doing justice to religious pluralism and to the dogma of the Christian faith.

The Indian Approach to Theology and the Transcendental Christology of Karl Rahner

Continuity and Plurality of the Indian Religious Consciousness and the Transcendental Christology of Karl Rahner

Studies of the cultural, racial, and caste traditions of India have established a continuity and unity in the development of the religious traditions of India. This is the result of a long process of interaction, adaptation, and integration. Many important elements of the religion of the Dravidians are indebted to the religion of the Indian aborigines, and many elements of the religion of the Aryans (Hinduism) are indebted to the Dravidian religion. Hinduism is related in terms of its origin and development not only to the religion of the Indian aborigines and of the Dravidians but also to the religions of the Greeks, Mesopotamians, and ancient Europe. Thus we find not only continuity and unity in the development of religious faith in the Indian subcontinent, but also a relationship to the religious experience of other parts of the world. On the unity in the variety of religions and the mutual influence among various religious traditions Abhedananda says,

> You have already seen how Christianity and Mohammedanism grew from the soil of Judaism, influenced by the Zoroastrianism of Persia. Again, Zoroastrianism has its roots in the vedic religion of the ancient Hindus. Judaism in its turn gradually was developed from the polytheistic beliefs of the different tribes of Asia, of the Babylonians, Chaldeans and Phoenicians, influenced by the Zoroastrianism of Persia. Christianity was influenced by the Aryan religion, Buddhism, as also by the philosophy and religion of ancient Greece.[44]

Religious experience evolves from the prehistoric period toward the fullness of experience and realization of the absolute self-communication of the Absolute in history together with the evolution and the development of culture and civilization. It is in this context that the statement of Rahner that "Chalcedon is not the end, but the beginning" is more understandable. We can find meeting points between the philosophy of Aurobindo Ghosh and Teilhard de Chardin, who state that the entire cosmos evolves toward the Absolute, and Rahner's idea of "Christology in the context of an evolutionary worldview." Aurobindo's concept of "involution" and "evolution" can be compared to Rahner's concept of God and the human being as transcendence.

According to Max Müller, Indian religious thought spread to Italy, Rome, Greece, France, Germany, and Palestine.[45] Therefore, if we consider the history of religious experience in different parts of the world as a single whole and the history of the world as a single human history, it is possible to understand the relevance of Rahner's transcendental theology in the context of the continuity and unity of the religious consciousness of the Indian subcontinent. Pluralism exists today in India's culture, caste, race, and religious confessions. The nature of Hinduism as a religion and as a philosophy is pluralistic and inclusive. This continuity and unity in the development of the religious experience and traditions of India from the prehistoric period onward accord with Rahner's concept of one world history, one salvation and revelation history, and one absolute savior. The concept of an absolute savior who is the transcendental Christ of Rahner's transcendental theology and Christology can be considered in the context of the experience of continuity and unity in Indian religious experience as the culmination of revelation and of the experience of salvation. The history of religious experience in India has a place for the concept of an absolute savior.

The Hindu Theological Position and the Christology of Karl Rahner

Rahner's Transcendental Christology Promotes Dialogue with Hinduism

The concept of salvation history as world history acknowledges the presence of God in each person and each cultural tradition. This promotes a dialogue with the Hindu concept of the individual as having the indwelling presence of God, which must be awakened through knowledge (*jnāna*) and loving devotion (*bhakti*). Abhedananda clarifies the Hindu theological position:

> This is the position of Vedānta. Christ alone did not say that truth. Long before Christ Buddha said: Truth is one. Know it and realize it, and then you will be free; emancipation of the soul comes to you.[46]

Therefore there are many mediators, according to Hinduism. At the same time, Hinduism recognizes the unity of Reality: the human being is united with the absolute.

For Rahner, the human being is a transcendental being. The concept of human personality as "transcendental" expresses the richness of our personality. "Transcendental revelation" is the general presence of God in us, while "categorical revelation" is revelation expressed through words, events, and peoples. The idea of transcendental revelation is very close to the idea of the human person in Hinduism.

Rahner does not affirm a substantial difference between philosophy and theology.[47] In Indian thinking there is no difference between theology and philosophy. The theology of Rahner originates from his own personal spiritual experience and is based on the Ignatian spirituality of finding God in everything.[48] Theology in the Indian and oriental traditions is the expression of personal spiritual experience (*anubhava* and *darśana*). The starting point of the transcendental Christology of Rahner in human experience, and the anthropological nature of transcendental Christology as transcendental anthropology, seem similar to the Indian approach to theology, since the latter is grounded in human experience, culminating in the experience (*anubhava*) of the Absolute (*Ātman*) in the self (*ātman*).

Transcendental Christology Integrates the Hindu Approach to Christ

Because of the universalism in Hinduism, Hindus can accept Christ as God incarnate (*avatār*). Many believers of popular Hinduism do not find any difficulty in going to Christian churches to pray, without converting to Christianity. The great Hindu reformer and philosopher Vivekananda could understand and accept Christ and his message in spite of his commitment to the Hindu vision of reality:

> If I, as an oriental, am to worship Jesus of Nazareth, there is only one way left to me, that is to worship him as God, and nothing else. Do you mean to say that we have no right to worship him in that way? If we bring him

> down to our own level and simply pay him a little respect, as a great man, why should we worship at all? Our scriptures say, These great Children of Light who manifest the light, are light themselves; they being worshipped become one with them.[49]

This approach of Vivekananda, the founder of the Ramakrishna Mission as a reform movement in Hinduism, is reflected naturally in the religious life of the Hindus. In some Hindu homes we see the picture of Christ on the wall beside those of Rama and Krishna. The problem that Rahner's transcendental Christology has with Hinduism is the Hindu acceptance of other "lords and gods." Vivekananda says,

> Let us, therefore, find God not only in Jesus of Nazareth, but in all the great ones that have preceded him, in all that came after Him, and all those who are yet to come. Our worship is unbounded and free. They are all manifestations of the same infinite God. They are all pure and unselfish; they struggled and gave up their lives for us poor human beings. They each and all suffer various atonement for every one of us, and also for all that are to come hereafter.[50]

This pluralism and inclusivism existed long before the pluralistic and inclusivists thought of today's theologians. Vivekananda asserts the oriental origin of Jesus Christ: "Many times you forget that the Nazarene Himself was an Oriental of the Orientals."[51] "So we find Jesus of Nazareth, in the first place, the true son of the orient, intensely practical."[52] The pluralistic and inclusivist nature of Hinduism is also exemplified in the writings of Abhedananda and the philosophy of Radhakrishnan.

The difference is that this pluralism exists on the phenomenal level of experience, with many different manifestations of the Absolute. The challenge is to liberate Christ from this phenomenal understanding of Hinduism and raise it to the noumenal level of Christian experience. Rahner does this through his transcendental theology. According to the Christian faith, there is only one absolute savior, Jesus the Christ; Rahner defends this Christian dogma philosophically.

The observations of S. J. Samartha seem relevant in this context. He reminds us that a parallel to the Christian claim about Jesus' uniqueness can be found in the Hindu scriptures:

> Bhagavad Gita, faced with the possibility of many *mārgās* (paths of God), suggested that those who worship other gods, in reality worship Krishna alone, but not properly (B.G. IX. 23) or worship him unknowingly (B.G. IX. 24). Does not this remind one of certain Christian attitudes today? The Gita goes even further. Krishna says, "Whatever form

> any devotee wishes to worship, I make that faith of his steady" (B.G. VII. 21). Also: "in whatever way persons approach Me, in the same way do I accept them" (B.G. IV. 11). Christians can speak of the unknown Christ of Hinduism, the Hindus too can talk of the "unknown Krishna of Christianity.[53]

Rahner himself was once confronted with a similar question: when asked whether Hindus and Buddhists could consider Christians to be anonymous Hindus or anonymous Buddhists, Rahner's reply was positive. To consider the believers of other religions as anonymous believers of one's own religion is to accept others in faith, hope, and love. Such an understanding and acceptance by followers of different religions will help us to live together, pray together, and adore the one God who is the savior of all. In the context of such an openness toward the other, it is possible to discern the historical incarnation of the absolute savior as a result of religious experience and as the result of a life of witness in faith, hope, and love.

Abhedananda interprets and experiences Jesus Christ in the context of *advaita* and integrates the person and the religion (message) of Christ into his own religion:

> You will become like Christ, like God. In fact Christ means a state—a divine state. It means that an individual who reached the state of Christhood becomes Christ. Christ will be born in you, and that means you will attain that perfect state. Christ also explained that, but his disciples and followers did not understand him, and that is the reason why there is so much trouble in Christian theology. Theology goes in one direction, while Christ's religion is entirely different. You must remember that when you understand the true spirit of Christ, Christ will be born in you and you will be able to realize the same truth that Christ realized when he said: "I and my Father are one."[54]

Abhedananda can accept Christ as God, but he understands Christ's teachings in the context of the *advaita* philosophy of Sankara, the mainstream of Hindu philosophy today. He does not pay attention to categorical Christology or to the historical Christ, but to the preaching and teachings, and to the person of Christ presented in the Gospels. A discussion of the Christ of faith without any reference to the Jesus of history is acceptable to Hindu theologians like Abhedananda because the historicity of the Hindu incarnations is not decisive for Hinduism. Abhedananda continues,

> In that second spiritual birth, the old ideas and thought forms are all rejected, and new ideals and thought forms are created, and then the person begins to think differently and live differently. . . . Through spiritual exercise he developed a spiritual personality which was contradictory to his physical personality.[55]

Abhedananda speaks in terms of a spiritual transformation, but it is the pluralistic nature of Hinduism that dominates his views: "As Christians cannot think of their religion without Christ, so the Buddhists or Mohammedans cannot think of their religion without Buddha or Mohammed."[56] But in the light of our theological discussions it is possible to draw on Rahner's transcendental theology to analyze the experience of different manifestations of God on the phenomenal (*prātibhāsika*) level and to search for one absolute savior on the noumenal (*paramārthika*) level.

Hick and Samartha affirm that their pluralistic theology offers a new approach to the theology of religions, to Christ, and to other religions. It is interesting to compare their attitude with the approach of Hindu religious leaders and theologians. Hinduism integrates all the other religions into itself through the concept of universal righteousness and universal religion (*Sanātanadharma*), whereas the theocentric theology of Hick and Samartha understands all religions as equal, independent, and parallel entities, with only God above them. Rahner's transcendental theology recognizes other religions and approaches without compromising the experience of the uniqueness of Christ. For him, Christianity is not the Hindu *Sanātanadharma* (universal righteousness), because Christianity does not include all other religions. Yet Christianity can be called universal righteousness because the fullness of grace is available in Christ and in the church.

The self-consciousness of Hinduism as universal righteousness can include all religions in the general framework of Hinduism. Although Rahner recognizes and accepts the validity of all religious traditions, he does not include other religions in Christianity, but affirms absolute and final revelation of God in the absolute savior, Jesus Christ. Rahner arrives at this conclusion of the absolute revelation of God in the person of Jesus of Nazareth philosophically, logically, and anthropologically by analyzing human experience via the method of transcendental hermeneutics. Modern Hindu theologians such as Vivekananda and Abhedananda also recognize the absolute revelation of God in Jesus of

Nazareth; this is not theologically impossible for a Hindu. They also maintain the validity of revelation in the non-Christian religions and affirm the same absoluteness of revelation in many other individuals that Christians affirm in Jesus of Nazareth: God reveals himself absolutely whenever he wishes. As Saphir P. Athyal says, "Hinduism basically held the view of the equality of religions for two millenniums before Ernst Troeltsch spelled it out and John Hick and many others elaborated on it with reference to Christianity."[57] In the context of the transcendental theology of Rahner we may conclude that our common belief in one God who saves everyone unites us. This unity is the starting point for the mutual coexistence of the believers and the followers of different religious traditions.

Rahner's Theology of Incarnation in Dialogue with the Hindu Concept of "Avatār"

The Sanskrit word *avatār* is used in Hinduism to designate the concept of incarnation or the concept of God becoming a human being. There is a difference between the understanding of the concept of *avatāra* in Christianity and the understanding in Hinduism, but this same word is used in many Indian languages by Christians to designate the incarnation. Many consider the hymn *Purushasūkta*[58] of the *Vedas* of 1000 B.C.E. as the first theological germ of the doctrine of *avatār* in Hinduism.[59] The word *avatār* does not occur in the classical Upanishads. Even in the *Bhagavad-Gīta* the word *avatār* does not occur. The compiling of many fragmentary songs of the *Bhagavad-Gīta* is dated to 300 B.C.E., while the *Gīta* in its present structure and form was composed in 200 C.E.[60] It is here that we see the first reference to the concept of *avatār*. The concept of God descending to the world occurs in the *Bhagavad-Gīta*.[61] The idea of incarnation developed in Hinduism along with the devotional (*bhakti*) traditions after 600 C.E.[62] It is the *Bhagavatpurāna* of the tenth century C.E. that describes clearly the doctrine of *avatār*. In different traditions from the sixth to the eighth centuries C.E. and onward, such as the Saivaite devotional (*bhakti*) traditions of Alvars, Appar, or Tirunavukkarasar, Sambandhar, Manikkavachakar, and Sundharar, we see the development of the veneration of Krishna as the incarnation (*avatār*) of God. The writings of Sankara (eighth century), Ramanuja (eleventh century), Madhva (twelfth century), Vallabha (1481), Chaitanya (1486–1534), Kabir (1440?–1518), Dadu (1544–

1603), and the different Puranas from the sixth to the tenth centuries developed the doctrine of incarnation (*avatār*). The Krishna *Agnirasa* mentioned in Rig Veda[63] and Krishna *Devakiputra* in the Chandogya Upanishads[64] are not Krishna the incarnation (*avatār*). The concept of incarnation (*avatār*) had developed in Hinduism by 500 C.E. It is the *Adhyātmarāmayana* of the Middle Ages and *Ramacharitamānasa* of Tulasidas (1543–1623) that describe Rama as incarnation (*avatār*). Until the tenth century C.E., there is no clear reference of the worship of Rama as incarnation (*avatār*).

Thus we may conclude that the development of the concept of incarnation (*avatār*) in Hinduism is of very late origin. Before the sixth century C.E. we do not find a clearly developed theology of incarnation (*avatār*) and the veneration of Krishna and Rama as incarnation (*avatār*) of God.[65]

The development of the concept of *avatār* in Hinduism is very late. But the concept of incarnation in Christianity existed long before the development of *avatār* in Hinduism, from the first century onward, in fulfillment of the Jewish expectation of the Messiah. This concept was declared a dogma at the Council of Chalcedon in 451. The spread of Christianity in South India from the first century onward through the preaching of the apostle Thomas, and in North India because of the preaching of the apostle Bartholomew especially in Kalyan,[66] and the fact that high castes were converted to Christianity and enjoyed the first rank in the society are sufficient reason to see unity and continuity in India in the development of the concept of incarnation (*avatār*).

Although today theologians speak of "Buddhology," "Krishnology," and "Muhammadology," it is in Hinduism that we clearly find the idea of incarnation parallel to the concept of Christian incarnation. Its theo logical and scriptural roots in the ancient Hindu scriptures parallel Old Testament passages that support the fulfillment of God's self-communication and revelation in Jesus Christ. The *Bhagavad-Gīta* gives an answer to Raimundo Panikkar's concept of the *Unknown Christ of Hinduism:* "for it is I who of all acts of sacrifice am Recipient and Lord. But they do not know me as I really am."[67]

The scriptural formulation of the Christian concept of incarnation (*avatār)* is in John 1:14: the *Logos* becoming flesh. But while there are many incarnations (*avatārs*) in the *Gīta,* in Christianity there is only one incarnation (*avatār*), that is, the incarnation of Jesus the Christ, once and for all. In the *Gīta* the incarnations (*avatārs*) are for the protection of the good and for the destruction of the wicked. But the purpose of

Christ is to bring life and not to destroy (John 3:16). Again, the *Bhagavad-Gīta* speaks of partial incarnations (*avatārs*) and complete incarnations (*avatārs*), whereas in the Bible there is only one incarnation—Christ. In Hinduism incarnations (*avatārs*) come to the earth for a short time, whereas Christians believe in the continuing manhood of Jesus.[68] Robin Boyd uses the concept of perfect incarnation (*purnāvatāra)* to defend the Christian concept of incarnation, in line with Rahner's concept of incarnation:

> Christ is the (*Purnāvatāra*); he comes once and once only; he comes to bring fullness of life, not destruction; he is fully God and fully man. Perhaps one of the most helpful aspects of the *avatāra* conception, as Chakkrai saw, is that it takes Christology away from categories of substance and person—out of the realm of being into the realm of action; for Jesus came to seek, to save, to suffer, to die, to rise again and to indwell in bhaktas.[69]

Christianity does not employ the concepts of full and partial incarnation. Rahner points out that "for modern people, it is not credible, without further ado, that the event of incarnation should have taken place just once."[70] It is essential for the kerygma that we present an understanding of the world in which the hypostatic union could have taken place only once.[71] Thus the questions about incarnation, which so interested the fathers and later theologians, seem to take on renewed importance today.

Samartha arrives at a very different conclusion about the development of *avatār* in Hinduism and in the Indian traditions, possibly because he is influenced by European pluralistic theology, which developed in the context of European analytical philosophy:

> The theory of multiple *avatārās* seems to be theologically the most accommodating attitude in a pluralistic setting, one that permits recognizing both the Mystery of God and the freedom of the people to respond to divine initiatives in different ways at different times.[72]

We do not find in other religions a clear development of the doctrine of incarnation prior to its development in Christianity. Direct and indirect references to the doctrine of incarnation in other, earlier religious traditions cannot be regarded as more important than the messianic expectations of the Old Testament. The presence of this doctrine in various religions is due to the mutual interaction between cultures and religious traditions. Here we must also bear in mind the evolutionary aspect of the development of religious consciousness.

Instead of considering other "lords and saviors" as equals to Christ, or relativizing Christ as merely one of these "lords and saviors," Rahner's transcendental Christology invites us to see the presence of the universal savior, our Lord Jesus Christ, in every race, culture, ethos, and religion, in different ways and forms which permit non-Christians to experience grace through faith, hope, and love and to be saved, thanks to the universal salvific will of God.

Pre-Sixteenth-Century Traditions of the St. Thomas Christians and the Christology of Karl Rahner

The Christian life and worship of the early Indian Christians were certainly based in theology, but all theological documents of a systematic theology akin to the European type among Indian Christians before the sixteenth century are lost. This is why the word "tradition" is used here to designate their theological conception. The St. Thomas Christians were friendly and cooperative with other religious and social communities of India. They were "addressed as *Nazarāni māppilas* (if not as 'sons of the kings' or 'first kings')."[73] They were indebted from very early times to the Persian church in matters of worship and to Hinduism for the architectural style of their churches and for their social customs.[74] A. M. Mundadan (1923–), a renowned historian and theologian of the Syro-Malabar Church, writes about the theological consciousness of the St. Thomas Christians in his criticism of the synod of Diamper:

> The synod of Diamper mentions among others one particular "error." The St. Thomas Christians are said to have held: "Each one can be saved in his own law, all laws are right." The synod is right in attributing this "error" to the contacts the St. Thomas Christians maintained with their Hindu neighbors. It would be centuries before the Europeans would acquire a life-experience of non-Christian religions, before a theology of the religions of the world would emerge which would give due respect to the positive elements in those religions and their providential salvific role for millions of people. But the Indian Christians had been already living for centuries in a positive encounter with the high-caste Hindus and had developed a theological vision of the Hindu religion which was more positive and liberal. Today in the light of modern theological approaches to non-Christian religions one must admit that the vision of the Indian Christians was a more enlightened one than that of their European contemporaries.[75]

The St. Thomas Christians lived among the followers of other religious professions in tolerance and mutual recognition. This does not mean that their theological vision was that of the pluralistic theologies of Hick or Samartha. They did not make a choice among exclusivism, pluralism, and inclusivism; it may be easiest to define their attitude in the context of the unity and continuity of revelation of God in history, drawing also on Rahner's transcendental Christology. M. M. Thomas (1916–1996), a well-known theologian of the Mar Thoma Church, says that the St. Thomas Christians had the Eucharist as the center of their life, while also considering the religions of the non-Christians as valid ways of salvation:[76]

> It is signifying that the first theologically meaningful decision came under the pressure of the Portuguese Catholic mission led by the Archbishop Menezes of Goa in 1599 in the synod of Udayamperur (Diamper) that the St. Thomas Christians had to renounce their conviction that each human being—even Hindus—can obtain salvation in their religion. What the synod tried to compel through its decrees has gained acceptance later after two hundred years within the influence of the Anglican missionaries by a priest called Abraham Malpan in a reform movement which finally followed the foundation of the Mar Thoma Church.

Christianity appeared in the Roman world as a new "way" (Acts 9:2) proclaiming loyalty to Jesus Christ, the Son of God, a way of salvation (Acts 16:17). It was condemned by Roman emperors. It was to be persecuted and destroyed. The new "way" appeared in India during the same period, as a different and a distinct way called *Mārthōma mārgam* (the way of St. Thomas), on the pattern of other ways of salvation (*mārgas*). It was integrated into the religious life of Indian society. The St. Thomas Christians spoke of the way of St. Thomas, the way of St. Peter, the way of the Portuguese,[77] and so on, on the pattern of the *mārgās* (ways) in Hinduism; they also accepted the other ways as valid for salvation. But they never spoke of the way of Christ (*Christu mārga)* or relativized Christ as one among the other religious leaders. The followers of non-Christian religious traditions could accept this theological position; for this reason, and thanks to their high caste, the St. Thomas Christians enjoyed privileged positions in society. The uniqueness of Christ remained for the St. Thomas Christians on the experiential level, as an experience of transcendence: the universality of Christ was to be personally encountered and experienced. This is ultimately an experience of mystery that can be attained by the followers of other ways too, even though they do not experience and proclaim it in the historical person of Jesus. This transcendental approach is closer to the approach of Rahner.

Neither Hick nor Samartha takes into account the presence of Christianity in India and the experience of Christ from the first century onward, and its powerful influence on Indian society (at least in Kerala). Hick says: "But we should never forget that if the Christian Gospel had moved east, into India, instead of the west, into the Roman empire, Jesus' religious significance would probably have been expressed by considering him within Hindu culture as a divine *avatar*."[78] But Christianity did move to the East, into India, in the same period as it came to Rome. In many Indian languages Jesus is called as *avatār*, but not in the sense Hick means. Nor do they identify the *avatār* (incarnation) of Jesus with the Hindu concept of *avatār*. Jesus is the only *avatār,* since he is the perfect *avatār*. This understanding corresponds to Rahner's anthropological interpretation of the incarnation of Jesus as the climax of creation, the full actualization of human reality, the climax of human possibility, and as a self-transcendence which only Jesus of Nazareth can realize, because he is the Word made flesh.

The Theocentric Christology of John Hick and the Transcendental Christology of Karl Rahner

Hick himself claims that the theocentric model of his Christology is a "Copernican revolution" in Christian theology, because it is a revolutionary change from "Ptolemaic theology" (centered on one's own religion) to a "Copernican" (world-centered) view of the religious life of mankind. This change from "christocentrism" to "theocentrism" takes God rather than Christ as the center. Rahner's transcendental Christology is likewise an attempt to interpret the Christian faith today in the light of contemporary philosophical thought; one of his fundamental intentions was to promote the Christian faith and help the magisterium by defending the Catholic faith theoretically and philosophically. Hick belongs to the Presbyterian Church, but one cannot see any affinity with a specific religious confession in his theological writings; he remains more a philosopher of religion than a theologian. Despite its wide influence, Hick's theology is not acceptable to Christian churches, whereas

Rahner is considered one of the greatest twentieth-century theologians. We shall not offer a detailed comparison of the theologies of Hick and Rahner, but only highlight some of Hick's basic assumptions and claims, showing how these differ from the views of Rahner.

Basic Difference in the Understanding of Many Theological Concepts

Rahner had no direct contacts with believers of non-Christian religions, as Hick did in England, India, and Sri Lanka; nor did he study systematically the philosophy of other religious traditions as Hick did. Hick's pluralistic theology did not, however, develop directly as a result of the encounter with non-Christian religions; it is a product of European post-Enlightenment rationalism. His pragmatic approach to the interpretation of religions and the influence of analytical philosophy generate a rationalist and secularist pluralistic religious theory. According to Hick, the concept of God is an idea.[79] Since Christian experience of Christ is only one experience of Jesus, it is also possible for Jesus to be experienced as someone else:[80] the Christian experience is relative. Rahner's theology takes a radically different stance: God is not an idea but a reality, a person, a mystery, and Jesus is Christ, the Son of God, the *Logos* incarnate. Hick's comparison of religion with civilization[81] and the concept of religion as a human and ethnic reality[82] are not acceptable to Rahner. According to Rahner, the basis of religion is the experience of divine revelation, so that religion is not merely a secular reality.

Hick's understanding of religion as developing streams[83] seems to be comparable to what Rahner says about the transcending and evolutionary dimension of religious experience.[84] However, this concept does not lead Hick to any idea of mutual relationship and continuity in the development of the religious idea and religious revelation. Hick proposes global and human theologies that assert the equality of all religions.[85] Hick's concept of Christianity as one of the religions and Christ as one of the mediators[86] contradicts his own view of religion as developing streams because he denies any unity and continuity in the development he recognizes.[87] Rahner cannot accept the type of rethinking in Christianity which Hick suggests,[88] since the price to be paid is the uniqueness of Christ.

Hick's view of the concept of Christ as Son of God as fifth-century creation[89] contradicts the faith experience of the Christians, which is documented in the first five centuries. He denies the uniqueness of

Christ and the unique salvific role of the church for salvation.[90] According to him the idea of God incarnate is a myth and a metaphor: Jesus is only an inspired human being, and Christ is not preexistent. Jesus has no universal significance. Jesus himself did not claim to be God or God incarnate. All these ideas of Hick contradict the faith-experience of Christians and the confession of the faith of the Catholic Church.

Rahner's Interpretation of Chalcedon: A Critique of Hick's Critique

John Hick quotes Karl Rahner's statement, "Chalcedon is not an end but only a beginning, not goal but means, truth which opens the way to the ever-greater Truth," in support of his own view of Jesus as an inspired human being.[91] But Rahner does not deny the divinity of Jesus; all he suggests is that we must "work out a fresh concept of substantial and hypostatic unity."[92] Rahner understands the "essence" of human beings as being "unbound" or "indefinable." "To be human beings in the fullest sense (which we never attain)" is "God's presence in the world."[93] In the transcendental theology of Rahner, Jesus Christ is the fullest self-communication of God, who becomes a human being only once in human history.[94]

Rahner's statement that Chalcedon is not the end but a beginning must be understood within his own theological context. He understands the formulas of the magisterium as the result of the centuries-long work of the church in prayer, reflection, and struggle concerning God's mysteries. Their goal is to preserve religion from error, but if the end product is to be true, it must at the same time also be a beginning, opening out onto the unlimited.[95] Rahner considers this dogma to be a revelation that invites us to communion with God, just as other revelations do. "Because all the truth of the self-revealing God is given as a path and encouragement to direct communion with God, an opening onto the immeasurable, a beginning of that which is unlimited."[96] The goal of the Chalcedonian dogma is the experience of the self-communication of God in Jesus Christ. It invites us to experience this. Even in the act of being formulated, the Chalcedonian dogma "is left behind for a new reality."[97] This opens up a wider horizon for theology, but without contradicting the development of christological speculations and dogma.[98] Rahner's own interpretation and understanding of what he writes is the key to understanding Rahner and interpreting Hick's critique.

Hick's Critique of the "Anonymous Christian"

In contrast to Rahner's conclusion that Jesus is worshiped under different names, Hick says that a number of different beings are worshiped under the name Jesus or Christ. "In one sense it is true to say that he has been worshipped by millions; and yet in another sense, in terms of subjective 'intentionality,' a number of different beings, describable in partly similar and partly different ways, have been worshipped under the name Jesus or under the title of Christ."[99] Hick does not see many conflicting historical and metaphysical truth claims between religions[100] and the religious traditions of India and the Semitic world.[101] On the presence of Christ in non-Christian religions, Hick says:

> And further, it may be that Christ is also present in these other religions, and their several awarenesses of God likewise present in Christianity; so that, whilst a single world religion may well be impossible, nevertheless there may, in our communicationally unified world, be an increasing interpenetration of religious traditions and a growing of them closer together.[102]

In the essay "Christianity and the non-Christian religions" (1969), Hick appreciates Rahner's struggle to do justice to the believers of other religions but complains that Rahner has not been able to face the Copernican revolution that is required, thus contributing only "yet another ingenious epicycle to the old Ptolemaic theology."[103] Hick offers a positive view of Rahner when he writes:

> The best known attempt is that of Karl Rahner, with his concept of the "anonymous Christian." Those who do not have an explicit Christian faith but who nevertheless seek, consciously or unconsciously, to do God's will can be regarded as, so to speak, honorary Christians—and this even though they do not so regard themselves and even though they may insist that they are not Christians but Muslims, Jews, Hindus, or whatever. Rahner's is a brave attempt to attain an inclusivist position which is in principle universal but which does not thereby renounce the old exclusivist dogma.[104]

Hick holds that Rahner's concept of "anonymous Christians" was adopted by the Second Vatican Council, though without using Rahner's terminology, and that Rahner's view is reiterated by Pope John Paul II in his first encyclical *Redemptor Hominis* (1979), which declares that "every man without any exception whatever has been redeemed by Christ, and . . . with man—with every man without any exception whatever—Christ is in a way united, even when man is unaware of it."[105] The doctrine of "anonymous Christian" provides a new vision of religious pluralism.[106] In Hick's view, "an 'inclusivism' according to which non-Christians are included in the sphere of Christian salvation probably represents the nearest approach to a consensus among Christian thinkers today."[107] In spite of this appreciation of Rahner's understanding, Hick moves in the opposite direction, considering religions as independent ways and religious leaders as inspired human beings.

The Concept of Incarnation

Hick believes that "a Christian acceptance of religious pluralism must involve the rethinking of the doctrine of Incarnation." Rahner is "a prime example of one who was faithful to his own tradition but who at the same time accepted a responsibility to reformulate its affirmations in ways which are relevant and intelligible to the modern world."[108] Hick refers to Rahner's attempt to correct the popular misconception of incarnation and to "recognize the genuine humanity of Christ." Otherwise Jesus would be "God who is active among us in human form and not the true man who can be our mediator with respect to God in genuine human freedom."[109] Hick quotes Rahner and explains his view of incarnation as the "uniquely perfect instance of that relationship" of God to the human being, the "absolute peak of the relation of the created spiritual beings to God in Christ."[110] Hick accepts Rahner's view of Christology as self-transcending anthropology, and anthropology as deficient Christology.[111]

Hick says, "Rahner can even see incarnation as the supreme instance of the operation of divine grace,"[112] "the total actualization of human reality,"[113] which "has only actually happened in one unique case: 'It is only in Jesus of Nazareth that one can dare to believe such a thing has happened and happens eternally.'"[114] Rahner is a theologian who is faithful to the Chalcedonian tradition, considering incarnation as "unique and absolute" and professing Jesus Christ as both genuinely human and at the same time God.[115] Rahner attempts to make this "traditional paradox"[116] acceptable by saying that God, as God, can do anything, and therefore can become a genuinely free and independent human being whilst remaining God. Hick comments:

> This is merely however, to reiterate the traditional dogma without doing anything either to recommend it or to render it intelligible. Rahner's

> faithfulness to his tradition, with its implied absolute claim, is reflected consistently in his own theology of religions.[117]

Thus Hick sees Rahner as exclusivist, in spite of his openness toward other faiths. Hick concludes that the theological position of many inclusivists is essentially that of Rahner, "namely that salvation, whenever and wherever it occurs, is exclusively Christian salvation, so that Jews, Muslims, Hindus, Buddhists, and so on, who are saved are saved, and can only be saved, by Christ whether or not they know the source of their salvation."[118] But at the same time Hick says that the Christology of Baillie, Lampe, Harnack, John Knox, Maurice Wiles, Norman Pittenger, Karl Rahner, Edward Schillebeeckx, and Hans Küng provides "the basis for an authentically theocentric development of Christianity that is compatible with genuine religious pluralism."[119] In that case, we could say that Hick's development of Rahner, based on Rahner's own theological foundations (viz., transcendental theology) means that Hick considers the different religious traditions as independent realities whereas Rahner would consider them as parts of an ongoing process, development, and evolution into the unique and full revelation of God, which takes place when the *Logos* becomes incarnate in the person of Jesus of Nazareth.

For Rahner, Jesus Christ is the unique incarnation, the fullness of God's self-communication and self-revelation. Since human history is revelation history and salvation history, Jesus Christ is the center of human history. Thus, Rahner's conclusion is the opposite of Hick's.

The Attitude toward Non-Christian Religions

Hick considers the attitude of the Catholic Church, reflected in the council declaration that the church "rejects nothing that is true and holy in [non-Christian] religions" and respects in them the ray of that truth which enlightens all human beings, as magnificently open and charitable, but he complains that the "Vatican Council has not made the Copernican revolution that is needed in the Christian attitude to other faiths."[120] He does not agree with the teaching of *Lumen Gentium* that "salvation is only in Christ and his Church."[121] But he is happy with the new attitude: "This new thinking begins before pronouncement of the Second Vatican Council and goes beyond it, and starts with Karl Rahner's 1961 essay, prior to the Council, on 'Christianity and non-Christian religions.'" Rahner's concept of "anonymous Christian" is a struggle "to do justice to the reality of religious faith outside Christianity." but Rahner is not revolutionary enough "to face the Copernican revolution that is required."[122]

However, Rahner's transcendental theology shows that this kind of Copernican revolution is not necessary, in order to recognize and accept the religious convictions and experiences of the believers of other faiths. Nor is it correct from the perspective of the history of religious ideas or of the philosophy of religion.

Revised Christology of Stanley J. Samartha and the Christology of Karl Rahner

Samartha's theological conclusions are similar to those of Hick, although his theological background is entirely different. Samartha has two goals: a theology of religion that is theocentric and a theology of liberation. He combines these in his theocentric theology, which presents a revised or "bullock-cart" Christology.

Different Approaches to the Same Problem

Samartha theologizes in the context of his involvement in interreligious dialogue, which leads him to appeal for a revision of theological understanding and a revised Christology. He considers that salvation is possible also in names other than Jesus.[123] Samartha does not search (like Rahner) for a philosophical basis for the experience of salvation in Jesus of Nazareth, nor is his starting point in the history of religions. From his experience of religious pluralism, Samartha concludes that salvation is possible through mediators other than Jesus Christ. In the light of the theology of the *Vedas* he argues that the experience of the Mystery, response to it, and salvation are plural.[124] Samartha sees the possibility of many christologies through cross-cultural hermeneutics as responses to historical contexts and as spiritual sources for the struggle against injustice. He develops a theocentric or mystery-centered Christology which denies any exclusive claim for Christians on behalf of Christ: exclusivism is fundamentalism, a "disaster" and a "tragedy."[125] This pluralistic Christology denies the uniqueness of Jesus Christ and the claim that he is the "Son of God."

The Concept of Incarnation

For Samartha, Jesus is only one among many incarnations. He sees the Christian concepts of incarnation and of the "Son of God" as later developments in the Councils of Nicaea and Chalcedon; he does not discuss the Christian experience and belief in Jesus "Son of God" from the first century onward. At the same time, this "later development" in Christianity is the starting point of an idea of incarnation in the history of religions. The development of the concept of incarnation and its dogmatization in Hinduism and in other religions are later than its existence in Christianity. This too is disregarded by Samartha. This means that the Christian claim of the uniqueness of Jesus, which Rahner defends and interprets, can be justified.

Samartha's Interpretation of Christianity in the Context of Pluralism

Samartha attempts to construct a relevant Indian Christian theology that takes into consideration the factors of religious pluralism and oppression. In essence, it is another version of "Hindu inclusivism," and does not differ from the Hindu theological vision represented by Vivekananda, Abhedananda, or Radhakrishnan. This interpretation accords Christianity the status of a group in Hinduism like Vaishnavism or Saivaism, which are considered valid movements, each with its own unique features. But Christianity understands itself neither as one among many religious movements with its own religious leaders and symbols nor as a universal world vision in which all other religions have equal status. The first approach would consider Christianity as a part of Hinduism, while the second would lead only to conflict. A Hindu believer would not recognize a claim of equality. According to the Hindu worldview, the term *Sanātanadharma* (universal righteousness) is applicable only to Hinduism. But a transcendental worldview and a transcendental Christology which emphasizes the transcending and evolving nature of reality neither questions the basic claim of Hinduism nor accepts the Hindu world vision. In addition, an emphasis on the transcendental nature of reality does not contradict the Hindu view of reality. It views Christianity from an entirely different perspective. The use of Rahner's transcendental hermeneutics to interpret Christ and Christianity in the context of other religions and ideologies establishes the Christian vision of God, Christ, and the human being without contradicting the claims of other religious beliefs; and at the same time, Rahner defends the claims of Catholic belief.

The Relevance of the Approach of Rahner

It is true that the "christocentrism" and the "ecclesiocentrism" of Rahner are not acceptable to pluralists, nor his "transcendentalism" to many Catholic theologians, because of the symbolism and idealism these involve. Speaking of the "anonymous Christian," Rahner affirms that one will scarcely find a more adequate terminology to do justice to the reality of pluralism in religious experience and to the Christian experience of the absolute savior in Jesus of Nazareth. The Hindu vision of the human being, with its concept of the different levels of truth experience[126] and different levels of human self-realization, culminating in the experience of the Absolute, fits in better with the concept of transcendental experience and transcendentalism in theological thinking.

The Significance of Rahner's Approach in the Context of Catholic Doctrine

Many Indian Christian theologians from the sixteenth century onward have drawn on Indian philosophical and theological terminology in order to interpret the Christian faith, just as Karl Rahner used the terminology of Martin Heidegger or the terminology of Thomas Aquinas (who in turn used Greek terminology) to interpret Christian faith. The difference between Rahner and these Indian theologians is that Rahner tried to establish the presence of Christ in non-Christian religions dogmatically; nobody before or after Rahner has dared to attempt this challenge. Rahner's attempt to find an apt terminology to express the experienced truth and his efforts to remain faithful to the official teachings of the church caused criticism of his theology. Rahner accepts the believers of other religions on an equal basis without compromising his own faith. In this respect, his theological position may be considered unique among theologians. Given his attempts to make the Christian faith relevant in the context of multiple religious traditions, Rahner's approach should be given serious consideration. His transcendental Christology can supply the key for evaluating such theological concepts as "the universal Christ and the particular Christ"; "the historical and transhistorical Christ";[127] "Jesus is Christ; Christ is more than Jesus";[128] "absolute faith without absolute claims";[129] and so on.

The Relationship between Rahner's Theology and the Official Teaching of the Church

Rahner theologizes as a Catholic theologian, not as a philosopher or theologian of religions. His confession of the Catholic doctrines of faith, the truths of the Bible and the teachings of the church fathers, and his loyalty to the magisterium are reflected in his entire christocentric theology, where we see how Rahner defends his philosophical, theological, and logical openness to the world and to the natural sciences while at the same time manifesting his fidelity to the theological position of the church. We can also see how he makes theology a discipline compatible with other sciences. In Herbert Vorgrimler's words, "Karl Rahner is loyal to the Church and to the Church traditions at least as much as his critics are loyal to the Church."[130]

Traditional Christology from below begins with Jesus of Nazareth. But the starting point of Rahner's Christology from below is not the person of Jesus, but human experience.[131] Rahner makes it clear why we are interested in this Jesus of Nazareth rather than in Socrates, Buddha, or Gandhi. Although Rahner is faithful to the Catholic theological position, he emphasizes the human aspect involved in understanding and articulating the concept of revelation. Rahner maintains total loyalty to the magisterium and defends the Catholic theological position while at the same time opening up possibilities for accepting other articulations, religions, or professions of faith. He interprets and explains the Catholic faith which he professes, so as to make Catholic teaching acceptable in the present-day religious, theological, and philosophical context. He says that revelation in Jesus Christ "implies the concept of the church and the communion of believers," through which "the self-communication of God is handed on."[132] Therefore this conclusion of revelation is "an opening and an inauguration" of the absolute and unsurpassable self-communication of God to created spirits.[133] This conclusion of revelation is what is handed on through the church "in its development of the dynamics of the development of dogma."[134] Rahner attempts to explain and interpret the concept of revelation and the self-communication of God philosophically and anthropologically, while affirming that the eschatological finality of revelation in Jesus Christ cannot be explained in a purely natural way.[135]

The encounter between the gospel and a particular people involves not only elements of a natural knowledge of God in non-Christian religions but also supernatural elements of grace which God gives to the human being through Christ. This is why non-Christian religions should be understood as filled *a priori* with supernatural grace.[136] They should be considered in varying degrees as legitimate mediations of a relationship with God and instruments of salvation.[137] All persons in all times and all situations of human history, even outside the recognized religions, must have the possibility of a relationship with the God of salvation.[138] This does not, however, mean that every non-Christian religion is legitimate in the same way as the Old Testament.[139] Christians should consider non-Christians not as persons untouched by the grace and the revelation of God,[140] but as anonymous Christians.[141]

Another positive aspect of Rahner's transcendental Christology is that the Catholic catechism can be interpreted in the light of his transcendental theology and transcendental hermeneutics. Rahner's philosophical theology presents doctrines of Christian faith in a style that is understandable and acceptable to the intellectual world. The *Catechism of the Catholic Church* says, "The desire for God is written in the human heart, because man is created by God and for God" (27). This "desire for God" can be formulated in Rahnerian terminology as the transcendental openness of the human being or as the supernatural *existential* of the human being. The church affirms the possibility of knowing God on the basis of the world (cf. *Catechism* 32). Rahner develops this concept on the basis of his experience of Ignatian spirituality and mysticism and reaches the conclusion that one can find Christ through the experience of God in the world.[142] "God willed both to reveal himself to man, and to give him the grace of being able to welcome this revelation in faith" (*Catechism* 35). Rahner calls this the "self-communication" of God to every human being.[143] The church fosters "dialogue with other religions, with philosophy and science, as well as with unbelievers and atheists" (*Catechism* 39), and this is the main thrust of Rahner's theological task.[144] The church understands the Incarnation as the culmination of the self-revelation of God, and Rahner substantiates this by means of his transcendental Christology.[145]

The International Theological Commission has criticized the "soteriological theocentrism" that denies the universal salvific significance of

Jesus and considers incarnation a metaphor. The document considers inclusivism an approach acceptable to the Catholic Church. It is evident that inclusivism is not understood in this document in the Hindu sense (i.e., including non-Hindu religions in Hinduism); we are told that inclusivism means not only a "thematization of the transcendence" but the "intensive realization of the same," in which the human being is called to radical decision. The document considers the proclamation of the Word of God as directed to all cultures and races. This "inclusivism" is closer to the transcendentalism of Rahner. The terminology of the document, especially the "thematization of the transcendence" and the statement that the other expressions and understandings are perhaps "derived from the same transcendental event," clearly shows a transcendental approach. The term inclusivism is understood and interpreted by the International Theological Commission from the perspective of Christ's role in the dispensation of universal salvation.

Nostra Aetate says that non-Christian religions possess rays of truth.[146] But the council does not say that they are included in Christianity. Instead, the Catholic Church acknowledges the presence of Christ in non-Christian religions[147] along the lines of Karl Rahner's theological understanding.

Pope John Paul II writes in *Fides et Ratio* that faith remains charged with mystery: "Faith alone makes it possible to penetrate to mystery in a way that allows us to understand it coherently. . . . Faith is said first to be an obedient response to God. This implies that God be acknowledged in his divinity, transcendence and supreme freedom" (13). The concept of mystery, transcendence, and hope in this encyclical is similar to Rahner's understanding of God as mystery and transcendence and human transcendental experience of the mystery in faith and freedom. The encyclical refers to the teachings of the two Vatican councils and says:

> Revelation has set within history a point of reference which cannot be ignored if the mystery of human life is to be known. Yet this knowledge refers back constantly to the mystery of God which the human mind cannot exhaust but can only receive and embrace in faith. Between these two poles, reason has its own specific field in which it can inquire and understand, restricted only by its finiteness before the infinite mystery of God (14).

This idea is in harmony with Rahner's concept of an absolute savior as absolute revelation within history, as the climax and reference point in the history of salvation and revelation. The relationship between the "mystery of human life," "mystery of God," and "faith" expressed in the encyclical can be explained with the help of the anthropological theology of Rahner. The pope writes: "The truth of Christian Revelation, found in Jesus of Nazareth, enables all men and women to embrace the 'Mystery' of their own life" (15). This relationship between the truth of the Christian revelation in Jesus of Nazareth and the mystery of one's own life is in harmony with Rahner's concept of incarnation and his Christology from below.

Rahner's philosophy and that of *Fides et Ratio* complement each other. Since Rahner wrote in the context of church tradition and patristic teaching, with the purpose of interpreting and defending Catholic doctrine both philosophically and logically, his theology supports Catholic doctrines.

Rahner's Transcendental Christology in the Context of the Current Trends in the Catholic Theology of Religions

Concerning theologians' attempt to go beyond Rahner in the interpretation of Christ and Christian dogma in the context of religious pluralism, we must ask whether these efforts to develop Rahner have in fact abandoned him. Recent approaches in favor of pluralism abandon the christocentrism and ecclesiocentrism implied in Rahner's transcendentalism. A theocentrism which denies christocentrism is not a Catholic theology of religions. Pluralism considers different religious traditions as independent units with an equal claim to validity. A pluralist does not consider the unifying elements in different religious traditions and the continuity in the development of human religious traditions.

Exclusivism, as generally understood, is not a Catholic position. Yet the term "inclusivism" is confusing, since it is an accepted expression for the Hindu concept of reality and theology of religions. Even a new word may not be fully satisfying. As Rahner says concerning his expression of an anonymous Christian, our attempt should be to find the most suitable term until a better one is discovered. Rahner's transcendentalism clearly unites inclusivism, pluralism, and theocentrism into a single concept by using the term transcendence to interpret the human being, God, and Christ.

Felix Wilfred says that the theology of religions today goes beyond settled foundations, viz., beyond the concept of inclusivism.[148] "The radical new Indian theology of religions" abandons, in the context of dialogue, "the sensitive and delicate question of uniqueness of Jesus."[149] He wants to maintain the "relationship between unity and plurality" in interpreting Christian dogma in the cultural context.[150] He says, "How are we to reconcile the unity of faith represented by the dogmas and the plurality that will result if the Christian mystery and dogma are interpreted and expressed starting from different cultural horizons, with different resources, presuppositions, etc."[151] Joseph Pathrapankal asks whether the inclusive approach sufficiently recognizes the positive meaning of other religions. Is the meaning of other religions conditioned and controlled by Christ and Christianity?[152] He says,

> Hence more and more theologians are moving away from the inclusivist position of viewing Christianity as the necessary and unique fulfillment and norm for all other religions to a more pluralistic model which affirms the possibility that other religions are equally valid and relevant as Christianity itself. They are beginning to admit that other religious personalities may be carrying out, in different ways, revelatory and salvific roles analogous to that of Jesus Christ.[153]

Raimon Panikkar says, "The Christ of every Christian generation is more than a remarkable Jewish teacher who had the fortune or misfortune of being put to death rather young."[154] Paul F. Knitter reinterprets the understanding of the uniqueness of Jesus Christ[155] by saying that Jesus is "God's truly but not only saving word."[156] D'Costa attempts to use the concept of "christocentric trinitarianism" to interpret Christ and the Christian faith in the pluralistic predicament.[157]

M. Amaladoss finds the three paradigms of exclusivism, inclusivism, and pluralism unsatisfactory,[158] since the ecclesiocentrism of inclusivism, the negative attitude of the exclusivists toward other religions, and the neglect of the "otherness" of other religions by the pluralists (which they reduce to nominalism) are all problematic.[159] He proposes a phenomenological approach in terms of "absolute" and "relative" relationships.[160] He says, "this pluralism is integrated within the one plan that God has for the world. The unity of the plan of God is a unity of relationships, neither of identity nor of simple plurality. Relationship implies a plurality of roles and functions within a totality."[161] The profound meaning of affirming that Christ is the universal savior is that God is really the savior of all the peoples.[162]

Hans Küng, who has devoted much attention to constructing a global ethics, says,

> Thus I have tried to walk the difficult *via media* between two extremes. On the one hand I wanted to avoid a narrow-minded, conceited *absolutism* (of Christian and Islamic provenience), which sees its own truth as "absolute," that is, detached from the truth of the others. I have aimed to defend neither a *standpoint of exclusivity,* which issues a blanket condemnation of the non-Christian religions and their truth, nor a *standpoint of superiority,* which rates my own religion as a priori better (in doctrine, ethics, or system).[163]

But Küng's theology of religious pluralism is criticized by the Hindu theologian Bibhuti S. Yadav: "Küng is in search of words which could gently show that the world is smaller than the Vatican."[164] But Küng does not let God be God.[165] "Küng's theology is a methodology of absolutising a particular form of life."[166]

Catholic theologians who deal with the reality of religious pluralism do not doubt the need for evolving a new Catholic theology of religions, acceptable not only to Catholics but also to non-Christians. This is why the main trend in contemporary Catholic theology in India has been the Christian interpretation of non-Christian religions and involvement in interreligious dialogue. Kuncheria Pathil says, "Dialogue and collaboration should be based on the principle and right of pluralism which calls for equality of status and dignity and respect for the other as the other. Christianity has to recognize the other religions as "religions," as "ways of salvation" to their believers.[167] "Shall we not say that the universal plan of God and his effective salvific will penetrate the whole of human history including all peoples, their cultures and religions? Shall we not say that all authentic religions have a salvific role in so far as they are activated by the same saving Spirit of God?" Ignatius Puthiadam emphasizes the greatness of God. He confesses, "But I know well God is greater than Christianity, greater than Jesus Christ and it is in Him all religions find their ultimate center. I will remain in dialogue with all of them and work together with them for the creation of a new society."[168] Raimon Panikkar says, "both the myths, Christianity's religious superiority and the Church's cultural immunity, are in crisis today."[169] Theologians now investigate the possibility of theologizing in the multireligious context of pluralism without denying the Catholic dogma of the uniqueness and universality of Jesus Christ.

An attempt to integrate christocentrism and theocentrism is made by Jacques Dupuis, who says that an African or Asian Christology can no longer dispense with serious reflection on the encounter of Jesus Christ with the religions:[170] "In a Christian theology of religions, Christocentrism and theocentrism go hand in hand; indeed they are inseparable. There can be no Christian theocentrism without Christocentrism; but neither can there be a genuine Christocentrism that will not at the same time be theocentric." He suggests a combination of deductive and inductive methods; "the hermeneutic key of a Christian theology of religion is not a Christ without Jesus, but Jesus-the-Christ."[171] "A Christian theology of religion is Christology. Far from fostering exclusivism, Christian Christocentrism is capable of integrating, in their difference, all religious experiences into a truly catholic-inclusive and universal-theology." Thus Dupuis clearly defines his theological position as christocentrism.

Another noteworthy contribution is the attempt to define the "universally unique and uniquely universal" significance of Jesus Christ in the religious pluralistic context.[172] Subhash Anand says, "Jesus is God's loving presence within history. A human being can be in history only once. Hence this presence of God within history in and through Jesus is once for all, but it is for all."[173] Sebastian Athappally states clearly that the claim of the uniqueness of Jesus Christ is a *skandalon* with which we have to live, without any compromises.[174] But according to Francis X. D'Sa "the traditional notion of uniqueness which is dogmatic and one-sided cannot do justice" to the multireligious experience of today:[175]

> What makes difficulties for Christians (especially of the western variety) is that their understanding of uniqueness derives from the western world-view of history where uniqueness is perceived numerically: hence it is understood exclusively. But some Indian Christian theologians are beginning to look at uniqueness from a different angle. They would find it difficult to maintain the kind of uniqueness of Jesus which does not tolerate the uniqueness of, for example, the Buddha. The uniqueness which states that, the Buddha is unique, Jesus cannot be unique, would not be acceptable to these theologians because their concept is of inclusive uniqueness.[176]

D'Sa suggests a "more comprehensive hermeneutic principle for the development of a Christian theology in India." He compares the unique role of Jesus Christ with the unique role of a sense in the body. The eye alone can see. The mouth can speak. The skin can feel. Each one has a unique *dharma.* The uniqueness of each organ is grounded in the uniqueness of the human person. He says,

> Similarly the uniqueness of each religion is grounded in the absolute uniqueness of the Ultimate Mystery. It is the uniqueness of the Ultimate Mystery. It is this uniqueness that manifests itself in the unique dharma of the cosmic body. The uniqueness of Jesus has to be seen in this light because of our multi-religious context.

Anand Amaladoss writes: "I think that Indians are not so much interested in the metaphysical composition of Jesus' personality or the complexities of his divine-human psychology as in his significance for our life today. They try to explore this significance through images like the '*guru,*' the 'liberator,' the 'man of sorrow,' the 'cosmic dancer,' etc."[177]

A worshiper of Christ who lives in the Indian religious situation of *jnana* (contemplation), *bhakti* (devotion), and *karma* (action) and who practices *bhakti* and *prapatti,* contemplation and action, which is a purely Christian way of life, may indeed ask whether so much debate on the conceptualization of faith doctrines is necessary; thousands of believing Christians are not concerned about the validity of non-Christian religious traditions or the absolute validity of Christianity. They believe in Christ, love him, participate in liturgical life and try to follow him. They live in a world beyond conceptualization. In this context we can dream of a "theology of humble waiting" in joyfully and faithfully sharing the Christ-experience.[178] On this, Francis Vineeth says, "This theology, therefore, moves with the spirit of a basic search with its own faith in Jesus Christ, desirous of delving deep into the very mystery of Christ which though appeared in 'certain fullness' will appear in 'capital fullness' only at the end of time."[179] This transcendental openness and eschatological claim provide new paths for a theology of religions. Vineeth says, "But the economy of salvation wrought in Christ is really Catholic and thus all pervading. Until the final fullness of Christ is manifested in that eschatological moment, in which everything will be gathered in Christ, the Church will keep on unveiling new dimensions of Christ in and through her encounter with their religions."[180]

D. S. Amalorpavadass devoted his life to the Indianization of the Christian church through theological, liturgical, and catechetical programs. Describing his efforts as the "christianization of Hinduism,"[181] he concentrated on experiencing the presence of Christ in the Indian religious, theological, and cultural contexts and on imparting this experience to the faithful and to the believers of other religions.

A transcendental approach to the interpretation of Christian dogma in the context of religious pluralism seems the best model for a Catholic theology of religions; this approach should be linked closely to Rahner's transcendental hermeneutics. The mirror image of Christ reflected in the *Vedas*, Brahmasutras, Ithihasas, and so on is better understood and interpreted in the language of Rahner and his idea of an *a priori* Christ. Panikkar's interpretation of Christ, his Christology based on the concept of *Īswara* of the Brahmasutras[182] and the development of the *cosmotheandric* Christ in his interpretation of Christ from a *theandropocosmic* viewpoint,[183] Bede Griffith's understanding of Christ based on the concept of *Purusa,*[184] and Abhishiktananda's interpretation based on the concept of *Saccidānanda* of *Vedāntha*[185] can be easily integrated into the frame of a transcendental Christology. Yet at the same time, these theologies can integrate within themselves Rahner's transcendental theology. Panikkar says,

> A pluralistic Christian will not confess many saviors. That would be a non-pluralistic assertion, since the faith experience of savior is unique for each believer and cannot be multiplied. A pluralistic Christology will begin by saying that the mystery of Christ cannot be reduced to a quantitative understanding. While believing that the mystery of Christ is of far-reaching significance, I cannot possibly say that it is only important to my own personal salvation, my own church, or my church's doctrinal tradition. Yet it would be improper to absolutize my own limited understanding in such a way that I monopolize this mystery.[186]

Panikkar affirms the universal significance of Christ, but without absolutizing his own personal conviction.

A theology based on Christian experience of the person of Jesus Christ should be fostered. Christians experience Jesus as the Lord, the *Logos* incarnate. A Christology based on the personal experience of the person of Jesus Christ (Acts 2:14–36) can be supported and verified through an analysis of the human experience. Karl Rahner does this against the background of the Bible, traditions, the fathers, conciliar documents, and church dogmas. The sacramental life and the experience of the eucharistic celebration promote the encounter with the person of Jesus Christ and deepen one's personal experience of him. Christians believe and preach what they experienced (Acts 4:11–13). At the same time, a genuine experience will help Christians to recognize and accept the religious experience of our brothers and sisters of other faiths. A genuine faith will inspire Christians to live in accordance with their experience of the truth.

A transcendental approach to reality will foster brotherhood and mutual acceptance. A transcendental hermeneutics to interpret the religious reality of the world realizes the transcendental experience of the absolute savior, who is Jesus the Christ. Rahner's transcendental theology can assist believers today, just as in the past the theology of an Augustine and an Aquinas helped in interpreting and defending the faith.

Conclusion

THE AIM OF THIS STUDY was not the construction of an entire theology of religious pluralism. Any attempt to interpret the Christian faith in terms of one approach to religious pluralism—that is, exclusivism, inclusivism, christocentrism, ecclesiocentrism, soteriocentrism, relativism, the psychological interpretation of religious experience, and so on—would of necessity be limited; nor is it easy to suggest a better terminology. While a provisional validity can be perceived in many such concepts, the abandoning of the christocentric concept of salvation is a denial of the Christian faith and traditions. Our task is to interpret the Christian faith in the present context without denying the Christ-experience of Christians and the dogmatic, biblical, and theological traditions, which have a significant position and role in the history of human religious experience.

There is a correspondence between Karl Rahner's Christology, on the one hand, and the continuity and plurality present in Indian religious consciousness and the pre-sixteenth-century theology of the St. Thomas Christians, on the other. This makes Rahner's theological approach and transcendental Christology appropriate instruments for interpreting Christian faith in the context of religious pluralism, especially in India.

An evaluation of the approaches of Hick and Samartha and a presentation of the challenges which they raise underlines the importance of going beyond exclusivistic rigidity and pluralistic relativism to encompass reality, while at the same time recognizing what we might call a provisional exclusivism and pluralism. Rahner's transcendental Christology is a theology that goes beyond inclusivism. Using Rahnerian terminology, we call this approach transcendentalism; this entails a provisional inclusivism. A concept closer to this in the Indian language may be the theology of *anubhava* (experience).

The relationship of this work to the history of religions and to the philosophy of religion may be seen through a study of the anthropological and the transcendental approach in hermeneutics. This is in accord with Rahner himself, since he presents the philosophy of religion as the ontology of the *potentia oboedientialis* for revelation; the philosophy of religion is "the inner moment of general ontology" dependent on the history of religions.[1] Each human being has the "capacity to hear" the Word of God, and thus the potential to be a theologian through the grace which empowers one to receive this Word as it appears in history.[2] This essential and undeniable relationship between philosophy of religion and theology generates two aspects of metaphysics, both based on metaphysics, in the sense that theology deals with the *a priori* possibility of the human being to hear the Word of God (revelation that subsists in the very essence of the human being), while the philosophy of religion appeals to reason by considering metaphysics as general ontology of the knowledge of God. Revelation is historical, although it seems to be essentially "supratemporal" and "suprahistorical." The philosophy of religion is metaphysical because it deals with a religion independently of its historical existence, in its universality and newness.[3] Since the philosophy of religion is "natural metaphysics," it is the only basis for theology.[4]

The theologies of Hick and Samartha have their own positive elements as responses to the reality of pluralism in religions. But the theocentrism they propose is not acceptable. Their consideration of incarnation as myth and metaphor contradicts the Christian experience of Jesus Christ. If Indian theologians attempt to interpret the Christian faith in the light of the pluralistic theology of Hick and his followers, who work against the background of postmodern European Enlightenment, this will offend Indian religious traditions. Indian philosophical and religious traditions provide sufficient foundation for a theology of religions that will provide better answers to our many theological questions.

The fact that Rahner is a European theologian who interpreted the Christian faith in the light of European philosophy is not to be neglected. But his theology can go beyond the limitations of European philosophy, since his universal outlook and openness toward other religious experiences are able to integrate the "rays of truth" in other religions and to accept these as valid ways of salvation. We do not deny that an interpretation of the Christian faith in the light of Indian philosophy can perhaps answer the problems of religious pluralism better and easier. Pope John Paul II says, "In India particularly, it is the duty of Christians now to draw from this rich heritage the elements compatible with their faith, in order to enrich Christian thought" (*Fides et Ratio* 72). However, Rahner's transcendental approach and transcendental method, by their very nature, go "beyond" experience and can help us to understand the transcending nature of religious experience and of the human being. According to Rahner, the human being of its very nature transcends toward the Absolute. Jesus Christ is absolute transcendence, the perfect human being, the *Logos* made flesh, God incarnate. Rahner's theological position complements the "trinitarian christocentrism" formulated by the Congregation for the Clergy.[5]

Rahner's theology is christocentric and ecclesiocentric. Through his transcendental Christology, he makes an ontological defense of the universal possibility of salvation. He accepts the unity of human history and the unity of salvation and revelation: natural human history is also salvation history and revelation history. Non-Christian religions belong to the universal salvific plan of God just as Christianity does. The unique role of the church is the result of the unique self-communication and self-revelation of God and of his grace.

Rahner states that Jesus Christ is the fulfillment of God's self-communication and self-revelation; at the same time, he recognizes the availability of the experience of Christ and his presence in non-Christian religions, though in a way different from Christian experience through the church. For this reason, Rahner's christocentric and ecclesiocentric transcendentalism, developed in the light of the Christology of the Bible, the fathers, the conciliar documents, the encyclicals, and documents of the magisterium, interprets the Christian faith with the help of contemporary philosophy. It also makes Christian faith reasonable and understandable, while expressing an openness to dialogue with other religions, ideologies, natural sciences, and philosophies.

Notes

Introduction

1. See G. Evers, "Trends and Conferences in the Field of Inter-Religious Dialogue," *Studies in Inter-Religious Dialogue* 8, no. 2 (1998): 244, 245.

2. Ibid., 246.

3. The description of Herbert Vorgrimler of the life of Karl Rahner seems to provide the substance of Rahner's theology. Vorgrimler says, "A life with God: This life was in a circle around that which we call God, a search for God, a wrestling with God, a salvage for God, a continuous exposition of idols, a destruction of wrong pictures of God, a blind touch to the silent mystery, and certainly, some times, a rejoicing overcome in the bliss of this mystery" (*Karl Rahner verstehen* [Freiburg/Basel/Vienna, 1985], 12).

4. See K. Rahner, *St. Theresa of Avila: Doctor of the Church, Opportunities of Faith*, trans. E. Quinn (New York, 1970), 123–26.

5. See K. Lehmann, "Philosophisches Denken im Werk Karl Rahners," in *Karl Rahner in Erinnerung*, ed. A. Raffelt (Düsseldorf, 1994), 10–28, esp. 11, 18; B. J. Hilbreath, *Karl Rahner*, 61.

6. See H. Vorgrimler, *Karl Rahner: Leben, Denken, Werke* (Munich, 1963), 35, 49, 59.

7. See K. Rahner, "Hat unser Dialog reale Bedeutung?" in *Sehnsucht nach dem geheimnisvollen Gott*, ed. H. Vorgrimler (Freiburg/Basel/Vienna, 1990), 73–77.

8. See K. Rahner, "Dogmengeschichte in meiner Theologie," in *Dogmengeschichte und katholische Theologie*, ed. W. Löser. K. Lehmann, and M. Lutz-Bachmann (Würzburg, 1985), 323–28.

9. Rahner's approach in developing his themes in *Geist in Welt, Hörer des Wortes, Theos im Neuen Testament, Probleme der Christologie von heute,* etc. is very philosophical.

10. *Worte ins Schweigen* (Innsbruck, 1947) is a good example of Rahner's philosophical style with a deep spiritual insight.

11. P. Knitter, *No Other Name?* (New York, 1984), 131.

12. Ibid., 133.

Chapter 1
The Reality of Religious Pluralism and the Challenge of a Pluralistic Theology

1. See A. Peelman, *Christ Is a Native American* (New York, 1995), 104.

2. See J. Kadiba, "In Search of a Melanesian Theology," in G. W. Trompf, *The Gospel Is Not Western: Black Theologies from the Southwest Pacific* (New York, 1987), 139–48, esp. 146, 147.

3. In the context of African cultures and traditions Christ is understood as Jete-Ancestor (E. J. Pénoukou), Nana-great ancestor (J. S. Pobee), the elder Brother (H. Sawyerr), the head and the master (A. T. Sanon), the healer (Aylward Shorter), proto-ancestor (Bénézet Bujo), etc. See C. Nyamiti, "African Christologies Today," in *Faces of Jesus in Africa*, ed. R. J. Schreiter (New York, 1995), 3–24, esp. 3ff.; J. M. Éla, *My Faith as an African* (New York, 1988; London, 1989; originally published as *Ma foi d'Africain* [Paris, 1985]), 13ff.

4. See K. B. Douglas, *The Black Christ,* 3rd ed. (New York, 1994), 1ff.

5. R. Panikkar, *The Unknown Christ of Hinduism* (London, 1964).

6. S. J. Samartha, *Hindus vor dem universalen Christus: Beiträge zu einer Christologie in Indien* (Stuttgart, 1970).

7. M. M. Thomas, *The Acknowledged Christ of Indian Renaissance* (London, 1969).

8. Continuity has been confirmed by the research of the following authors: M. Eliade, *History of Religious Ideas,* vol. 1, 125ff.; K. K. Klostermaier, *A Survey of Hinduism*, 31ff.; G. E. Moore, *History of Religions* (Edinburgh, 1971; first published, 1914), 243ff.; P. D. Mehta, *Early Indian Religious Thought,* 20ff.; E. Hardy, *Indische Religionsgeschichte* (Leipzig, 1896), 19ff.; M. Coppieri, "Ist die Induskultur wirklich verschwunden?" *Anthropos* 60 (1995): 719–62; W. Koppers, "Zentralindische Fruchtbarkeiten und ihre Beziehungen zur Induskultur," *Geographica Helvetica* 1 (1946): 165–77. Such a continuity has been observed also in Africa, and the need for safeguarding the continuity has been asserted by Jean Marc Éla, writing on ancestors and Christian worship: "The subject of this chapter—relationship between the ancestors and the Christian faith—is meaningless for a form of Christianity that merely transfers dogmas, rites and customs formed overseas for African traditions, which are then violently cast off. But discussion of this relationship becomes a very important question for a faith that can accept, with discernment, all the signs of an existing culture. Of course such openness requires an effort to purify and liberate" (*My Faith as an African*, 13). John Hick, the well-known prophet of pluralistic theology, himself affirms a continuity in the religious consciousness of mankind as a universal human relationship to God. "If God is the God of the whole world, we must presume that the whole religious life of mankind is part of a continuous and universal human relationship to him. . . . However instead of thinking of religion as existing in mutually exclusive systems perhaps we should see the religious life of mankind as a dynamic continuum within which certain major disturbances have from time to time set up new fields of force, of greater or lesser extent, displaying complex relationships of attraction and repulsion, absorption, resistance and reinforcement. These major disturbances are the great creative religious movements in human history from which the distinguishable religious traditions have stemmed" (*God and the Universe of Faiths* [London, 1993; first published, 1973]), 101, 102; Hick says, "Christians have become increasingly conscious of the continuing reality of the other great religious traditions" (*Problems of Religious Pluralism* [London, 1985; repr., Wiltshire, 1995], 31).

9. See H. Crowland, *Cambridge Ancient History,* vol.1 (Cambridge, 1967), 2–47.

10. The Negritto and Proto-Australoid people of India, who were conquered by the Dravidians around the third millennium B.C.E. founded the village system, and it was their contribution to the world. Their well-developed religion was centered on their village system for its practices. The same people were living in this period also in Indonesia and further India. See Mehta, *Early Indian Religious Thought,* 20–21.

11. Many descendants of this people are living today in an underdeveloped situation.

12. The word *Samhita* means "collection." It is a collection of hymns. *Rigveda,* a collection of 1,017 hymns distributed in ten books, is the first monument of Indian genius, which is also the earliest literature produced within the Indo-European family of peoples. See J. N. Farquhar, *An Outline of the Religious Literature of India* (Delhi/Patna/Varanasi, 1964; first published, Oxford, 1920), 6.

13. The religious philosophy of contemporary Hinduism is mainly *Advaita, Viśistadvaita* and *Dvaitā.* The *bhakti* traditions are the most popular trend of contemporary Hinduism. *Advaita,* the religious philosophy of Sankaracharya (788–820), is in the words of Dr. S. Radhakrishnan "a system of great speculative daring and logical subtlety," which considers salvation as the union of the individual self with the ultimate self (realization) through the means of self-knowledge (*Jnana*) having the supreme role of continuing and influencing the later religious thought of the sub-continent. See S. Radhakrishnan, *Indian Philosophy,* vol. 2 (New York, 1945), 1. *Viśistadvaita,* the religious philosophy of Ramanuja (1017–1137), which teaches the distinction between the individual self and the ultimate self, has been regarded to be a more graspable interpretation for the common people. According to this school of thought, salvation is the union of the individual self with the ultimate self through devotion (*bhakti*). In the understanding of the nature of the union with the Absolute and in the concept of the means of salvation *Viśistadvaita* philosophy differs from the *Advaita* of Sankara. *Dvaitā,* the religious philosophy of Madvacharya (1197–1276), accepting two distinct principles, considers salvation through action (*karma*) and devotion (*bhakti*). All the three of these great thinkers, namely, Sankara, Ramanuja, and Madva defend their thesis by commenting on the *Prastānatrāyas*, the three important teachings of Hindu traditions, namely, *Upanisads, Bhagavadgīta and Brahmasūtras.* Some of the saints of the *bhakti* traditions are Manikkavachakar (ca. 650–700), Appar, Sambandhar, and Sundarar of the seventh and the eighth century, Kabir (1440–1518), Nanak (1469–1538), Dadu, Daidas, Dhana, and Sena, of the fifteenth and the sixteenth century, Chaitanya (1485–1533), Tulasidas (1532–1623) and Mirabai (ca. 1420).

14. Mehta, *Early Indian Religious Thought,* 31; J. Hick, *God and the Universe of Faiths,* 133, 134.

15. Pope John Paul II writes, "My thoughts turn immediately to the lands of the East, so rich in religious and philosophical traditions of great antiquity. Among these lands, India has a special place. A great spiritual impulse leads Indian thought to seek an experience which would liberate the spirit from the shackles of time and space and would therefore acquire absolute value. The dynamic of this quest for liberation provides the context for great metaphysical systems. In India particularly, it is the duty of Christians now to draw from this rich heritage the elements compatible with their faith, in order to enrich Christian thought" (*Fides et Ratio*, 72); John Paul II, *Encyclical Letter Fides et Ratio of the Supreme Pontiff John Paul II to the Bishops of the Catholic Church on the Relationship between Faith and Reason* (Vatican City, 1998), 105, 106.

16. M. Amaladoss, *Becoming Indian: The Process of Inculturation* (Rome/Bangalore, 1992), 47.

17. They have been in India since the eighteenth century, mainly in Gujarath and Bombay, engaged in business. See Farquhar, *An Outline of the Religious Literature of India,* 4.

18. From the eighth century C.E. onward Muslims started to settle in South India (Kerala). But the occupation of Punjab by Mohammed of Gazni and the establishment of the Delhi Sultanate in 1206 marked the forceful propagation of Islam in India. In spite of the subjugation of Hinduism by Muhammadans, the destruction of Hindu culture and temples and the rule of Muslim kings in major parts of the country, Muslims could bring about only 11 percent of the whole population to Islam, which means it is not easy to destroy the continuity, unity, and the pluralistic nature and the character of coexistence in culture and life of the Indians.

19. The Jews who settled in Bombay believe that their ancestors came to the Konkon coast in 175 B.C.E. to escape the persecutions of Antiochus Epiphanes, the Greek overlord who was persecuting them. Those who settled in Cochin, Kerala, trace their origin to 70 C.E., when Roman Emperor Titus destroyed the Second Temple in Jerusalem. See S. J. Samartha, *One Christ—Many Religions* (New York, 1994; first published, 1991), 202; Klostermaier, *Survey of Hinduism*, 45.

20. Namadeva (thirteenth century), Kabir (fifteenth century), Ramananda (sixteenth century), Tulasidas (1532–1623), Ekanatha (sixteenth century), Tukaram (seventeenth century), and Ramadasa (seventeenth century) are some of the important Vishnavite saints.

21. The *Śaivite Āgamās* are the *Śaivasidhanta* of Tamilnadu, *Lingayats* of Karnataka and Kashmir *Saivites*.

22. The *Śakti Tantrās* are the left hand *Śaktās* and the right hand *Śaktās*.

23. His important book is *The Precepts of Jesus, the Guide to Peace and Happiness* (Calcutta, 1820).

24. See M. M. Thomas, *Christus im neuen Indien: Reform-Hinduismus und Christentum* (Göttingen, 1989), 30–51; F. Wilfred and M. M. Thomas, *Theologiegeschichte der dritten Welt, Indien* (Munich, 1992), 29.

25. Ibid., 56ff.

26. Ibid., 146–47; see also M. K. Gandhi, *All Religions Are True,* ed. A. T. Hingorani (Bombay, 1962), 4, 20, 53ff.; *In Search of the Supreme,* vol. 3, ed. V. B. Kher (Ahmedbad, 1962), 17; *Gandhi: Essential Writings,* ed. V. V. R. Murthy (New Delhi, 1970), 101.

27. Swami Abhedananda, *Attitude of Vedānta Towards Religion* (Calcutta, 1947), 143.

28. The pluralism in Hinduism is seen in its theology, culture, and worship. We can understand this by observing the Hindu worship in different parts of the country and by different Hindu groups.

29. The approach of the Catholic theologian Raimon Panikkar (1918–) was a pioneer step in this regard (*The Unknown Christ of Hinduism* [London, 1964]).

30. W. C. Smith, *The Meaning and End of Religion* (New York, 1964); idem, *Towards a World Theology* (Philadelphia, 1981).

31. John Harwood Hick (1922–)—born an Anglican, ordained a Presbyterian in 1953; excluded from the ministry in the Presbyterian Church in 1962 because of his controversial theological writings; formerly Assistant Professor of Philosophy, Cornell University (1956–1959); Stuart Professor of Christian Philosophy, Princeton Theological Seminary (1959–1964); H. G. Wood Professor of Theology, University of Birmingham (1967–); Lecturer in the Philosophy of Religion, University of Cambridge; Danforth Professor of Philosophy of Religion at the Claremont Graduate School, California (1979-)—is at

present a fellow of the Institute for Advanced Research in the Humanities at Birmingham University, U.K.

32. See J. Hick, *The Rainbow of Faiths: Critical Dialogues on Religious Pluralism* (London, 1995), 37.

33. Ibid., 43, 44.

34. Hick refers to the agnostic John Stuart Mill's *Utility of Religion* and the rationalist Bertrand Russell's *Why I Am Not a Christian.* See Hick, *God and the Universe of Faiths,* 18–21.

35. Hick calls his theology a "Copernican revolution" because his theology demands a radical change in awareness, approach, and attitude, just as the Copernican revolution demanded a radical change in our world vision. See Hick, *God and the Universe of Faiths,* x, xix, 120–28, 195; idem, *The Second Christianity* (London, 1994; first published, 1968, as *Christianity at the Centre*), 81, 82.

36. See Hick, *God and the Universe of Faiths,* xi.

37. See Hick, *Interpretation of Religion,* 11.

38. See Hick, *God and the Universe of Faiths,* 22.

39. Ibid.

40. See Hick, *Interpretation of Religion,* 140; idem, *Problems of Religious Pluralism,* 19–20.

41. Hick, *Interpretation of Religion*, 140.

42. Hick, *Problems of Religious Pluralism,* 21.

43. Ibid., 23–25.

44. Ibid., 25.

45. John Hick, *The Metaphor of God Incarnate* (London, 1993), 8.

46. Hick, *Rainbow of Faiths,* 82.

47. Hick, *Problems of Religious Pluralism,* 14.

48. See Hick, *God and the Universe of Faiths,* 102.

49. Hick, *Problems of Religious Pluralism,* 28.

50. Ibid., 29.

51. Hick, *God and the Universe of Faiths*, 102.

52. See Hick, *Rainbow of Faiths,* 26–28.

53. Ibid., 47.

54. Hick, *Interpretation of Religion*, 2.

55. See Hick, *Problems of Religious Pluralism,* 86.

56. Hick, *God and the Universe of Faiths*, 101.

57. Ibid., 103.

58. Ibid., 106.

59. John Hick and L. C. Hempel, eds., *Gandhi's Significance Today: The Exclusive Legacy* (London, 1989), 88; see also John Hick, *Disputed Questions in the Theology and the Philosophy of Religion* (London, 1993), 90–91.

60. Ibid., 77–101.

61. Ibid., 88.

62. See Hick, *Metaphor of God Incarnate*, 169.

63. Hick, *Rainbow of Faiths*, 46.

64. Hick, *Problems of Religious Pluralism,* 42.

65. There may be many points on which Küng and Schillebeeckx agree, but neither author is basically in agreement with the theological Copernican revolution of Hick. Hick refers to Küng's *On Being a Christian* (H. Küng, *Christsein* [Munich, 1976]) and Schille-

beeckx's *An Experiment in Christology* (London, 1983). See Hick, *Second Christianity,* 71.

66. Ibid.

67. Hick, *Disputed Questions,* 2.

68. J. Hick cites from E. P. Sanders, *Jesus and Judaism* (London/Philadelphia, 1985), 240. See Hick, *Metaphor of God Incarnate,* 32.

69. Hick, *Metaphor of God Incarnate,* 5.

70. Hick, 4; see also p. 7.

71. Hick, *Problems of Religious Pluralism,* 35.

72. See Hick, *Rainbow of Faiths,* 88–92.

73. Hick, *Second Christianity*, 17.

74. Ibid., 15.

75. See Hick, *Disputed Questions,* 58ff.

76. "For Christianity's implicit or explicit claim to an unique superiority, as the central focus of God's saving activity on earth, has come to seem increasingly implausible within the new global consciousness of our time" (Hick, *Metaphor of God Incarnate,* 7; see also *Disputed Questions,* 35–36).

77. Hick, *Metaphor of God Incarnate*, 8.

78. Ibid., 24.

79. Ibid., 24.

80. See Hick, *God and the Universe of Faiths*, 111.

81. Ibid., 112.

82. See Hick, *Disputed Questions,* 42–43.

83. See Hick, *God Has Many Names*, 72.

84. See ibid; also idem, *Metaphor of God Incarnate,* 31.

85. Ibid., 9, 10.

86. Hick, *Rainbow of Faiths,* 95, 96.

87. Ibid., 91.

88. Hick, *Metaphor of God Incarnate,* 168, 177.

89. Ibid., 48.

90. See Hick, *Second Christianity*, 9–14.

91. Hick, *Rainbow of Faiths,* 87.

92. Cited by Hick (*Metaphor of God Incarnate,* 11) from K. Rahner, *Theological Investigations,* vol. 2, 2nd ed. (New York, 1965), 149.

93. This question is discussed in detail in the fourth chapter.

94. Hick, *Problems of Religious Pluralism,* 11.

95. See Hick, *Rainbow of Faiths*, 105, 106.

96. See Hick, *Metaphor of God Incarnate,* 78.

97. Ibid., 88.

98. See Hick, *Second Christianity,* 31, 32.

99. See Hick, *Disputed Questions,* viii.

100. Hick, *God and the Universe of Faiths,* 151.

101. Ibid., 152; see also idem, *Disputed Questions,* 49.

102. See Hick, *God and the Universe of Faiths*, 159.

103. Ibid., 163.

104. See Hick, *Problems of Religious Pluralism,* 11, 12; idem, *Rainbow of Faiths,* 91, 95, 126; idem, *Second Christianity,* 27, 28; idem, *God and the Universe of Faiths*, 12; idem, *Disputed Questions,* viii.

105. Ibid., xii.

106. Hick, *Rainbow of Faiths*, 95.

107. Ibid., 91.

108. Hick quotes Mark 1:14; Matt. 5:43–45; 6:25, 29; 8:21–22; 10:39; 16:24; 18:3; Luke 18:22; etc., which show, according to him, that Jesus was a preacher of God. See Hick, *Disputed Questions,* 37, 38.

109. Hick quotes from G. Vermes, *Jesus and the World of Judaism* (London, 1983), 43.

110. See Hick, *God Has Many Names,* 99–106. G. H. Carruthers, *The Uniqueness of Jesus Christ in the Theocentric Model of the Christian Theology of World Religions*, 89ff.

111. Hick, *Metaphor of God Incarnate,* 40–41.

112. Hick, *Disputed Questions,* 96.

113. Ibid., 47.

114. See Hick, *Rainbow of Faiths,* 94; idem, *God Has Many Names,* 100ff.; idem, "Jesus and the World Religions," 171ff.; idem, *Metaphor of God Incarnate,* 36, 175, 177.

115. Stanley Jedidiah Samartha (1920–) was Principal of Serampore College (1966–1968), Associate Secretary in the Department of Studies on Mission and Evangelization of the World Council of Churches (1968–1971), Director of the Council's Program on Dialogue with the People of Living Faith and Ideologies (1971–1980) and at present he is consultant to the Christian Institute for the Study of Religion and Society (CISRS) and visiting professor at the United Theological College, Bangalore. See WCC Central Committee, "Tribute to Doctor Stanley J. Samartha," *Current Dialogue* 1 (1980–81): 7; W. M. Choy, *For a Christology in Dialogue: A Critical Examination of Stanley J. Samartha's Attempt at a Christology in a Religiously Plural World* (Rome, 1993), 10.

116. Catholic theologians such as Roberto de Nobili (1577–1656) adopted the lifestyle of an Indian *sanyāsi* and *guru* and tried to contextualize Christian faith in the Indian cultural and religious milieu; Pierre Johannes (1882–1955) considered the fulfillment of *Vednta* in Christianity; Brahmabandhav Upadhyaya (1861–1907) interpreted *Vedānta,* especially the *Advaita Vedānta* in a Thomistic frame; Swami Parama Arubi Anandam (Jules Mochanin, 1895–1957) gave a *vedāntic* interpretation of Trinity; Swami Abhishiktananda (Henri le Saux, O.S.B. [1910–1973]) tried to share his conviction of communicating the Christian faith in the language of *advaitic* experience; Swami Dayananda (Bede Griffiths [1906–1993]) developed a Christian *Vedānta* and Duraiswamy Simon Amalorpavadass (1932–1990) attempted through his writings, activities in the National Biblical Catechetical and Liturgical Centre (N.B.C.L.C.) and through his *Anjali Ashram* to christianize Hinduism. Protestant theologians like William Müller (1838– 1923) and Alfred G. Hogg (1890–1954) taught that Christ has his own place in the general history of salvation; Bernard Lukas (1860–1920) believed that in Hinduism we can find the work of Christ and his Spirit; John Nichol Farquhar (1861–1940) considered the evolution of all religions in the direction of Christianity and Christianity as the fulfillment of Hinduism; Krishna Mohan Banerji (1813–1885) attempted to build up the relationship between the *vedic* religion and Christianity and pointed out that Christianity fulfills many important teachings of *vedic* religion; Lal Behari Day (1824–1894) brought for the first time the idea of a national church and founded the basis for the faith in Jesus Christ and respected the other believers; Nehemiah Nilakanth Shatri Goreh (1825–1895) defended the Christian doctrine of Trinity against *Advaita;* Arumugam S. Appaswamy (1848–1926) and his son Aiyadurai Jesudasan Appaswamy (1891–1975) promoted an Indian interpretation of Christianity emphasizing the importance of *Dhyāna,* and *Yoga;* Pandita Ramabai (1858–1922)

engaged herself in the liberation of the Hindu women; Narayan Vaman Tilak (1862–1919) interpreted Christ as *Yogaswara* (the lord of Yoga) in the light of Marati *bhakti* tradition; Susil Kumar Rudra (1861–1925) was convinced and conveyed that Jesus Christ is the center and the basis of all the Indian religions; Vedanayagam S. Azariah (1874–1945) emphasized ecumenism and the role of the church in the society; K. T. Paul (1876–1931) represented perhaps for the first time a theology mentioning the role of the church and Christianity in the Indian society of religious pluralism; Vengal Chakkarai (1880–1958) advocated a Christology in the light of *Vedānta* considering Jesus as the only *avatār* (incarnation); Savarirayan Jesudason (1882–1962) proclaimed Jesus as the perfect incarnation and adopted Hindu traditions in theology and worship; Pandippedi Chenchiah (1886–1959) tried to interpret Christ against the background of the integral *Vedānta* of Sri Aurobindo and suggested the Hindu scriptures for the Old Testament; Sadhu Sundar Singh (1889–1929) lived the life of a Hindu and Sikh mystic with Christian faith and R. C. Das (1887–1967) interpreted Christ in the light of the Hindu *bhakti* tradition. See Wilfred and Thomas, *Theologiegeschichte der dritten Welt,* 27–207, 257–67; J. Parappally, *Emerging Trends in Indian Christology* (Bangalore, 1995), 17–37; Samartha, *Hindus vor dem Universalen Christus,* 132–41; R. Boyd, *Indian Christian Theology* (Madras, 1971), 1ff.

117. See "Inter-Religious Relationships in the Secular State," in T. F. Dayanandan and F. J. Balasundaram, *Asian Expression of Christian Commitment* (Madras, 1992), 128–36, esp. 128; S. J. Samartha "Dialogue in a Religiously Plural Society," in I. Selvanayakam, *The Multi-Faith Context of India* (Bangalore, 1992), 1–14, esp. 8; idem, "The Progress and Promise of Inter-Religious Dialogue," *Journal of Ecumenical Studies* 9, no. 3 (1972): 463–74, esp. 468, 469.

118. See S. J. Samartha, "The Lordship of Jesus Christ and Religious Pluralism," in G. H. Anderson and T. F. Stansky, *Christ's Lordship and Religious Pluralism* (New York, 1983), 19–37, esp. 32; S. J. Samartha, *Courage for Dialogue: Ecumenical Issues in Inter-Religious Dialogue* (Geneva, 1981; New York, 1982), 30.

119. S. J. Samartha, "Religious Pluralism and the Quest for Human Community," in *No Man Is Alien: Essays on the Unity of Mankind,* ed. J. R. Nelson (Leiden, 1971), 129–49, esp. 143. See also idem, *Courage for Dialogue,* 100.

120. See S. J. Samartha, "Guidelines on Dialogue," *The Ecumenical Review* 31, no. 2 (1979): 155–62, esp. 159.

121. See S. J. Samartha, "Ganga and Galilee: Hindu and Christian Responses to Truth," *Jeevadhara* 11, no. 65 (1981): 335–51, esp. 345.

122. See S. J. Samartha, "Dialogue and the Politicization of Religions in India," *International Bulletin of Missionary Research* 8, no. 13 (1984): 104–7, esp. 105, 107.

123. See Samartha, "Religious Pluralism and the Quest for Human Community," 145.

124. S. J. Samartha, "Indian Realities and the Wholeness of Christ," *Missiology* 10, no. 3 (1982): 301–17, esp. 303.

125. Samartha, "Religious Pluralism and the Quest for Human Community," 144; see also idem, "The World Council of Churches and Men of Other Faiths and Ideologies," *Ecumenical Review* 22, no. 3 (1970): 190–98, esp. 191ff.

126. S. J. Samartha, "Religion, Language and Reality: Towards a Relational Hermeneutics," *Biblical Interpretation* 2, no. 3 (1994): 341–62, esp. 341–43.

127. Samartha, "Dialogue in a Religiously Plural Society," 10.

128. Ibid., 13.

129. S. J. Samartha, "Quest for Salvation and Dialogue between Religions," *International Review of Missions* 57, no. 228 (1968): 424–32, esp. 426.

130. Ibid., 424–31.

131. Ibid., 428.

132. Ibid., 429.

133. Ibid., 430, 431.

134. S. J. Samartha, "The Cross and the Rainbow: Christ in a Multi-Religious Culture," in R. S. Sugirtharajah, *Asian Faces of Jesus* (New York, 1993), 104–27, esp. 107. See also Samartha, *One Christ—Many Religions,* 4, 79.

135. Samartha, "Cross and the Rainbow," 108; idem, *One Christ—Many Religions,* 4, 80.

136. Samartha, *One Christ—Many Religions,* 4.

137. Ibid., 113.

138. Ibid., 58, 74, 85.

139. Ibid., 58–61.

140. Ibid., 84. See Samartha, "Quest for Salvation and the Dialogue between Religions," 424ff.

141. See Samartha, "Cross and the Rainbow," 113, 74; idem, *One Christ—Many Religions,* 84, 112, 115.

142. Samartha, *One Christ—Many Religions,* 6. To support this view he cites H. Berkoff, "Crisis in the Authority of the Scriptures," *Judson Bulletin* n.s. 6 (1987): 34–40; E. Schillebeeckx, *Jesus: An Experiment in Christology* (London, 1983), 573ff.; idem, *Jesus in Our Western Culture* (London, 1987); D. Cupitt, *The Debate about Jesus Christ* (London, 1979), 54ff.; A. Nolan, *Jesus before Christianity* (New York, 1985), 54ff.; see S. J. Samartha, "Mission in a Religiously Plural World," *International Review of Mission* 68 (1988): 311–24, esp. 315.

143. Samartha, *One Christ—Many Religions,* 92.

144. Ibid., 33, 44. See also "Religion, Culture and the Struggle for Justice," 383ff.

145. Ibid., 2, 94, 95.

146. Ibid., 43.

147. Samartha, *One Christ—Many Religions,* 104.

148. Ibid., 96, 97.

149. Samartha, "Dialogue: Significant Issues in the Continuing Debate," 335.

150. See Samartha, "Lordship of Jesus," 29, 30.

151. See Samartha, *One Christ—Many Religions,* x. Samartha concludes in the light of the studies of Kenneth Cracknell and S. Wesley Ariarajah that the Jews and the early Christians recognized a pluralistic theology, as this is presented in the Bible. See Samartha, "Religion, Language and Reality," 341ff.; idem, "Lordship of Jesus," 26ff.

152. Samartha, *One Christ—Many Religions,* xi.

153. Ibid., 76.

154. See Samartha, "Religion, Culture and the Struggle for Justice," 386–89.

155. Ibid., 359–62.

156. See Samartha, "Dialogue and the Politicization of Religions," 104–7.

157. Ibid.

158. See Samartha, "Ganga and Galilee," 345.

159. Ibid., 96; Samartha, "Inter-Religious Relationships in the Secular State," 135.

160. Ibid.; Samartha, *One Christ—Many Religions*, 93.

161. Samartha, "Dialogue in a Religiously Plural Society," 13.

162. See Samartha, "Cross and the Rainbow," 104.

163. Samartha, "Ganga and Galilee," 344.

164. See Samartha, "Cross and the Rainbow," 113.

165. See Samartha, "Religious Pluralism and the Quest for Human Community," 130.

166. Ibid., 134.

167. Ibid., 138.

168. Ibid., 146.

169. Ibid., 140.

170. See Samartha, *One Christ—Many Religions,* 2, 3. Samartha refers to A. Nandi, "Cultural Frames for Social Transformation," *Alternatives* 12 (1987): 113–14; P. Bruckner, *The Tears of the Whiteman: Compassion as Contempt,* trans. W. R. Beer (New York, 1986), quoted in *New York Times Book Review,* December 4, 1986, 4.

171. Samartha, *One Christ—Many Religions,* 81.

172. See S. J. Samartha, "Religious Imperatives and Social Concerns," *Religion and Society* 30, no. 334 (1983): 104–14, esp. 111; idem, "Religious Pluralism and the Quest for Human Community," 133.

173. S. J. Samartha, "Indian Realities and the Wholeness of Christ," 302. For Samartha's recognition of other ways of truth, see "Unwrapping the Gift of Life," *Ecumenical Review* 33, no. 2 (1981): 104–6, esp. 108.

174. Quoted in Samartha, "Ganga and Galilee," 346, from Harward R. Burkle, "Jesus Christ and Religious Pluralism," *Journal of Ecumenical Studies* 16, no. 3 (1979): 460.

175. Samartha, "Ganga and Galilee," 347.

176. Samartha says that although the witness of the New Testament writers is "Christocentric," Jesus Christ himself is "theocentric." He quotes John 10:30; 14:1, 28; 17:3; 1 Cor. 15:28; etc. See Samartha, "Lordship of Jesus," 27; idem, *One Christ—Many Religions*, 86, 87; idem, "Dialogue in a Religiously Plural World," 12, 13; idem, "The Holy Spirit and the People of Other Faiths," *Ecumenical Review* 42 (1990): 250–63, esp. 255.

177. See Samartha, *One Christ—Many Religions,* 86, 87; idem, "Dialogue in a Religiously Plural World," 12, 13.

178. Ibid.

179. Samartha, *One Christ—Many Religions,* 89.

180. See Samartha, "Dialogue: Significant Issues," 335; idem, *One Christ—Many Religions,* 88, 89, 90.

181. Ibid., 106, 116. In spite of his observations of inclusive and exclusive ideas of God in the Bible, Samartha emphasizes a pluralistic idea of God's revelation and incarnation: see "This Delivery Is Not for the Wise," *One World* 79 (1982): 18–19, esp. 19.

182. On this point Samartha quotes Acts 3:13 and 3:15, see Samartha, "Lordship of Jesus and Religious Pluralism," 26.

183. See Samartha, *Hindus vor dem Universalen Christus*, 159–61.

184. See S. J. Samartha, "The Significance of the Historical in Contemporary Hinduism," *Indian Journal of Theology* 16 (1967): 97–105, esp. 105; idem, "Religion Imperatives and Social Concerns", 109–14.

185. See Samartha, *Hindus vor dem Universalen Christus*, 113–15.

186. Ibid. See also Samartha, "The Holy Spirit and the Revelation of God," in *Emerging India and the Word of God,* ed. P. Puthenangady (Bangalore, 1991), 31.

187. Samartha, *One Christ—Many Religions,* 131.

188. Cited from Daya Krishna, "Religion and the Cultural Consciousness," *New Quest* [Bombay] (July-August 1978): 144, in Samartha, "Cross and the Rainbow," 121. See also Samartha, "Indian Realities and the Wholeness of Christ," 311, 312; idem, "Contrast, Controversy and Communication," 20; idem, "The Unknown Christ Made Better

Known," *Religion and Society* 30, no. 1 (1983): 52–61, esp. 54. This is a review article of R. Panikkar, *The Unknown Christ of Hinduism,* revised and enlarged edition (London, 1981).

189. Samartha, "Unknown Christ Made Better Known," 55.

190. Ibid., 118.

191. Ibid., 119.

192. Quoted in ibid., from V. Chakkarai, *Jesus the Avatar* (Madras, 1930), 210.

193. See Samartha, *One Christ—Many Religions,* 120, 121. On this point Samartha cites from D. Cupitt, *Debate about Christ*, 99.

194. Samartha, *One Christ—Many Religions.*

195. Ibid., 121. Here Samartha radically develops his early view of Paul's Christ-experience. See *Hindus vor dem Universalen Christus,* 184–88.

196. Cited in Samartha, *One Christ—Many Religions,* 123, from A. J. Appasamy, *The Johannine Doctrine of Life* (London, 1934), 2–3; S. W. Ariarajah, *The Bible and the People of Other Faiths* (New York, 1989), 21.

197. See Samartha, *One Christ—Many Religions,* 124.

198. Ibid., See also idem, "Dialogue in a Religiously Plural Society," 12; idem, "Mahatma Gandhi: Non-Violence in a World of Conflict," 55, 56.

199. Ibid., 94.

Chapter 2
Karl Rahner's Transcendental Christology and His Concept of the Transcendental Christ

1. In *Grundkurs des Glaubens,* Rahner himself uses this terminology and calls his theology a theology of the spirit and theology of the intellect. See Gk., 13.

2. Gk., 14. The theology of Karl Rahner is rooted in his Christian devotion, which he experienced in his Ignatian retreats, according to J. Sudbrack, "Karl Rahner und die Theologie der Exerzitien," in *Gott neu buchstabieren: Zur Person und Theologie Karl Rahners,* ed. H. D. Mutschler (Würzburg, 1994), 37. On the influence of the spirituality of St. Ignatius of Loyola on Rahner, see A. Zahlauer, *Karl Rahner und sein "produktives Vorbild" Ignatius von Loyola*, 21ff.; M. Schneider, "*Unterscheidung der Geister*": *Die ignatianischen Exerzitien in der Deutung von E. Przywara, K. Rahner und G. Fessard* (Innsbruck, 1983), 95ff.; R. Miggelbrink, *Ekstatische Gottesliebe im tätigen Weltbezug: Der Beitrag Karl Rahners zur zeitgenössischen Gotteslehre* (Altenberge, 1989), 26ff.

3. *Hörer des Wortes* originated in Rahner's lectures in Salzburg in 1937. It was published in 1941 and revised by Johannes Baptist Metz with the approval of Karl Rahner in 1963.

4. See Gk., 22.

5. See ibid.

6. Rahner quotes St. Anselm: "*irrationalia rationaliter cogitare.*" See "Glaube zwischen Rationalität und Emotionalität," in *Schriften*, XII:45–111, esp. 106. For a detailed analysis of spirit and rationality in Rahner, see F. Brüngel, "Erfahrung des Geistes: Rahners Modell der Auseinandersetzung mit Modernismus und Humanismus," in *Wagnis*, 21–34.

7. See B. J. Hilberath, *Karl Rahner,* 38. Nikolaus Knoepffler finds the word "transcendental" 26 times in *Hörer des Wortes* and 24 times in *Geist in Welt,* and the word

"transcendence" 116 times in *Hörer des Wortes* and 10 times in *Geist in Welt.* See N. Knoepffler, *Der Begriff "transzendental" bei Karl Rahner: Zur Frage seiner Kantischen Herkunft* (Innsbruck, 1993), 33. The concepts "transcendental" and "categorical" play a central role in the philosophy and theology of Karl Rahner and in the methodological forms of his total thought pattern: see L. B. Puntel, "Zu den Begriffen 'transzendental' and 'kategorial' bei Karl Rahner," 189. Ansgar Ahlbrecht considers the concept of "transcendental" by Rahner not as a thematically conceived and consciously reflected concept, but as a theological reflection that Rahner made from the starting point of the day-to-day experience of the human being: "Karl Rahners Theologie und die ökumenische Basis," in *Wagnis,* 123–32, esp. 125. Lambert Gruber defends the transcendental philosophy, transcendental philosophical thinking in theology named transcendental theology and transcendental method of Rahner against the criticism of Eberhard Simons that Rahner orients one-sidedly toward the "transcendental foundation of the knowledge of the objects" and neglects the interpersonal aspect inside this foundation: *Transzendentalphilosophie und Theologie bei Johann Gottlieb Fichte und Karl Rahner,* 1–25, 303–5. For Rahner's own reference to the use of this concept in his writings, see "Wissenschaftlichkeit der Theologie und Begegnung mit Gott: Karl Rahner im Gespräch mit Alfred Benzer, München, 1979," in *Glaube in winterlicher Zeit,* 72–78, esp. 74.

8. See L. Dümpelmann, *Kreation als ontisch-ontologisches Verhältnis: Zur Metaphysik der Schöpfungstheologie des Thomas von Aquin* (Freiburg/Munich, 1969), 62–75, 85–91; G. W. Volk, *Sein als Beziehung zum Absoluten nach Thomas von Aquin* (Würzburg, 1964), 92–98, 190–93; G. Rivera, *Konnaturales Erkennen und vorstellendes Denken* (Freiburg/Munich, 1967), 92–95; F. Greiner, *Die Menschlichkeit der Offenbarung: Die transzendentale Grundlegung der Theologie bei Karl Rahner* (Munich, 1978), 22, 28.

9. For Maréchal's concept of "transcendental," see J. Maréchal, *Le point de départ de la métaphysique* (Paris, 1944), Cahier III, 116–20, 182–85, 220ff., Cahier IV, 11–353, Cahier V, 515–61; T. Sheehan, *Karl Rahner: The Philosophical Foundations* (Athens, 1987), 91–96; K. Rahner, *Grundlagen einer Erkenntnistheorie bei Joseph Maréchal*, in SW 2:373–406; P. Eicher, *Die anthropologische Wende: Karl Rahners philosophischer Weg vom Wesen des Menschen zur personalen Existenz*, 22–33; H. Verweyen, *Ontologische Voraussetzungen des Glaubensaktes: Zur transzendentalen Frage nach der Möglichkeit von Offenbarung* (Düsseldorf, 1969), 45, 116, 117.

10. *Geist in Welt*, SW 2:111ff.

11. Rahner wrote *Hörer des Wortes* under the influence of the philosophy of Maurice Blondel, Immanuel Kant, Joseph Maréchal, Thomas Aquinas, and Martin Heidegger. For a detailed discussion of the theme, see H. Verweyen, *Gottes letztes Wort* (Düsseldorf, 1987), 56ff.; A. Raffelt and H. Verweyen, *Karl Rahner*, 40ff.

12. See HW; SW 4:20–21, 48–49, 254–81; HW 1941, 19, 43, 212–29; HW 1963, 25, 48, 203–21; Knoepffler, *Der Begriff "tranzendental" bei Karl Rahner*, 28–40.

13. See HW; SW 4:76–79; HW 1941, 64; HW 1963, 68.

14. See HW; SW 4:82–83; HW 1941, 68; HW 1963, 71.

15. See Gk., 33.

16. See HW; SW 4:8ff.; HW 1941, 9ff.; HW 1963, 15ff.

17. See HW; SW 4:10, 11; HW 1941, 11, 12; HW 1963, 16, 17.

18. See HW; SW 4:12, 13; HW 1941, 14; HW 1963, 19.

19. Ibid.

20. See HW; SW 4:26–28; HW 1941, 23, 24; HW 1963, 29, 30.

21. HW; SW 4:60, 61; HW 1941, 50, 51; HW 1963, 55.

22. HW; SW 4:83; HW 1941, 68; HW 1963, 71.

23. Ibid.

24. See GW; SW 2:35; GW 1939, 16; GW 1957, 46.

25. GW; SW 2:36; GW 1939, 17; GW 1957, 47.

26. See GW; SW 2:55, 56; GW 1939, 35ff.; GW 1957, 71ff.

27. Ibid.

28. See GW; SW 2:68; GW 1939, 47; GW 1957, 90.

29. Gk., 54; "Geheimnis. II. Theologisch," in H. Fries, *Handbuch theologischer Grundbegriffe*, I (Munich, 1962), 447–52.

30. See Gk., 54.

31. See GW; SW 2:50, 64, 104, 145, 153, 154, 295; GW 1939, 32, 44, 139, 140, 292; GW 1957, 86, 137, 194, 205, 207, 401.

32. See GW; SW 2:55; GW 1939, 35, GW 1957, 73.

33. See GW; SW 2:56; GW 1939, 36, GW 1957, 74.

34. See HW; SW 4:78–83; HW 1941, 69–72; HW 1963, 68–70. See also GW; SW 2:60–68; GW 1936, 39–47; GW 1957, 78–90. On the concept of the being of Being as consciousness, see HW; SW 4:179; HW 1941, 146; HW 1963, 147.

35. See HW; SW 4:80–81; HW 1941, 66; HW 1963, 70.

36. See HW; SW 4:106–65.

37. See HW; SW 4:140.

38. See HW; SW 4:161; HW 1941, 131; HW 1963, 131.

39. GW; SW 2:54; GW 1957, 71.

40. GW; SW 2:54; GW 1957, 71.

41. See GW; SW 2:60, 61.

42. Ibid.

43. See GW; SW 2:54.

44. SW 2:55.

45. GW; SW 2:55; GW 1957, 72. See also GW; SW 2:56; GW 1957, 74.

46. HW; SW 4:83; HW 1941, 73; HW 1963, 71.

47. HW; SW 4:81; HW 1941, 71; HW 1963, 69.

48. HW; SW 4:83; HW 1941, 73; HW 1963, 71.

49. See HW; SW 4:86, 87; HW 1941, 71, 72; HW 1963, 74, 75; HW2, 43, 44.

50. See HW; SW 4:87; HW 1963, 74. This expression is not found in the 1941 edition.

51. HW; SW 4:86, 87; HW 1941, 71, 72; HW 1963, 74, 75.

52. HW; SW 4:86–89; HW 1941, 72; HW 1963, 75.

53. See HW; SW 4:249 ; HW 1941, 204; HW 1963, 199.

54. Ibid., HW 1963, 200.

55. See GW; SW 2:65; GW 1957, 85; GW 1936, 45.

56. GW; SW 2:73; GW 1936, 52; GW 1957, 97.

57. See GW; SW 2:63; GW 1957, 83.

58. GW; SW 2:63; GW 1957, 83.

59. See HW; SW 4:83; HW 1941, 73; HW 1963, 71.

60. See HW; SW 4:86, 87; HW 1941, 75; HW 1963, 74, 75.

61. See HW; SW 4:81; HW 1941, 66; HW 1963, 69, 70.

62. See HW; SW 4:86, 87; HW 1941, 72; HW 1963, 75; HW2, 44.

63. See HW; SW 4:88, 89.

64. Ibid. See also HW2, 46, 47.

65. See HW; SW 4:89–91; HW 1941, 73–75; HW 1963, 75–77.

66. See HW; SW 4:88, 89; HW 1941, 73; HW 1963, 76.

67. Ibid.

68. See HW; SW 4:90, 91; HW 1941, 74; HW 1963, 77.

69. Ibid.

70. See HW; SW 4:91–95; HW 1941, 76–79; HW 1963, 78–80.

71. See HW; SW 4:123; HW 1941, 101; HW 1963, 104.

72. See HW; SW 4:213ff.; HW 1941, 176; HW 1963, 173ff.

73. The reference in the last sentence to *Umwelt* and *Mit-welt* is an addition by Metz in the 1963 edition. See HW; SW 4:215; HW 1941, 178; HW 1963, 174.

74. GW; SW 2:86; GW 1939, 67; GW 1957, 115.

75. See GW; SW 2:297, 298; GW 1939, 294; GW 1957, 403, 404.

76. See Gk., 61.

77. See HW; SW 2:60–65; HW 1941, 49–51; HW 1963, 54–56. For a detailed study of Rahner's concept of "supernatural existential," see L. J. Smith, *Maurice Blondel and Karl Rahner on the Possibility of a Primary Experience of God: A Comparative Study* (Ann Arbor, 1992), 77ff.; E. K. Donald, *Karl Rahner's Doctrine of the Supernatural Existential* (Ann Arbor, 1971), 120ff.; W. Kues, *Werde, der du sein sollst: Impulse für religiös gedeutete Entscheidungen von Karl Rahner und C. G. Jung* (Frankfurt, 1996), 44ff.

78. See HW; SW 4:19; HW 1963, 23. See also "Wissenschaftlichkeit der Theologie und Begegnung mit Gott: Karl Rahner im Gespräch mit Alfred Benzer," in *Glaube in winterlicher Zeit*, 75.

79. See ibid. W. V. Dych, *Karl Rahner* (London, 1992), 37; W. Sandler, *Bekehrung des Denkens: Karl Rahners Anthropologie und Soteriologie als formaloffenes System in triadischer Perspektive* (Frankfurt, 1996), 236–38; N. Schwerdtfeger, *Gnade und Welt: Zum Grundgefüge von Karl Rahners Theorie der "anonymen Christen"* (Freiburg, 1982), 161–204; J. Herberg, *Kirchliche Heilsvermittlung: Ein Gespräch zwischen Karl Barth und Karl Rahner* (Frankfurt, 1978), 158; G. Friedemann, *Die Menschlichkeit der Offenbarung: Die transzendentale Grundlegung der Theologie bei Karl Rahner* (Munich, 1978), 186–98.

80. See Dych, *Karl Rahner,* 38.

81. See Schwerdtfeger, *Gnade und Welt,* 200.

82. See K. Rahner, "Würde und Freiheit des Menschen," in *Schriften*, II, 1960 (6. Auflage), 248–50.

83. Ibid., 252.

84. See HW; SW 4:155–57; HW 1941, 131, 132; HW 1963, 127, 128.

85. See HW; SW 4:120–21; HW 1941, 99; HW 1963, 102.

86. See HW; SW 4:19, 22, 23; HW 1963, 23, 25; HW 1941, 20; "Über das Verhältnis von Natur und Gnade," in *Schriften,* I, 1954, 323–47; "Natur und Gnade," in *Schriften,* IV, 209–36.

87. "Über das Verhältnis von Natur und Gnade," 325.

88. Ibid., 323–45; J. Speck, *Karl Rahners theologische Anthropologie: Eine Einführung* (Munich, 1967), 65; I. Bokwa, *Christologie als Anfang und Ende der Anthropologie: Über das gegenseitige Verhältnis zwischen Christologie und Anthropologie bei Karl Rahner* (Frankfurt, 1989), 57.

89. "Natur und Gnade," 209–36.

90. See Dych, *Karl Rahner*, 9.

91. "Würde und Freiheit des Menschen," 251.

92. Ibid., 250.

93. Ibid., 252.

94. Ibid., 259.

95. "Über die Erfahrung der Gnade," in *Schriften,* III, 1962, 105–15, esp. 108. On Rahner's understanding of the human being as spirit, see G. Neuhaus, *Transzendentale Erfahrung als Geschichtsverlust? Der Vorwurf der Subjektlosigkeit an Rahners Begriff geschichtlicher Existenz an eine weiterführende Perspektive transzendentaler Theologie* (Düsseldorf, 1982), 69–74; Speck, *Karl Rahners theologische Anthropologie,* 110–23.

96. See Gk., 37, 39.

97. See Gk., 43.

98. See Gk., 45.

99. See Gk., 42, 44, 49.

100. See Gk., 46–48.

101. See Gk., 48, 49.

102. "Zur Theologie der Menschwerdung," in *Schriften,* IV, 137–57, esp. 142.

103. "Über den Begriff des Geheimnisses in der katholischen Theologie," 68, 69.

104. Ibid., 74.

105. Ibid., 75.

106. See HW; SW 4:110–19, 125; HW 1941, 92–98, 103; HW 1963, 94–100, 105. For a discussion on the concept of God as absolute transcendence by Rahner, see M. W. Petty, *A Faith that Loves the Earth: The Ecological Theology of Karl Rahner* (London, 1996), 86–97.

107. See HW; SW 4:153; HW 1941, 128; HW 1963, 126. See also "Über den Begriff des Geheimnisses in der katholischen Theologie," 55ff.

108. See HW; SW 4:123; HW 1941, 101; HW 1963, 103.

109. See HW; SW 4:167; HW 1941, 139, 140; HW 1963, 138, 139.

110. See HW; SW 4:181; HW 1941, 149; HW 1963, 181.

111. See "Theos im Neuen Testament," in *Schriften,* I, 91–169, esp. 120.

112. See Gk., 42–46.

113. *Schriften*, III, 455–72, esp. 455ff.

114. See Gk., 67.

115. Gk., 69.

116. See Gk., 69, 70.

117. "Bemerkungen zum Begriff der Offenbarung," in K. Rahner and J. Ratzinger, *Offenbarung und Überlieferung*, Quaestiones Disputatae 25 (Freiburg, 1965), 11–25, esp. 13, 14. According to Rahner, there is a transcendental necessity of the experience of God in the structure of the human categorical experience. See Schneider, "*Unterscheidung der Geister,*" 11–85.

118. Ibid., 13–15.

119. See HW; SW 4:261–63; HW 1941, 214, 215; HW 1963, 207, 208.

120. See HW; SW 4:265; HW 1941, 218; HW 1963, 210.

121. See HW; SW 4:265ff.; HW 1941, 218ff.; HW 1963, 210ff.

122. See "Die zwei Grundtypen der Christologie," in *Schriften,* X, 1973, 227–41, esp. 227ff.

123. Ibid., 228.

124. See M. Vekathanam, *Christology in the Indian Anthropological Context: Man–History–Christ: An Evaluative Encounter with K. Rahner and W. Pannenberg* (Frankfurt, 1986); J. Donceel, *Philosophical Anthropology* (New York, 1967); Speck, *Karl*

Rahner's theologische Anthropologie; Eicher, *Die anthropologische Wende;* K. P. Fischer, *Der Mensch als Geheimnis: Die Anthropologie Karl Rahners* (Freiburg, 1974).

125. See B. Tyrell, *The New Context of the Philosophy of God in Lonergan and Rahner* (Dublin, 1972); V. F. Branick, *An Ontology of Understanding: Karl Rahner's Metaphysics of Knowledge in the Context of Modern German Hermeneutics* (St. Louis, 1971); R. Lapointe, "L'Ontologie de Karl Rahner," *Dialogue* 8 (1970): 592–611.

126. See A. Gerken, *Offenbarung und Transzendenzerfahrung: Kritische Thesen zu einer künftigen dialogischen Theologie* (Düsseldorf, 1969); K. Baker, *A Synopsis of the Transcendental Philosophy of Emerich Coreth and Karl Rahner* (Bookstore, 1965); idem, "Rahner: The Transcendental Method," *Continuum* 2 (1964): 52–59.

127. See W. V. Donald, *Karl Rahner's Doctrine of the Supernatural Existential,* 212ff.

128. See Gk., 31, 32.

129. See Gk., 45.

130. See Gk., 32; on the experience of transcendence in the individual, see also *Das dynamische in der Kirche,* Quaestiones Disputatae 5 (Freiburg, 1960), 136ff.

131. See Gk., 32.

132. See Gk., 32, 70ff.

133. See Gk., 153, 155, 175.

134. Ibid. See also Knoepffler, *Der Begriff "transzendental" bei Karl Rahner*, 96.

135. "Naturwissenschaft und vernünftiger Glaube," in *Schriften,* XV, 1977, 24–63.

136. Ibid., 42.

137. See HW; SW 97; HW 1941, 8; HW 1963, 82; See also HW2, 46–49.

138. Ibid.

139. "Über die Erfahrung der Gnade," in *Schriften,* III, 105–11, esp. 105.

140. Ibid., 106–7.

141. Ibid., 108–9; see also "Grundlinien einer systematischen Christologie," in K. Rahner and W. Thüsing, *Christologie systematisch und exegetisch*, Quaestiones Disputatae 55 (Freiburg/Basel/Vienna, 1972), 11–25, esp. 15.

142. See Gk., 83.

143. See Gk., 62.

144. Vol. 8 of the collected works presents all of Rahner's writings on the theology of creation: *Sämtliche Werke*, Bd. 8, *Der Mensch in der Schöpfung,* bearbeitet von K. H. Neufeld, Hrsg., Karl Rahner Stiftung (Freiburg/Zurich, 1988).

145. See "Über den Begriff des Geheimnisses in der katholischen Theologie," 69, 70.

146. See Gk., 143ff.; "Vom Offensein für den je größeren Gott," in *Schriften,* VII, 1966, 32–54, esp. 51; "Überlegungen zur Methode der Theologie," in *Schriften*, IX, 1970, 79–127, esp. 106, 112.

147. "Bemerkungen zum Problem des anonymen Christen," in *Schriften,* X, 531–47, esp. 539.

148. Ibid., 543.

149. See "Selbsterfahrung und Gotteserfahrung," in *Schriften*, X, 133–45.

150. Ibid., 139.

151. Ibid., 142.

152. "Anonymes Christentum und der Missionsauftrag der Kirche," in *Schriften*, IX, 498–519, esp. 507; "Bemerkungen zum Problem des anonymen Christen," 538; "Ist Kircheneinigung dogmatisch möglich?" in *Schriften*, XII, 547–68, esp. 556.

154. See GW 1957, 404ff.; *Sendung und Gnade* (Innsbruck, 1959), 296ff.; "Bemerkungen zum Begriff der Offenbarung," 25, 17, 18.

155. "Glaubensakt und Glaubensinhalt," in *Schriften,* XV, 1983, 152–63, esp. 157.

156. HW; SW 4:117–19; HW 1941, 97, 98; HW 1963, 99, 100.

157. See HW; SW 4:45, 105, 117, 135, 165, 167, 169, 171, 233, 243.

158. HW; SW 4:139; HW 1941, 114, 116; HW 1963, 116, 117.

159. HW; SW 4:139; HW 1941, 114, 116; HW 1963, 116, 117.

160. Gk., 145; "Offenbarung, II. Theologische Vermittlung," in SM, III (Freiburg/Basel/Vienna, 1963), 832–43, esp. 840.

161. Gk., 157–77; Hilberath, *Karl Rahner*, 38.

162. Gk., 143–77; Hilberath, *Karl Rahner*, 42.

163. Gk., 173.

164. "Überlegungen zur Methode der Theologie," in *Schriften*, IX, 79–127.

165. Ibid., 112.

166. "Rede des Ignatius von Loyola an einen Jesuiten von heute," in *Schriften*, XV, 373–409.

167. "Bemerkungen zum Begriff der Offenbarung," 12.

168. Gk., 179.

169. See Gk., 204, 205, 224.

170. See Gk., 195.

171. See Gk., 193.

172. Gk., 193. See also Gk., 90, 91.

173. See Gk., 193.

174. Ibid.; see also *Foundations*, 193.

175. See Gk., 194.

176. See Gk., 194.

177. See Gk., 195.

178. See Gk., 193.

179. See Gk., 196–97.

180. See K. Rahner, "Gotteserfahrung heute," in *Schriften*, IX, 161–77.

181. Ibid., 170–71.

182. Ibid., 171.

183. Ibid., 171, 172.

184. Ibid., 174.

185. Ibid., 175.

186. See "Christologie im Rahmen des Selbst- und Weltverständnisses," in *Schriften,* IX, 227–41.

187. "Probleme der Christologie von heute," in *Schriften,* I, 169–223, esp. 207.

188. Ibid., 208.

189. Ibid., 207.

190. See HW; SW 2:50ff.; HW 1941, 42ff.; HW 1963, 48ff.

191. See GW; SW 2:54, 55; GW 1957, 71.

192. See GW; SW 2:54; GW 1957, 71.

193. See GW; SW 2:55; GW 1957, 72; Peter Eicher gives a detailed analysis of the transcendental method of Rahner in *Die anthropologische Wende,* 50–58. See also O. Muck, *Die transzendentale Methode in der scholastischen Philosophie der Gegenwart* (Innsbruck, 1964), 206; G. Coreth, *Metaphysik: Eine methodisch systematische Grund-*

legung (Innsbruck, 1964), 698; E. G. Farrugia, *Aussage und Zusage: Zur Indirektheit der Methode Karl Rahners veranschaulicht an seiner Christologie,* 198–216; Sandler, *Bekehrung des Denkens,* 79–93.

194. See K. Rahner, "Überlegungen zur Methode der Theologie," 79–80.

195. See HW; SW 4:53, 91; HW 1963, 49, 77; "Über die theoretische Ausbildung künftiger Priester heute," in *Schriften,* VI, 139–71, esp. 157; GW; SW 2:142, 143, 166, 172, 173, 213; GW 1957, 189, 190, 223, 232, 287; Eicher, *Die anthropologische Wende,* 61; H. Holz, *Transzendentale Philosophie und Metaphysik: Studie über Tendenz in der heutigen philosophischen Grundlagenproblematik* (Mainz, 1966), 16.

196. See K. Rahner, "Über die theoretische Ausbildung der künftigen Priester," 157.

197. See HW; SW 4:113; "Religionsphilosophie und Theologie," 288; "Über das Verhältnis von Natur und Gnade," 327.

198. See HW; SW 4:112–13, 178–79; HW 1941, 93, 147; HW 1963, 95, 96, 147.

199. See HW4, 1963, 88.

200. See "Religionsphilosophie und Theologie," 288; HW; SW 4:113.

201. See GW; SW 2:297, 298; GW 1957, 404.

202. See "Über das Verhältnis von Natur und Gnade," 237–329.

203. See "Naturwissenschaft und vernünftiger Glaube," 55ff.; "Die ewige Bedeutung der Menschheit Jesu für unser Gottesverhältnis," in *Schriften,* III, 47–61, esp. 57ff.; "Ideologie und Christentum," in *Schriften,* VI, 1965, 59–77, esp. 71; Gk., 143.

204. Ibid., 202.

205. Ibid., 208; see also "Probleme der Christologie von heute," 206–8.

206. "Überlegungen zur Methode der Theologie," 100, 101.

207. See Gk., 36.

208. See G. Vass, *Understanding Karl Rahner,* vol. 1, *A Theologian in Search of Philosophy,* 24.

209. On Heidegger's relevance to theology, see J. Macquarrie, *Heidegger and Christianity* (London, 1994), 16–63; idem, *Principles of Christian Theology* (London, 1997; first published 1966), 70, 71, 77.

210. See Puntel, "Zu den Begriffen 'transzendental' und 'kategorial' bei Karl Rahner," 189–99; S. Athappally, *Glaube und Welt* (Graz, 1985), 51–159; A. Losinger, *Orientierungspunkt Mensch: Der anthropologische Ansatz in der Theologie Karl Rahners* (St. Ottilien, 1992), 28ff.

211. See K. Rahner, "Transzendentaltheologie," 986; "Bemerkungen zum Begriff der Offenbarung," 15.

212. "Überlegungen zur Methode der Theologie," 96; Gk., 36; Neuhaus, *Transzendentale Erfahrung als Geschichtsverlust?* 17, 42, 348.

213. See A. Raffelt and K. Rahner, "Anthropologie und Theologie," in *Christlicher Glaube in moderner Gesellschaft,* ed. F. Böckle, F. X. Kaufmann, K. Rahner, and B. Welte, vol. 24 (Freiburg, 1981), 8–55, esp. 12.

214. See Rahner, "Transzendentaltheologie," 989.

215. Ibid., 987.

216. Ibid.

217. Ibid.

218. See "Um das Geheimnis der Dreifaltigkeit," in *Schriften,* XII, 320–25; "Überlegungen zur Methode der Theologie," 105; "Transzendentaltheologie," 990.

219. See "Der dreifaltige Gott als transzendentaler Grund der Heilsgeschichte," in

Mysterium Salutis, II, *Die Heilsgeschichte vor Christus*, 370, 383, 382; "Transzendentaltheologie," 990.

219. See "Überlegungen zur Methode der Theologie," 107, 108.

220. See "Theologie und Anthropologie," in *Schriften*, VIII, 1967, 43–66, esp. 43.

221. Theocentrism as understood by Rahner is entirely different from the "theocentrism" meant by John Hick.

222. "Theologie und Anthropologie," 43.

223. Ibid., 94.

224. Ibid., 44.

225. Ibid., 45.

226. Ibid., 65; see also "Christologie heute?" in *Schriften*, XII, 355–70.

227. See "Würde und Freiheit des Menschen," 253.

228. "Naturwissenschaft und vernünftiger Glaube," in *Schriften*, XV, 24–63, esp. 50.

229. Ibid., 52.

230. Ibid., 80.

231. Ibid., 95.

232. See Gk., 178.

233. See "Christologie heute?" 353–77.

234. Ibid., 360.

235. See Knoepffler, *Der Begriff "transzendental" bei Karl Rahner*, 118–19.

236. Gk., 179; see also "Wissenschaftlichkeit der Theologie und Begegnung mit Gott: Karl Rahner im Gespräch mit Alfred Benzer," 76.

237. See Gk., 179.

238. See Gk., 203.

239. See "Grundlinien einer systematischen Christologie," 20; Gk., 206–7.

240. See Gk., 206–7; "Grundlinien einer systematischen Christologie," 21, 22, 24.

241. See HW; SW 4:16, 17; HW 1941, 16; HW 1963, 21; HW2, 4, 5.

242. "Zur Theologie der Menschwerdung," 150ff.

243. See "Probleme der Christologie von heute," 192; "Grundlinien einer systematischen Christologie," 63.

244. Ibid., 174, 175. Rahner refers to *Humani Generis* 2 (DZ 3014).

245. "Probleme der Christologie von heute," 175.

246. Ibid.

247. Ibid., 189.

248. See "Transzendentaltheologie," 886–91; "Grundlinien einer systematischen Christologie," 17ff.; "Beiträge aus dem Handbuch der Pastoralentheologie," in SW 19:47–496, esp. 416; Hilberath, *Karl Rahner*, 129.

249. See Raffelt and Rahner, "Anthropologie und Theologie," 10, 11.

250. Ibid., 14, 16, 19.

251. Ibid., 14–19.

252. See "Probleme der Christologie von heute," 189.

253. Ibid., 186.

254. See HW; SW 4:8–89; "Religionsphilosophie und Theologie," 285–91; "Über den Begriff der Transzendenz in der katholischen Theologie," 68ff.

255. See "Anthropologische Voraussetzung für die Selbstvollzug der Kirche," in SW 19:184.

256. See "Beiträge aus dem Handbuch der Pastoralentheologie," SW 19:416.

257. See "Anthropologische Voraussetzungen für den Selbstvollzug der Kirche," 185.

258. Ibid., 187.

259. See "Theologische Anthropologie," in LThK 1:619.

260. See "Anthropologische Voraussetzungen für den Selbstvollzug der Kirche," 186.

261. See "Theologische Anthropologie," in LThK 1:626.

262. See Gk., 205.

263. Gk., 223.

264. See Gk., 298.

265. See Gk., 299.

266. This terminology is not used by Rahner.

267. See "Zur Frage der Dogmenentwicklung," in *Schriften*, I, 80.

268. Ibid., 78.

269. *Gefahren im heutigen Katholizismus* (Einsiedeln, 1950), 74.

270. See "Chalkedon: Ende oder Anfang?" in A. Grillmeier and H. Bacht, eds., *Das Konzil von Chalkedon: Geschichte oder Gegenwart*, vol. 3 (Würzburg, 1954), 3–59, esp. 54; "Probleme der Christologie von heute," 174.

271. See "Probleme der Christologie von heute," 169.

272. See Gk., 196, 197, 280.

273. See "Chalkedon Ende oder Anfang," 54.

274. "Das kirchliche Lehramt in der heutigen Autoritätskrise," in *Schriften,* XIII, 69–73 esp. 70.

275. Ibid. See also "Lehramt und Theologie," in *Schriften*, XIII, 69–93, esp. 70.

276. "Das kirchliche Lehramt in der heutigen Autoritätskrise," 345; "Lehramt und Theologie," 70; K. Lehmann, "Karl Rahner und die Kirche," in K. Lehmann, ed., *Vor dem Geheimnis Gottes den Menschen verstehen*, ed. K. Lehmann (Munich, 1984), 120–36, esp. 122–24.

277. K. Rahner, "Kirchliches Lehramt und Theologie nach dem Konzil," in *Schriften*, VIII, 111–33, esp. 112.

278. Ibid., 117, 118.

279. Gk., 158.

280. Gk., 159.

281. Gk., 159, 160. See also *Sendung und Gnade*, 301, 302.

282. Gk., 175.

283. Gk., 176.

284. Gk., 177, 178.

285. "Ideologie und Christentum," 70.

286. Ibid.

287. See Gk., 211, 212; *Ich glaube an Jesus Christus* (Einsiedeln, 1968), 45. For studies on Rahner's concept of Christ as the self-communication of God, see Herberg, *Kirchliche Heilsvermittlung*, 159; M. Blechschmidt, *Der Leib und das Heil: Zum christlichen Heilsverständnis der Leiblichkeit in Auseinandersetzung mit R. Bultmann und Karl Rahner*, 217.

288. See Gk., 221; on Rahner's concept of Jesus as revelation of God in history, see Friedemann, *Die Menschlichkeit der Offenbarung,* 289–94; K. Rahner, *Gabe der Weihnacht* (Freiburg, 1980), 24–27.

289. "Überlegungen zur Dogmenentwicklung," in *Schriften,* IV, 11–51, esp. 16, 17; G. Baudler, "Göttliche Gnade und menschliches Leben," in *Wagnis*, 35–51, 39; Gk., 122–42.

290. See "Über die Frage einer formalen Existentialethik," in *Schriften,* II, 227–47, esp. 242.

291. See R. Siebenrock, "Gnade als Herz der Welt," 36; Neufeld, *Die Brüder Rahner*, 84; Hilberath, *Karl Rahner*, 98.

292. See K. Rahner, "Probleme der Christologie von heute," 195, 202; *Exerzitienbetrachtungen*, 105.

293. "Grundlinien einer systematischen Christologie," 72–77.

294. "Zwei Grundtypen der Christologie," 232.

295. See ibid., 233; *Gott ist Mensch geworden*, 69.

296. See "Zwei Grundtypen der Christologie," 233.

297. See *Gott ist Mensch geworden*, 51; *Glaube, der die Erde liebt*, 35; Gk., 222.

298. See *Gott ist Mensch geworden*, 30; Gk., 222.

299. See *Gott ist Mensch geworden*, 40. "Weihnacht im Licht der Exerzitien," in *Schriften*, XII, 329–35, esp. 329, 330.

300. See Gk., 222.

301. In *Geist in Welt* and *Hörer des Wortes,* Rahner understands Being as "self-presence." See GW; SW 2:62, 63; HW; SW 4:77; HW 1941, 71; HW 1963, 68, 69.

302. See HW; SW 4:77; HW 1941, 71; HW 1963, 68, 69.

303. HW; SW 4:78–81; HW 1963, 70; HW2, 39, 40.

304. See HW; SW 4:76–83; HW 1941, 70, 72; HW 1963, 68–70.

305. See HW; SW 4:80; HW 1941, 72; HW 1963, 70; See also HW1, 41.

306. "Zur Theologie der Menschwerdung," 142; *Exerzitienbetrachtungen*, 105.

307. Ibid., 143; Gk., 216, 217.

308. Ibid.

309. Gk., 216.

310. Gk., 222.

311. "Zur Theologie der Menschwerdung," 144, 145.

312. Ibid., 147, 148.

313. Ibid., 151.

314. "Probleme der Christologie von heute," 217.

315. See Gk., 213; "Zur Theologie der Menschwerdung," 140.

316. "Probleme der Christologie von heute," 186.

317. Ibid., 186–87.

318. Ibid., 187.

319. "Die zwei Grundtypen der Christologie," 223.

320. See "Probleme der Christologie von heute," 185; *Exerzitienbetrachtungen*, 105ff.

321. "Zur Theologie der Weihnachtsfeier," in *Schriften,* III, 35–47, esp. 43, 44.

322. "Zur Theologie der Weihnachtsfeier," 44.

323. "Ich glaube an Jesus Christus," in *Schriften*, VIII, 213–18, esp. 215; see A. Röper, *Karl Rahner als Seelsorger* (Innsbruck, 1987), 123–26.

324. See K. Rahner, "Würde und Freiheit des Menschen," in *Schriften*, II, 247–79, esp. 253, 259.

325. Ibid., 258; *Exerzitienbetrachtungen*, 105, 106.

326. "Würde und Freiheit des Menschen," 248.

327. Ibid., 249.

328. See Gk., 197.

329. "Probleme der Christologie von heute," 188.

330. Ibid., 204.

331. Ibid., 205.

332. Ibid.

333. "Theologie und Anthropologie," 43.

334. Ibid.

335. "Zur Theologie der Weihnachtsfeier," 39. On Rahner's concept of incarnation as self-transcendence, see Petty, *A Faith that Loves the Earth*, 163–65. For a critical evaluation of Rahner's concept of "self-transcendence," see J. Moltmann, *The Way of Jesus Christ: Christology in Messianic Dimensions*, trans. M. Kohl (London, 1990), 297–301.

336. See K. Rahner, "Christologie innerhalb einer evolutiven Weltanschauung," 184.

337. Ibid., 196.

338. Ibid., 187.

339. Ibid., 187, 188.

340. Ibid., 186.

341. Ibid., 186, 187; see also Gk., 183.

342. "Christologie innerhalb einer evolutiven Weltanschauung," 194.

343. Ibid., 188.

344. Ibid., 189.

345. Ibid., 192.

346. Ibid., 195.

347. Ibid., 199.

348. Ibid., 201.

349. Ibid., 200–205.

350. Ibid., 204; see also Gk., 196.

351. "Christologie innerhalb einer evolutiven Weltanschauung," 206, 207.

352. Ibid., 202, 203; see also Gk., 185.

353. "Christologie im Rahmen des modernen Selbst- und Weltverständnisses," 239.

354. See "Wissenschaftlichkeit der Theologie und Begegnung mit Gott: Karl Rahner im Gespräch mit Alfred Benzer," 75; K. Rahner, "Naturwissenschaft und vernünftiger Glaube," 52.

355. See H. Gehring, "*Suchende Christologie,*" 287.

356. See Gk., 225.

357. See Rahner, "Probleme der Christologie von heute," 206.

358. Ibid.

359. "Menschliche Aspekte der Geburt Christi," in *Schriften*, X, 203–9.

360. *Gott ist Mensch geworden*, 20, 21.

361. Ibid., 31.

362. Ibid., 18.

363. "Probleme der Christologie von heute," 206.

364. "Die ewige Bedeutung der Menschheit Jesu für unser Gottesverhältnis," in *Schriften,* III, 62.

365. Ibid., 59.

366. "Weltgeschichte und Heilsgeschichte," in *Schriften* V, 115–36, esp. 134.

367. "Über den Absolutheitsanspruch des Christentums," in *Schriften,* XV, 171–85, esp. 171ff., 176–77; *Exerzitienbetrachtungen*, 113, 114.

368. See Gk., 177.

369. See Petty, *A Faith that Loves the Earth*, 123–28, 132–36. On Christ as the incarnation of God, see A. Ackley, *The Church of the Word: A Comparative Study of the Word, Church and Office in the Thought of Karl Rahner and Gerhard Ebeling* (Frankfurt, 1993), 42–43.

370. See *Gott ist Mensch geworden*, 60.

371. See A. Schilson, "Christologie im 20. Jahrhundert," in LThK³, II, 1170–73, esp. 1172.

372. See "Probleme der Christologie von heute," 200.

373. See Gk., 224; "Probleme der Christologie von heute," 201; "Grundlinien einer systematischen Christologie," 55; *Gott ist Mensch geworden*, 19, 65; *Glaube, der die Erde liebt,* 23.

374. See *Gott ist Mensch geworden*, 36; *Glaube, der die Erde liebt*, 23.

375. "Über den Versuch eines Aufrisses einer Dogmatik," 12; see also Gk., 160.

376. See Gk., 143.

377. See Gk., 143–44.

378. See Gk., 145, 146.

379. See Gk., 146.

380. See Gk., 161; see also *Ich glaube an Jesus Christus* (Einsiedeln, 1968), 31.

381. "Profangeschichte und Heilsgeschichte," in *Schriften,* XV, 10–24, esp. 12.

382. Ibid., 16, 17.

383. Ibid., 18; Gk., 177.

384. Ibid.

385. "Profangeschichte und Weltgeschichte," 19.

386. "Naturwissenschaft und vernünftiger Glaube," 59.

387. Ibid., 60.

388. Ibid., 61.

389. See Gk., 149, 150.

390. See Gk., 151, 157, 160.

391. See Gk., 160, 161.

392. See Gk., 162.

393. "Grundkurs des Glaubens," in *Schriften*, XIV, 53, 54.

394. "Kleine Anmerkungen zur systematischen Christologie heute," 132–33.

395. See Gk., 288.

396. See Gk., 174.

397. See Gk., 176.

398. See Gk., 177.

399. "Probleme der Christologie von heute," 206; HW 1961, 67.

400. Gk., 194ff.

401. Gk., 204ff.

402. "Die deutsche protestantische Christologie der Gegenwart," in SW 4:299–312, 302, 303.

403. "Bemerkungen zum Begriff der Offenbarung," 16, 17; G. Vass, *Understanding Karl Rahner,* vol. 3, *A Pattern of Doctrines 1, God and Christ* (London, 1996), 162.

404. See Gk., 204, 205.

405. J. B. Metz, *Glaube in Geschichte und Gesellschaft: Studien zu einer praktischen Fundamentaltheologie* (Mainz, 1992; first published 1972), 28, 37.

406. W. V. Dych, "Theology in a New Key," 15.

Chapter 3
The Philosophical and Theological Foundations of the Idea of the Presence of Christ in Non-Christian Religions according to Karl Rahner

1. Gk., 303. See K. Rahner, "Jesus Christus in den nichtchristlichen Religionen," in *Schriften,* XII, 1975, 370–86, esp. 370.

2. This article was originally published in a volume edited by Gerd Oberhammer. See K. Rahner, "Jesus Christus in den nichtchristlichen Religionen," in *Offenbarung: Geistige Realität des Menschen*, ed. Gerd Oberhammer (Vienna, 1974), 2:189–98.

3. "Jesus Christus in den nichtchristlichen Religionen," 370; Rahner refers in the footnotes to his works "Bemerkungen zum Problem des »anonymen Christen«," 531–46, and *Christologie—systematisch und exegetisch*, Quaestiones Disputatae 55 (Freiburg, 1972), 15–78.

4. Gk., 304.

5. See "Anonymer und expliziter Glaube," in *Schriften*, XII, 76–85, esp. 76, 77, 80; "Theologische Überlegungen zu Säkularisation und Atheismus," in *Schriften*, IX, 117–197, esp. 177–197. Rahner argues on the basis of the teachings of *Lumen Gentium* 16, *Gaudium et spes* 22, and *Ad gentes* 7. See "Heilsbedeutung der nichtchristlichen Religionen," in *Schriften*, XIII, 341–353, esp. 343.

6. "Das Christentum, eine Religion für die gesamte Menschheit? Karl Rahner im Gespräch mit Jarczyk, Paris, 1983," in *Glaube in winterlicher Zeit*, 200–204; "Ist das Christentum eine absolute Religion," in K. Rahner, *Gnade als Freiheit* (Freiburg, 1968), 155–161, esp. 155, 156; Gk., 313–76; "Weltgeschichte und Heilsgeschichte," 140–41; "Das Christentum und die nichtchristlichen Religionen," in *Schriften,* V, 136–58, esp. 138.

7. "Christologie heute?" 217–24.

8. "Das Christentum und die nichtchristlichen Religionen," 143ff.

9. Gk., 144–47; "Über die Heilsbedeutung der nichtchristlichen Religionen," 341–53; "Das Christentum und die nichtchristlichen Religionen," 152, 153; H. Vorgrimler, *Karl Rahner. Leben, Denken, Werke,* 57.

10. Ibid., 43, 59.

11. E.g., on baptism, see "Die Gliedschaft in der Kirche nach der Lehre der Enzyklika Pius XII. «Mystici Corporis Christi»," in *Schriften*, II, 7–95, esp. 31.

12. See also "Heilsbedeutung der nichtchristlichen Religionen," 340ff.

13. "Welt in Gott: Zum christlichen Schöpfungsbegriff," in *Sein und Offenbarung in Christentum und Hinduismus,* ed. A. Bsteh (Mödling, 1992; first published 1984), 69–83, esp. 69.

14. "Die ignatianische Mystik der Weltfreudigkeit," in *Schriften*, III, 329–49, esp. 331.

15. F. Kard. König, "Erinnerung an Karl Rahner als Konzilstheologen," in *Karl Rahner in Erinnerung*, ed. A. Raffelt (Düsseldorf, 1994), 149–65, esp. 158.

16. Ibid., 159; see also K. Rahner, "Die bleibende Bedeutung des II. Vatikanischen Konzils," in *Schriften,* XIV, 303–19.

17. See "Das Christentum eine Religion für die gesamte Menschheit," 201; *Theologische und philosophische Zeitfragen im katholischen deutschen Raum (1943),* 99, 100.

18. See "Über den Dialog in der pluralistischen Gesellschaft," in *Schriften,* VI, 46–59, 46ff.; "Kleine Frage zum heutigen Pluralismus in der geistigen Situation der Katholiken

und der Kirche," in *Schriften* VI, 34–46, esp. 34; "Glaubensbegründung heute," in *Schriften*, XII, 17–41, esp. 21; "Glaube zwischen Rationalität und Emotionalität," in *Schriften*, XII, 45–111, esp. 101–3; "Die eine Kirche und die vielen Kirchen," in *Schriften*, XII, 531–47, esp. 535; "Kirche, Kirchen und Religionen," in *Schriften*, VIII, 355–74, esp. 355ff.; "Über die theologische Problematik der neuen Erde," in *Schriften*, VIII, 580–93, esp. 581; "Aspekte europäischer Theologie," in *Schriften*, XV, 84–104, esp. 85–94; "Der Pluralismus in der Theologie und die Einheit des Bekenntnisses in der Kirche," in *Schriften*, IX, 11–34, esp. 11ff.; Gk., 387ff.

19. See Gk., 18, 19.

20. See ibid., 386.

21. See ibid., 387.

22. See ibid., 391, 392.

23. See ibid., 392.

24. See "Aspekte europäischer Theologie," 85–87; "Der Pluralismus in der Theologie und die Einheit des Bekenntnises in der Kirche," 11.

25. See Gk., 425.

26. See *Horizonte der Religiosität*, ed. G. Sporschill (Munich, 1984), 127–29.

27. See "Einheit der Kirche Einheit der Menschheit," in *Schriften*, XIV, 385–403, esp. 382–88.

28. See "Das Christentum und die nichtchristlichen Religionen," 136.

29. Ibid., 138; K. Rahner and N. Greinacher, "Theologische Deutung der Gegenwartssituation als Situation der Kirche," HBPTh, II, 1 (Freiburg, 1966), 233–55; A. Zahlauer, *Karl Rahner und sein "produktives Vorbild" Ignatius von Loyola*, 320.

30. K. Rahner, "Perspektiven der Pastoral in der Zukunft," in *Schriften*, XVI, 143–59.

31. "Über die gute Meinung," in *Schriften*, III, 127–55, esp. 137.

32. Herbert Vorgrimler points out that Karl Rahner is the real inspiration of the theology of liberation in Latin America. See H. Vorgrimler, "Ein Brief zur Einführung," 15, 16. The influence of Rahner can be seen in G. Gutiérrez, *Theologie der Befreiung* (Munich/Mainz, 1972).

33. See K. Rahner, "Kirche, Kirchen und Religionen," in *Schriften*, VIII, 355–74, esp. 370.

34. Ibid., 372.

35. "Das Christentum und die nichtchristlichen Religionen," 138.

36. "Einige Bemerkungen über die Frage der Konversion" in *Schriften*, V, 356–79, esp. 356ff.; "Das Christentum und die nichtchristlichen Religionen," 139–43.

37. Ibid., 154.

38. Ibid., 156–57.

39. Ibid., 158.

40. "Kirche, Kirchen und Religionen," 373.

41. See K. Rahner and K. H. Weger, *Was sollen wir noch glauben?* (Freiburg, 1979), 121–22.

42. See K. Rahner, "Über den theologischen Begriff der Konkupiszenz," in *Schriften*, I, 377–414, esp. 405–12; SW 8:25–30; "De deo elevante. Über Gott den Begnadiger," in SW 8:263–313, esp. 263ff.

43. "Über das Verhältnis von Natur und Gnade," in *Schriften*, I, 323–47, esp. 323ff.; "Über die Erfahrung der Gnade," in *Schriften*, III, 105–11, esp. 105ff.; "Weltgeschichte und Heilsgeschichte," in *Schriften*, V, 115–36, esp. 118ff.; Hilberath, *Karl Rahner*, 45, 89.

44. See Gk., 24.

45. See ibid., 26.

46. "Über das Problem des Stufenweges zur christlichen Vollendung," in *Schriften*, III, 11–35, esp. 20.

47. "Über die Erfahrung der Gnade," 105.

48. "Die Freiheit in der Kirche," in *Schriften*, II, 95–115, esp. 100.

49. "Vergessene Wahrheiten über das Bußsakrament," in *Schriften*, II, 143–85, esp. 145.

50. *Glaube in winterlicher Zeit*, 59; Hilberath, *Karl Rahner*, 89, 93.

51. See K. Rahner, "Theos im Neuen Testament," 97.

52. See HW; SW 4:81; HW 1941, 71; HW 1963, 68.

53. "Der Mensch von heute und die Religion," in *Schriften*, VI, 13–34.

54. See K. H. Neufeld, "Vorwort zur Neuausgabe," in M. Viller and K. Rahner, *Aszese und Mystik in der Väterzeit: ein Abriss der frühchristlichen Spiritualität* (Innsbruck, 1989; first published in 1939), 9.

55. On the influence of Ignatius of Loyola on Rahner, see Zahlauer, *Karl Rahner und sein "produktives Vorbild" Ignatius von Loyola,* 86ff.

56. K. Rahner, "Warum uns das Beten Not tut," *Leuchtturm* 18 (1924–25): 10–11.

57. "Le début d'une doctrine des cinq sens spirituels chez Origène," RAM 13 (1932): 113–45; "Die geistliche Lehre des Evagrius Ponticus: In ihren Grundzügen dargestellt," ZAM 8 (1933): 21–38; "La doctrine des 'sens spirituels' au Moyen-Age: En particulier chez St. Bonaventure," RAM 14 (1933): 163–299; "Der Begriff der ecstasis bei Bonaventura," ZAM 9 (1934): 1–19; "'Coeur de Jésus' chez Origène?" RAM 14 (1934): 323–36.

58. "Die geistliche Lehre des Evagrius Ponticus: In ihren Grundzügen dargestellt," 21–38.

59. "La doctrine des 'sens spirituels' au Moyen-Age: En particulier chez St. Bonaventure," 163–299.

60. "E latere Christi, Der Ursprung der Kirche als zweite Eva aus der Seite Christi des zweiten Adam: Eine Untersuchung über den typologischen Sinn von Jo 19, 34" (diss., Innsbruck, 1936).

61. See Viller and Rahner, *Aszese und Mystik in der Väterzeit*, 20.

62. Hans Urs von Balthasar, "Aszese und Mystik in der Väterzeit: Ein Abriss von Marcel Viller S.J. und Karl Rahner S.J.," *Stimmen der Zeit* 136 (1939): 334. See also Neufeld, "Vorwort zur Neuausgabe," 11.

63. K. Rahner, "Die ignatianische Mystik der Weltfreudigkeit," in *Schriften*, III, 329–49, esp. 344, 345.

64. Ibid., 346; H. Vorgrimler, "Gotteserfahrung im Alltag: Der Beitrag Rahners zur Spiritualität und Mystik," in *Vor dem Geheimnis Gottes den Menschen verstehen: Karl Rahner zum 80. Geburtstag,* ed. K. Lehmann (Munich/Zurich, 1984), 62–78. On the influence of Ignatius on the later thinking of Rahner, see K P. Fischer, "Gott als das Geheimnis des Menschen: Karl Rahners theologische Anthropologie, Aspekte und Anfragen," *Zeitschrift für die katholische Theologie* 113 (1991): 1–23, esp. 1ff.

65. See Vorgrimler, "Gotteserfahrung im Alltag," 62–78.

66. It is noteworthy in this context that, under the guidance of Rahner, Andreas Bsteh wrote a doctoral dissertation on the theme of the universality of salvation in the teachings of the church fathers of the second century. A. Bsteh, *Zur Frage nach der Universalität der Erlösung: Unter besonderer Berücksichtigung ihres Verständnisses bei den Vätern des*

zweiten Jahrhundertes (Vienna, 1966). Rahner's detailed study on the early history of penance is based on the fathers of the church. See *Schriften,* IX, *Frühe Bußgeschichte in Einzeluntersuchungen* (Zurich, 1973), 1–512.

67. On Rahner's contribution to Vatican II, see K. H. Neufeld, *Die Brüder Rahner*, 242; F. König, "Erinnerungen an Karl Rahner als Konzilstheologen," 149–55; H. Vorgrimler, *Karl Rahner verstehen*, 117ff.; P. F. Knitter, *No Other Name? A Critical Survey of Christian Attitude Towards the World Religions* (New York, 1985), 125; idem, *Jesus and the Other Names: Christian Mission and Global Responsibility* (New York, 1996), 6, 7; A. Race, *Christians and Religious Pluralism: Patterns in the Christian Theology of Religions* (London, 1983), 45; G. D'Costa, *Theology and Religious Pluralism: The Challenge of Other Religions* (Oxford, 1986), 80; Hilberath, *Karl Rahner*, 28, 29; Y. Congar, "Die Offenheit lieben gegenüber jeglicher Wahrheit: Brief des Thomas von Aquino an Karl Rahner," in *Mut zur Tugend: Von der Fähigkeit menschlicher zu leben,* ed. K. Rahner and B. Welte (Freiburg/Basel/Vienna, 1979), 124–33.

68. F. König, "Karl Rahners theologisches Denken im Vergleich mit ausgewälten Textstellen der dogmatischen Konstitution 'Lumen Gentium,' in *Glaube im Prozess: Christsein nach dem II. Vatikanum*, ed. E. Klinger and K. Wittstadt (Freiburg/Basel/Vienna, 1984), 121ff.; König, "Erinnerung an Rahner als Konzilstheologen," 134ff.

69. "Die Antwort heißt Gott: Karl Rahner im Gespräch mit Walter Tscholl," 11–26, esp. 17; "Zeuge des Konzils: Rahner im Gespräch mit Thomas C. Fox, Innsbruck, 1982," in *Glaube in winterlicher Zeit*, 93–99, esp. 93–95, 99; König, "Erinnerungen an Rahner als Konzilstheologen," 152–54; "Der Konzilstheologe," in *Karl Rahner: Bilder eines Lebens*, ed. P. Imhof and H. Biallowons (Freiburg/Basel/Vienna, 1985), 60–64; Y. Congar, "Erinnerungen an Karl Rahner auf dem Zweiten Vatikanum," in *Karl Rahner: Bilder eines Lebens*, 65–68.

70. Knitter, *Jesus and the Other Names*, 6.

71. See K. Rahner, "Theologische Grundinterpretation des II. Vatikanischen Konzils," in *Schriften,* XIV, 287–303, esp. 292, 293; "Die bleibende Bedeutung des II. Vaticanischen Konzils," in *Schriften,* XIV, 305–19, esp. 314–18.

72. See "Zeugen des Konzils: Karl Rahner im Gespräch mit Thomas C. Fox, Innsbruck, 1982," 93–98.

73. See König, "Erinnerungen an Rahner als Konzilstheologen," 156.

74. See H. Waldenfels, "Theologie der nichtchristlichen Religionen: Konsequenzen aus 'Nostra aetate,'" in *Glaube im Prozess: Christsein nach dem zweiten Vatikanum,* ed. E. Klinger and K. Wittstadt, 757–78, esp. 757ff., 761–63.

75. See Gk., 304.

76. See ibid., 323–33.

77. See Viller and Rahner, *Aszese und Mystik in der Väterzeit*, 12–22.

78. See Gk., 304.

79. See ibid., 305.

80. See ibid., 306.

81. See ibid., 305.

82. See ibid., 304.

83. See ibid., 15.

84. See ibid., 279.

85. See ibid., 307.

86. See H. Wolf, "Einleitung," in *Karl Rahner—Theologische und philosophische Zeitfragen im katholischen deutschen Raum (1943)*, ed. H. Wolf 18–80, 68.

87. Wolf, "Einleitung," 68; Wolf refers to M. Müller, "Zu Karl Rahners 'Geist in Welt,'" in *Bilder eines Lebens*, ed. Imhof and Biallowons, 28–31. See also K. Rahner, "Dogmengeschichte in meiner Theologie," in *Dogmengeschichte und katholische Theologie: Festschrift für H. Bacht, A. Grillmeier, und A. Schönmetzer*, ed. W. Loser, K. Lehmann, and M. Lutz-Bachmann (Würzburg, 1985), 323–28.

88. K. Rahner, "Über den Versuch eines Aufrisses einer Dogmatik," in SW 4:404–18, esp. 411.

89. Gk., 307.

90. Ibid.

91. Ibid., 305.

92. Rahner refers to *Lumen Gentium* 16; *Nostra Aetate* 1; *Ad Gentes* 7 and *Gaudium et Spes* 2, 10, 12, etc. See "Jesus Christus in den nichtchristlichen Religionen," 371.

93. See Gk., 305.

94. Ibid.

95. See ibid., 305.

96. See ibid., 309, 310.

97. See ibid., 177.

98. See ibid., 143.

99. See ibid., 143–44, esp. 146.

100. See ibid., 144.

101. See ibid., 145.

102. See ibid., 145–46.

103. See ibid., 146.

104. See ibid., 160–61.

105. Ibid., 305.

106. In "Der Gesetzesbegriff in der christlichen Offenbarung: Trialog zwischen Prof. Karl Rahner, Innsbruck, Pater Dr. Leopold Soukup, Seckau, und Pastor Dr. G. Milon, Wien," in *Gesetz und Wirklichkeit*, ed. S. Moser (Innsbruck, 1949), 247–54, esp. 252, Rahner tries to give a new understanding to the old interpretation of salvation (*extra ecclesiam nulla salus*). In this text Rahner refers for the first time to his concept of anonymous Christian. He says, "If a human being is genuine, is called by God and says yes to this call, he is an anonymous Christian."

107. See H. Vorgrimler, "Grundzüge der Theologie Rahners," in *Sehnsucht nach dem geheimnisvollen Gott*, ed. H. Vorgrimler (Freiburg, 1990), 32.

108. K. Rahner, "Der Christ und seine ungläubigen Verwandten," in *Schriften,* III, 419–51, esp. 427.

109. Ibid. See also "Die Gliedschaft der Kirche nach der Lehre der Enzyklika Pius XII. «Mystici Corporis Christi»," 1ff.

110. "Der eine Jesus Christus und die Universalität des Heiles," in *Schriften,* XII, 1975, 251–82; see also "Anonyme Christen und expliziter Glaube," in *Schriften*, XII, 76–85, esp. 80, 81; "Zur «Offenbarungsgeschichte» nach dem II. Vatikanum," in *Schriften,* XII, 241–51, esp. 243.

111. "Der Christ und seine ungläubigen Verwandten," 427.

112. See Gk., 123.

113. See ibid., 126; See also *Foundations*, 120.

114. See Gk., 123.

115. Ibid., 122.

116. K. Rahner, "Erfahrung eines katholischen Theologen," in *Karl Rahner in Erinnerung*, ed. A. Raffelt, 134–49, esp. 140.

117. Gk., 81, 126.

118. "Christologie im Rahmen der modernen Selbst- und Welt-verständnis," 227.

119. Gk., 92, 93.

120. Ibid., 93.

121. See J. P. Galvin, "The Invitation of Grace," in L. O'Donovan, *A World of Grace*, 70; 1 Timothy 2–4.

122. See J. B. Metz, "Karl Rahners Ringen um die theologische Ehre des Menschen," in *Karl Rahner in Erinnerung,* ed. Raffelt, 71, 72.

123. See Vorgrimler, "Grundzüge der Theologie Rahners," 22.

124. See Hilberath, *Karl Rahner*, 41.

125. See K. Rahner, "Zur Theologie der Weihnachtsfeier," 42; "Gnade als Mitte menschlicher Existenz: Ein Gespräch mit und über Karl Rahner aus Anlaß seines 70. Geburtstages," in *Herder-Korrespondenz* (1974): 77–92; "Gotteserfahrung heute," 167ff.; "Die Sinnfrage als Gottesfrage," in *Schriften,* XV, 201, 202; "Die menschliche Sinnfrage vor dem absoluten Geheimnis Gottes," in *Schriften*, XIII, 111–29, esp. 111ff. Vorgrimler, "Grundzüge der Theologie Karl Rahners," 22; Hilberath, *Karl Rahner*, 45.

126. Rahner, "Theos im Neuen Testament," 98.

127. Ibid.

128. Ibid., 103, 104.

129. Ibid., 106–7.

130. Ibid., 120–21; Acts 17:27–29; Eph. 4:6.

131. "Theos im Neuen Testament," 109.

132. Gk., 142; *Foundations*, 137.

133. God as mystery is one of the central themes of Rahner. See "Über den Begriff des Geheimnisses in der katholischen Theologie," 48, 68, 76ff., 80; "Frömmigkeit früher und heute," in *Schriften*, VII, 1–32, 30ff.; "Überlegung zur Methode der Theologie," 116–19, 250; "Zum Verhältnis zwischen Theologie und heutigen Wissenschaften," in *Schriften*, X, 104–15, esp. 107; "Glaubensbegründung heute," in *Schriften*, XII, 17–41, esp. 39; "Glaubende Annahme der Wahrheit Gottes," in *Schriften,* XII, 215–24, esp. 220; "Altes Testament und christliche Dogmatik," in *Schriften*, XII, 224–41, esp. 286, "Über die Verborgenheit Gottes," in *Schriften*, XII, 285–306, esp. 288ff., 298; "Die menschliche Sinnfrage von dem absoluten Geheimnis Gottes," in *Schriften*, XIII, 1978, 111–29, esp. 120.

134. See Gk., 23.

135. Ibid., 24.

136. "Die Gliedschaft in der Kirche nach der Lehre der Enzyklika Pius XII. «Mystici Corporis Christi»," 93.

137. Ibid., 84, 85.

138. Ibid., 93.

139. Ibid., 61.

140. Ibid., 62.

141. Ibid., 71.

142. See Gk., 61–64.

143. See ibid., 64, 65.

144. See ibid., 65.

145. See ibid., 61.
146. See ibid., 62.
147. See ibid., 63.
148. See ibid., 64.
149. See ibid., 65.
150. Ibid., 66; *Foundations*, 57.
151. See Gk., 66.
152. "Theos im Neuen Testament," 95, 96.
153. Ibid., 97.
154. "Anonymer und expliziter Glaube," 77, 83.
155. See N. Schwedtfeger, *Gnade und Welt*, 55; P. Eicher, "Wovon spricht die transzendentale Theologie? Zur gegenwärtigen Auseinandersetzung um das Denken von Karl Rahner," *ThQ* 156 (1976): 284–95, esp. 289; K. Fischer, "Wovon erzählt die transzendentale Theologie? Eine Erwiderung an Peter Eicher," in *ThQ* 157 (1977): 159–70, esp. 140.
156. K. Rahner, "Zur Theologie der Weihnachtsfeier," 39–40.
157. Gk., 89.
158. Ibid., 90.
159. GW; SW 2:54.
160. GW; SW 2:55.
161. GW; SW 2:56.
162. GW; SW 2:57.
163. See "Einführung in den Begriff der Existentialphilosophie bei Heidegger," in SW 2:319–49, esp. 326.
164. See "Erfahrung eines katholischen Theologen," 135.
165. "Theos im Neuen Testament," 93.
166. Ibid., 95.
167. Ibid., 120–21.
168. Ibid., 121.
169. Ibid., 115, 116.
170. Ibid., 117.
171. See Gk., 92.
172. See Gk., 90.
173. See HW; SW 4:34–245; HW 1941, 195–201; HW 1963, 192, 198.
174. See HW; SW4:235–45; HW 1941, 194–201; HW 1963, 190–97.
175. See HW; SW 4:245; HW 1941, 200; HW 1963, 197.
176. See HW; SW 4:245; HW 1941, 201; HW 1963, 198.
177. HW; SW 2:248, 249; HW 1941, 204; HW 1963, 199.
178. Herbert Vorgrimler says, "From his own personal experience Rahner had the basic theological conviction that God reveals himself in each human being and that is the real and the original form of revelation. . . . For Rahner it was the will of God himself that human beings learn to interpret and point out their God-experience just as the Jewish-Christian tradition had interpreted it." Vorgrimler, *Karl Rahner verstehen,* 36. Rahner's concept of a general supernatural revelation is very significant for the interpretation of the history of religions. See Vorgrimler, *Karl Rahner: Leben, Denken, Werke,* 55.
179. See A. E. Carr, "Starting with the Human," 27.
180. See Galvin, "The Invitation of Grace," in O'Donovan, *A World of Grace*, 76.
181. Ibid., 79, 80.
182. See Rahner, "Das Christentum und die nichtchristlichen Religionen," 140–43.

183. See Gk., 315; Hilberath, *Karl Rahner*, 95.
184. See Rahner, "Heilsbedeutung der nichtchristlichen Religionen," 345.
185. Ibid., 347.
186. Gk., 305.
187. Ibid., 304.
188. Gk., 51, 52.
189. See "Weltgeschichte und Heilsgeschichte," 115, 116.
190. Ibid., 116.
191. Ibid., 124.
192. Ibid., 125.
193. See "Vom Geheimnis des Lebens," in *Schriften*, VI, 83–221.
194. Gk., 123.
195. Ibid., 304.
196. See ibid., 304, 305.
197. See ibid., 274.
198. Ibid., 275.
199. See ibid., 280.
200. See ibid., 282–83.
201. See "Heilsbedeutung der nichtchristlichen Religionen," 396.
202. See "Zur Offenbarungsgeschichte nach dem II. Vatikanum," 243, 244.
203. "God, who creates and conserves all things by his word (cf. Jn. 1:3), provides men with constant evidence of himself in created realities (cf. Rom. 1:19–20). And furthermore, wishing to open up the way to heavenly salvation, he manifested himself to our first parents from the very beginning. After the fall, he buoyed them up with the hope of salvation by promising redemption (cf. Gen. 3:15); and he has never ceased to take care of the human race. For he wishes to give eternal life to all those who seek salvation by patience in well-doing (cf. Rom. 2:6–7). In his own time God called Abraham, and made him into a great nation (cf. Gen. 12:2). After the era of the patriarchs, he taught his nation, by Moses and the prophets, to recognize him as the only living and true God, as a provident Father and just judge. He taught them, too, to look for the promised Saviour. And so, throughout the ages, he prepared the way for the Gospel" (*Dei Verbum,* 3).
204. See Gk., 306, 307.
205. See ibid., 307. Rahner refers here to two articles: H. Fries, "Uroffenbarung," in SM, IV (Freiburg/Basel/Vienna, 1969), 1224–30; K. Rahner, "Offenbarung. II. Theologische Vermittlung," in SM, III (Freiburg/Basel/Vienna, 1963), 832–43.
206. K. Rahner, "Bemerkungen zum Begriff der Offenbarung," 17. See also "Das Christentum und die nichtchristlichen Religionen," 136–58, esp. 148, 153; "Anonymer und expliziter Glaube," 76; "Zur Offenbarungsgeschichte nach dem II. Vatikanum," 245.
207. See Gk., 307.
208. See "Über den Versuch eines Aufrisses einer Dogmatik," 25.
209. See "Zur Offenbarungsgeschichte nach dem II. Vatikanum," 246.
210. Ibid., 247.
211. Ibid.; *Das zweite Vatikanische Konzil,* LThK, I, 1966, 203–9; III, 1968, 351–55; 363ff., 391ff., 409, 461, 463.
212. See K. Rahner, "Zur Offenbarungsgeschichte nach dem II. Vatikanum," 242.
213. Ibid., 248.
214. "Über den Versuch eines Aufrisses einer Dogmatik," 24.
215. Gk., 306.

216. See ibid.
217. See ibid., 276.
218. See ibid., 277.
219. Ibid., 292.
220. See ibid., 293.
221. Ibid., 294.
222. See ibid., 306.
223. See ibid.
224. Ibid.
225. See Schwerdtfeger, *Gnade und Welt*, 19.
226. See K. Rahner, "Heilsbedeutung der nichtchristlichen Religionen," 342. See also "Das Christentum und die nichtchristlichen Religionen," 137, 138; J. Heislbetz, *Theologische Würde der nichtchristlichen Religionen* (Freiburg/Basel/Vienna, 1967), 9ff.
227. Ibid., 344, 345.
228. See K. Rahner, "Die Gliedschaft der Kirche nach der Lehre der Enzyklika Pius XII. «Mystici Corporis Christi»," 7–11.
229. Ibid., 31.
230. Ibid., 20–28.
231. Ibid., 29–30.
232. See Vorgrimler, "Grundzüge der Theologie Karl Rahners," 34.
233. Rahner, "Über die Heilsbedeutung der nichtchristlichen Religionen," 341–48.
234. "Theos im Neuen Testament," 99.
235. Gk., 306.
236. Ibid.
237. "Bemerkungen zum Begriff der Offenbarung," 19. For the question how salvation takes place in the non-Catholic churches, see *Vorfragen zu einem ökumenischen Amtsverständnis*, Quaestiones Disputatae 65 (Freiburg, 1974), 46ff.
238. See Gk., 306; "Das Christentum und die nichtchristlichen Religionen," 157, 158.
239. "Heilsbedeutung der nichtchristlichen Religionen," 347.
240. "Anonymer und expliziter Glaube," 76.
241. See Gk., 308.
242. See "Jesus Christus in den nichtchristlichen Religionen," 375; DZ 3008, 3009.
243. Ibid., 376; *Ineffabilis Deus*, DZ 2803, 1530.
244. Gk., 308.
245. Ibid.
246. Ibid., 310.
247. Ibid.
248. Ibid.
249. See ibid., 309; see also 260ff.
250. "Über Erfahrung der Gnade," *Schriften,* III, 105–111, esp. 108.
251. "Über den Begriff des Geheimnisses in der katholischen Theologie," 17.
252. "Würde und Freiheit des Menschen," 251.
253. "Die Freiheit in der Kirche," in *Schriften*, II, 95–115, esp. 108; Brüngel, "Erfahrung des Geistes," 21, 34. J. O'Donell, "*In Him and Over Him*"*: The Holy Spirit in the Life of Jesus* (Rome, 1989), 24–45.
254. Gk., 54.
255. See ibid., 79–83.
256. See HW; SW 4:71ff.

257. Gk., 313.
258. See ibid., 314.
259. See ibid., 315.
260. See ibid., 316.
261. See ibid., 317.
262. See ibid., 318.
263. See ibid., 320.
264. See ibid., 333.
265. See ibid., 366.
266. See ibid., 336.
267. See ibid., 354.
268. "Ist Christentum eine absolute Religion?" in K. Rahner, *Gnade als Freiheit*, 155–60.
269. See Gk., 154.
270. Ibid., 156.
271. Ibid.
272. Ibid., 157.
273. Ibid., 158.

Chapter 4
The Importance of the Theological Position of Karl Rahner in the Context of Religious and Theological Pluralism

1. See P. F. Knitter, *No Other Name? A Critical Survey of the Christian Attitudes Towards the World Religions* (New York, 1985); *One Earth Many Religions: Multifaith Dialogue and Global Responsibility* (New York, 1995); *Jesus and the Other Names: Christian Mission and Global Responsibility* (New York, 1996); *Horizonte der Befreiung: Auf dem Weg zu einer pluralistischen Theologie der Religionen*, ed. B. Jaspert (Frankfurt/Paderborn, 1997); *The Uniqueness of Jesus: A Dialogue with Paul Knitter*, ed. L. Swidler and P. Mojzes (New York, 1997); "Introduction: The Totally Other—The Utterly Necessary," in *Pluralism and Oppression. Theology in World Perspective*, ed. P. F. Knitter (New York, 1988), vii–xii.

2. This classification was first proposed by the Anglican theologian Alan Race. See A. Race, *Christians and Religious Pluralism,* 1ff.

3. For a detailed description of the exclusivist position, see K. Gnanakan, *The Pluralistic Predicament*, 8ff.; G. D'Costa, *Theology and Religious Pluralism*, 52ff.; Race, *Christianity and Religious Pluralism*, 10ff.; Knitter, *No Other Name*, 75ff.; S. J. Samartha, *One Christ—Many Religions*, 98–103; A. Amaladoss, "The Pluralism of Religions and the Significance of Christ," 85ff.; D. L. Okholm and T. R. Phillips, "Introduction," in J. Hick and C. H. Pinnonk, *More than One Name?* (Michigan, 1995); 17ff.; J. Pathrapankal, *Text and Context* (Bangalore, 1993), 66–71; P. Schmiedt-Leukel, *Theologie der Religionen,* 99–164; D. J. Krieger, *The New Universalism: Foundations for a Global Theology* (New York, 1991), 59ff.; H. Coward, *Pluralism, Challenge to World Religions* (New York, 1985), 25ff.

4. Knitter, *No Other Name?* 75.

5. Kraemer's important books are *Christian Message in a Non-Christian World* (Lon-

don, 1938); *Religion and Christian Faith* (London, 1956); *The Communication of the Christian Faith* (London, 1956); *World Culture and World Religions* (London, 1962); and *Why Christianity of all Religions* (London, 1965). The first volume of the *Church Dogmatics* of Barth deals mainly with his exclusivist theological position (see K. Barth, "The Revelation of God and the Abolition of Religions," in *Church Dogmatics*, vol. 1/2 [Edinburgh, 1956], 280–361). See S. Neil, *Christian Faith and Other Religions: The Christian Dialogue with Other Religions* (Oxford, 1970); idem, *Crisis of Belief,* rev. ed. (London, 1984); L. Newbegin, *The Open Secret* (New York, 1978); idem, *The Finality of Christ* (London, 1969); idem, *Christian Witness in a Plural Society* (London, 1977); N. Anderson, *Christianity and Comparative Religion* (London, 1971); idem, *The Mystery of Incarnation* (London, 1978); E. Brunner, "Revelation and Religion," in *Revelation and Reasons: The Christian Doctrine of Faith and Knowledge* (Philadelphia, 1946), 258–73.

6. See Gnanakan, *The Pluralist Predicament*, 83; Samartha, *One Christ—Many Religions*, 86, 88, 119.

7. According to Knitter, the mainline Protestant theologians are Paul Althaus, Emil Brunner, Paul Tillich, Wolfhart Pannenberg, Carl Heinz Ratschow, Carl Braaten, Lesslie Newbegin, Stephan Neill, Paul Devanandan, and M. M. Thomas. The mainline Protestant model accepts a general revelation but no salvation outside Christ. The Catholic model is represented by the Declaration of the Vatican II on the Relationship of the Church to the Non-Christian Religions, and so on. See Knitter, *No Other Name?* 97–145.

8. G. D'Costa, *Theology and Religious Pluralism*, 10.

9. M. Dhavamony, "Theology of Religion," in *Dictionary of Fundamental Theology*, ed. R. Latourelle and R. Fisichella (New York, 1994), 886–92, esp. 888.

10. See Acts 10:35; 14:16ff.; 17:22–31; Race, *Christians and Religious Pluralism*, 41.

11. See J. N. Farquhar, *The Crown of Hinduism* (Oxford, 1913). "This inclusivist note was echoed in later theology, especially in Roman Catholic circles, fulfilling Farquhar's position, with an emphasis on the fulfillment taking place through the Christian church and not in Christ alone. I shall call this paradigmatic approach 'inclusivist,'" says Gavin D'Costa (*Theology and Religious Pluralism,* 7). M. Müller, M. Monier Williams, and T. E. Slater are representatives of fulfillment theory. See W. Halbfass, "'Inklusivismus' und 'Toleranz' im Kontext der indisch-europäischen Begegnung," in *Inklusivismus: Eine indische Denkform*, ed. G. Oberhammer (Vienna, 1983), 29–61, 58, 59.

12. See E. Schillebeeckx, *Christ the Sacrament of the Encounter with God* (London, 1963); idem, *The Language of Faith: Essays on Jesus, Theology and the Church* (London, 1995). See H. Waldenfels, "Der Absolutheitsanspruch des Christentums und die großen Weltreligionen," *Hochland* 62 (1970): 202–17; idem, "Ist der christliche Glaube der einzige Wahre? Christentum und die nichtchristliche Religionen," *Stimmen der Zeit* 112 (1987): 463–75.

13. See P. Tillich, *What Is Religion?* (New York, 1969); idem, *The Future of Religions* (New York, 1966); idem, *Systematic Theology*, vol. 1 (1997; first published 1951), vol. 2 (1997; first published 1957), vol. 3 (1997; first published 1963); J. Robinson, *Truth Is Two-Eyed* (London, 1979).

14. See D'Costa, *Theology and Religious Pluralism*, 16.

15. See R. Panikkar, *The Unknown Christ of Hinduism* (London, 1964; Bangalore, 1981), 24ff.; idem, *Myth, Faith, Hermeneutics* (New York, 1979; Bangalore, 1983); idem, *Intra-Religious Dialogue* (New York, 1978; Bangalore, 1984); K. Klostermeier, *Hindu and Christian in Vrindavan* (London, 1969); idem, *Kristvidya* (Bangalore, 1967); S.

Abhishiktananda, *Hindu Christian Meeting Point in the Cave of the Heart* (Bangalore, 1969); idem, *Saccidananda: A Christian Approach to Advaitic Experience* (Delhi, 1974); B. Griffiths, *Return to the Centre* (London, 1978); idem, *The Marriage of East and West* (London, 1982); H. Schlette, *Towards a Theology of Religions* (London, 1966); Y. Congar, *The Wide World My Parish: Some Problems of the Understanding and the Application of Catholic Doctrine* (London, 1964; first published 1961); H. de Lubac, *Surnaturel* (Paris, 1946); idem, *Le mystère du surnaturel* (Paris, 1965); idem, *Histoire et Esprit* (Paris, 1950); J. Cobb, *Beyond Dialogue: Towards a Mutual Transformation of Christianity and Hinduism* (Philadelphia, 1982).

16. Knitter, *No Other Name?* 23.

17. See Gnanakan, *The Pluralistic Predicament*, 51.

18. See D'Costa, *Theology and Religious Pluralism*, 7; Gnanakan, *The Pluralistic Predicament*, 51, 144–45; Race, *Christians and Religious Pluralism*, 77ff.; Knitter, *No Other Name?* 25–27; J. Hick and B. L. Heblethwaite, *Christianity and Other Religions* (London, 1980), 14ff.

19. See E. Troeltsch, *The Absoluteness of Christianity* (London, 1972).

20. Hick and Heblethwaite, *Christianity and Other Religions*, 14ff.; Gnanakan, *The Pluralistic Predicament*, 155.

21. Race, *Christians and Religious Pluralism*, 72.

22. J. Moltmann, *The Church in the Power of the Spirit* (London, 1977), 153ff.

23. I. Puthiyadam, "The Theology of Religions in the Indian Context," 212.

24. See Hick, *The Rainbow of Faiths*, 20; idem, *The Second Christianity*, 80; idem, *The Metaphor of God Incarnate*, 140; Race, *Christians and Religious Pluralism*, 43, 45, 68; D'Costa, *Theology and Religious Pluralism*, 80ff.; Knitter, *Jesus and the Other Names*, 5ff.

25. P. Hacker, "Inklusivismus," in *Inklusivismus: Eine indische Denkform*, ed. G. Oberhammer (Vienna, 1983), 11–29, esp. 11.

26. RV X, 121.

27. "You are that"; see *Chandogya-Upanisad*, 6.

28. See B.G. 7:20–23; 9:23.

29. Hacker, "Inklusivismus," 12–26.

30. Ibid., 19.

31. Halbfass, "'Inklusivismus' und 'Toleranz,'" 35, 36.

32. Quoted by Halbfass, "'Inklusivismus' und 'Toleranz,'" 42, from Vivekananda, *Complete Works* (Calcutta, 1970–73), 251.

33. See S. Radhakrishnan, *The Hindu View of Life* (London, 1968; first published 1927), 18.

34. See HW; SW 4:20–21.

35. See K. Rahner, *Religionsphilosophie und Theologie,* 285–91; "Über den Begriff des Geheimnisses in der katholischen Theologie," 68.

36. See Gk., 143ff.

37. "Über das Geheimnis der Dreifaltigkeit," 320–25; "Überlegung zur Methode der Theologie," 105; "Tranzendentale Theologie," 990.

38. "Tranzendentale Theologie," 989.

39. "Überlegungen zur Methode der Theologie," 95.

40. Gk., 194.

41. "Probleme der Christologie von heute," 207.

42. Gk., 178.

43. J. Hick, *Disputed Questions in Theology and the Philosophy of Religion*, 143. Hick says that he finds inclusivism an unsatisfactory premise and therefore he moved to pluralism.

44. Abhedananda, *Attitude of Vedanta Towards Religion* (Calcutta, 1947), 131.

45. M. Müller, "On the Mygration of the Fables," *The Contemporary Review* 14 (1870): 572–98. There are a number of studies on the Hindu and Buddhist theological and moral concepts behind the teachings of Jesus which provide us another reason for a universal approach to the person of Jesus of Nazareth.

46. Abhedananda, *Attitude of Vedānta Towards Religion*, 26, 137.

47. K. Lehmann, "Philosophisches Denken im Werk Karl Rahners," in *Karl Rahner in Erinnerung*, ed. A. Raffelt, 10–28, esp. 11ff.

48. Schwerdtfeger, *Gnade und Welt*, 55; P. Eicher, "Wovon spricht die transzendentale Theologie?" 289; K. Fischer, "Wovon erzählt die transzendentale Theologie?" 140.

49. Vivekananda, *Christ the Messenger* (Calcutta, 1970), 22.

50. Ibid., 33.

51. Ibid., 10.

52. Ibid., 16.

53. S. J. Samartha, "The Cross and the Rainbow," 121, quoted from Dayakrishna, "Religion and the Cultural Consciousness," *New Quest* [Bombay] (July-August 1978): 144.

54. Abhedananda, *Yoga Psychology* (Calcutta, 1970), 64.

55. Ibid., 150.

56. Ibid., 81.

57. S. P. Athyal, "Foreword," in Gnanakan, *The Pluralistic Predicament* (Bangalore, 1992), iii–vii, esp. iii.

58. RV X, 90.

59. See G. Parrinder, *Avatār and Incarnation: A Comparison of Indian and Christian Beliefs* (New York, 1982; first published 1970), 16, 17; S. Dasgupta, *A History of Indian Philosophy*, vol. 2 (Delhi, 1975), 523ff.; R. Panikkar, *The Vedic Experience, Manthramanjari* (Pondichery, 1983), 73ff.; R. Mehta, *The Hindu Concept of Avatār* (Delhi, 1980), 22; M. Eliade, *Myth and Reality* (New York, 1963), 1–4; R. C. Zaehner, *Bhagavadgita* (London, 1973), 183, 184, 340.

60. See S. Radhakrishnan, *Indian Philosophy*, vol. 2 (New York), 520.

61. "To protect the righteous, to destroy the wicked, and to establish the kingdom of God, I am reborn from age to age" (B.G. 4:8); see Parrinder, *Avatār and Incarnation*, 32; Samartha, *One Christ—Many Religions*, 128; J. Neuner, "Das Christus-Mysterium und die indische Lehre von den Avatāras," in *Das Konzil von Chalkedon*, vol. 3, ed. A. Grillmeier and H. Bracht (Würzburg, 1954), 785ff.; M. Dhavamony, "Hindu Incarnations," in *Mediation in Christianity and Other Religions*, *Studia Missionalia* 21, 125ff.; P. Schoonenberg, "Christologie angesichts der *Avatār*-Lehre," in G. Oberhammer, *Epiphanie des Heils: Zur Heilsgegenwart in indischer und christlicher Religion* (Vienna, 1982), 179–92, esp. 179ff.

62. There is a theory that *Bhagavad-Gīta* was written by a Christian sage, because of parallels in Gita and Bible. Christ was born in a manger and Krishna in a prison. There are shepherds round about in the first case and cowherds in the other. The killing of the children in Bethlehem and in Gokul respectively was common to both stories. From this point of view, Weber, a Christian commentator of *Bhagavad-Gīta* says that *Gīta* was influ-

enced by Christianity. See R. D. Renade, *The Bhagavadgīta: The Philosophy of God-realization* (Bombay, 1965), 98, 99, 286.

63. RV VIII, 85:3–4.

64. *Chāndōgya upanishads*, III, 17:6.

65. See Parrinder, *Avatār and Incarnation*, 19ff.; Samartha, *One Christ—Many Religions*, 126–31; G. H. Schokker, "Menschwerdung Gottes," in G. Oberhammer, *Beiträge zur Hermeneutik indischer und abendländischer Religionstraditionen* (Vienna, 1991), 213–29; J. Neuner, "Das Christus-Mysterium und die indische Lehre von den *Avatāras,*" 785–824; P. Schoonenberg, "Christologie angesichts der *Avatāra*-Lehre," 179–92.

66. See A. M. Mundadan, *History of Christianity in India*, vol. 1 (Bangalore, 1984), 1–66; idem, *Sixteenth Century Traditions of St. Thomas Christians* (Bangalore, 1970), 38–67; idem, *Indian Christians: Search for Identity and Struggle for Autonomy* (Bangalore, 1984), 1ff.; A. C. Perumalil, *The Apostles in India* (Patna, 1971), 5ff.; E. Tisserant, *Eastern Christianity, in India: A History of the Syro-Malabar Church from the Earlier Time to the Present Day* (Bombay/Calcutta/Madras, 1957), 2ff.; B. Vadakara, *Origin of India's St. Thomas Christians: A Historiographical Critique* (Delhi, 1995), 16ff.; Perumalil concludes (pp. 139ff.) that the early North Indian Christians of St. Bartholomew were settled in Kalyan and continued as a separate Christian community until the coming of the Portuguese and then merged with the Christians of Bombay. See also G. M. Moraes, *A History of Christianity in India from Early Times to St. Francis Xavier: A.D. 52–1542* (Bombay, 1964), 44.

67. B.G. IX, 23.

68. See Boyd, *Indian Christian Theology*, 147–49.

69. Ibid., 148.

70. Rahner, "Probleme der Christologie von heute," 218, 219; *Investigations,* I, 197, 198.

71. See "Theos im Neuen Testament," 118, 198.

72. Samartha, *One Christ—Many Religions*, 131.

73. *Māppila* = *Mahā* + *pilla* = great son, royal son, prince. M. Mundadan, *Sixteenth Century Traditions of St. Thomas Christians* (Bangalore, 1970), 136ff.; idem, *Indian Christians: Search for Identity and Struggle for Autonomy* (Bangalore, 1984), 18; B. Vadakkekara, *Origin of India's St. Thomas Christians: A Historiographical Critique* (Delhi, 1995), 35ff.

74. See Mundadan, *Indian Christians*, 23, 28.

75. Ibid., 28; see also A. M. Mundadan, *Emergence of the Catholic Consciousness in India: St. Thomas Academy for Research, Documentation Nr. 7* (Aluva, 1985).

76. F. Wilfred and M. M. Thomas, *Theologiegeschichte der dritten Welt, Indien* (Munich, 1992), 27.

77. *Mārga* = way. *Mārthōma mārga* (the way of St.Thomas), *Parangi mārga* (the way of the Portuguese), and so on. See Mundadan, *Indian Christians*, 22, 26, 45, 133.

78. J. Hick, *The Myth of God Incarnate*, 176; see also idem, *God and the Universe of Faiths*, 117. The neglect of the powerful presence of early Christianity in India is a serious omission on the part of Samartha. See Samartha, *Hindus vor dem Universalem Christus*, 147.

79. See Hick, *An Interpretation of Religion,* 11.

80. Hick, *Problems of Religious Pluralism*, 25.

81. Hick, *God and the Universe of Faiths*, 102.

82. Hick, *Problems of Religious Pluralism*, 26–28; idem, *An Interpretation of Religion*, 2; idem, *The Second Christianity*, 78.
83. Hick, *God and the Universe of Faiths,* 102.
84. See Rahner, "Christologie innerhalb einer evolutiven Weltanschauung," 183ff.
85. See Hick, *God and the Universe of Faiths*, 106.
86. Hick, *The Rainbow of Faiths*, ix, 12.
87. Hick, *God and the Universe of Faiths*, 102.
88. Hick, *The Second Christianity*, 71.
89. Hick, *The Metaphor of God Incarnate*, 7, 9, 12.
90. Ibid., 7.
91. Ibid., 11.
92. See Rahner, "Probleme der Christologie von heute," 201.
93. Ibid., 205.
94. See "Überlegungen zur Dogmenentwicklung," 16ff.; "Zur Theologie der Menschwerdung," 142ff.; "Christologie innerhalb einer evolutiven Weltanschauung," 208ff.; "Zur Theologie der Weihnachtsfeier," 44ff.; Gk., 224ff.; 283ff.
95. See "Probleme der Christologie von heute," 169.
96. Ibid.
97. Ibid., 170.
98. See ibid., 170–87.
99. Hick, "Jesus and World Religions," 167.
100. Hick, *The Rainbow of Faiths*, 54–56.
101. Hick, *Problems of Religious Pluralism*, 68ff.
102. Hick, *God and the Universe of Faiths*, 107.
103. Ibid., 128.
104. Hick, *Problems of Religious Pluralism*, 32.
105. Hick, *The Myth of God Incarnate*, 87.
106. Hick, *Problems of Religious Pluralism*, 53, 58.
107. Hick, *The Myth of God Incarnate,* 88.
108. Hick, *Problems of Religious Pluralism,* 53.
109. Ibid., 55, quoting from *Investigations*, I, 160.
110. Hick, *Problems of Religious Pluralism*, 55, quoting from *Investigations*, I, 164.
111. Ibid.
112. Ibid., quoting from *Investigations*, I, 199, 200.
113. Hick, *Problems of Religious Pluralism,* 58.
114. Ibid., 56; *Investigations*, IV, 111.
115. Hick, *Problems of Religious Pluralism,* 59; *Investigations*, I, 173.
116. Hick, *Problems of Religious Pluralism.*
117. Ibid., 58.
118. Hick, *The Rainbow of Faiths*, 20.
119. Hick, *Disputed Questions in Theology and Philosophy of Religion*, 55; "Trinity and Incarnation in the Light of Religious Pluralism," 209.
120. Hick, *God and the Universe of Faiths*, 126.
121. Ibid., 127.
122. Ibid., 127, 128.
123. See Samartha, "Quest for Salvation and Dialogue between Religions," 430, 431.
124. See Samartha, "Cross and Rainbow," 107; *One Christ—Many Religions*, 4, 79ff.
125. See Samartha, "Inter-religious Relationships in the Secular State," 101.

126. *Prātibhāsikasatta, Vyavahārikasatta and Paramārthikasatta* are three different levels of reality-experience. *Annamayakūsa, Prānamayakūsa, manomayakūsa, Vinjānamayakūsa* and *Anandamayakūsa* are different levels of reality according to Hindu religious thought.

127. See Panikkar, *The Unknown Christ of Hinduism*, 37; idem, *Salvation in Christ: Concreteness and Universality. The Supreme* (Santa Barbara, 1972), 45ff.; idem, *Kerygma und Indien: Zur heilsgeschichtlichen Problematik der christlichen Begegnung mit Indien* (Hamburg, 1967), 17ff. See also J. Dupuis, *Jesus at the Encounter of World Religions* (New York, 1989; originally published as *Jésus-Christ à la rencontre des religions* [Paris, 1989]), 187, 188; Parappally, *Emerging Trends in Indian Christology*, 137–44.

128. See F. Wilfred, "Zum Verständnis Jesu Christi im heutigen Indien: Christologische Herausforderungen und Zukunftperspektiven," in R. Schwager, *Relativierung der Wahrheit? Kontextuelle Theologie auf dem Prüfstand* (Freiburg/Basel/Vienna, 1988), 77–106, esp. 97–99; Amaladoss, "The Pluralism of Religions and the Significance of Christ," 94, 95; E. Schillebeeckx, *Jesus in Our Western Culture* (London, 1987), 2, 3.

129. Knitter, *Jesus and the Other Names: Christian Mission and Global Responsibility*, 74–76.

130. Vorgrimler, *Karl Rahner, Leben, Denken, Werke*, 15.

131. See Hilberath, *Karl Rahner*, 48.

132. Ibid., 18, 19.

133. Ibid., 18.

134. Ibid., 19.

135. See K. Rahner, "Passion und Aszese," in *Schriften*, III, 73–105, esp. 83.

136. Ibid., 143.

137. Ibid., 148.

138. Ibid., 151.

139. Ibid., 153.

140. Ibid., 154.

141. Ibid., 156.

142. See Rahner, "Theos im Neuen Testament," 93; "Erfahrung eines katholischen Theologen," 135; Gk., 117; "Zur Theologie der Weihnachtsfeier," 39–40; "Anonymer und expliziter Glaube," 77ff.

143. See "Selbstmitteilung Gottes," SM, IV (Freiburg/Basel/Vienna, 1969), 521–24. See also Siebenrock, *Gnade als Herz der Welt*, 36.

144. See K. Rahner, "Über die Möglichkeit des Glaubens heute," in *Schriften*, V, 11ff.; "Das Christentum und die nichtchristlichen Religionen," 136ff.; "Über den Dialog in der pluralistischen Gesellschaft," 46ff.; "Theologische Überlegungen zu Säkularisation und Atheismus," in *Schriften*, IX, 117–97, esp. 177; "Zum Verhältnis zwischen Theologie und heutigen Wissenschaften," 104ff.; "Zum heutigen Verhältnis zwischen Philosophie und Theologie," 70ff.

145. See *Catechism* 51–65; Gk., 218ff.; *Gott ist Mensch geworden*, 45; "Probleme der Christologie von heute," 195ff.; "Grundlinien einer systematischen Christologie," 72ff.; "Zwei Grundtypen der Christologie," 232.

146. See *Nostra Aetate*, 2. See also *Das Christentum und die Religionen*, no. 81.

147. See *Das Christentum und die Religionen*, no. 84.

148. See F. Wilfred, *Beyond Settled Foundations: The Journey of Indian Theology* (Madras, 1993), 225.

149. See L. Anandam, *The Western Lover of the East: A Theological Enquiry into Bede Griffith's Contribution to Christianity* (Kodaikanal, 1998), 46.

150. F. Wilfred, "Dogma and Inculturation," in *Vidyajyoti Journal of Theological Reflection* 53, no. 7 (1989): 350–60, esp. 352.

151. Ibid.

152. J. Pathrapankal, *Text and Context in Biblical Interpretation* (Bangalore, 1993), 68; See also J. Pathrapankal, *The Christian Program* (Bangalore, 1999), 315–82. Perry Schmidt-Leukel considers the pluralistic option more reasonable for a theology of religions. See P. Schmidt-Leukel, *Theologie der Religionen: Probleme, Optionen, Argumente* (Neuried, 1997), 582; idem, "Skizze einer Theologie der Religionen," in *Wege der Theologie: An der Schwelle zum dritten Jahrtausend,* ed. G. Risse, H. Sonnenmans, and B. Thess, Festschrift für H. Waldenfels (Paderborn, 1996), 446–60; idem, "Christlicher Wahrheitsanspruch angesichts der Kritik und des heutigen Pluralismus," in *Christlicher Glaube in multireligiöser Gesellschaft: Erfahrungen, theologische Reflexionen, missionarische Perspektiven,* ed. A. Peter (Immensee, 1996), 249–67.

153. Ibid.

154. Panikkar, *The Unknown Christ of Hinduism*, 14.

155. Knitter, "Five Theses on the Uniqueness of Jesus," 4ff.

156. Ibid., 14.

157. D'Costa, "Christ, the Trinity and the Plurality," 16.

158. Amaladoss, "The Pluralism of Religions and the Significance of Christ," 86; see also "Pluralism of Religions and the Significance of Christ," *Vidyajyothi Journal of Theological Reflection* 53, no. 8 (1989): 85–104, esp. 101ff.

159. Ibid., 86, 87.

160. Ibid., 88, 89.

161. Ibid., 98.

162. Ibid., 100.

163. H. Küng et al., *Christianity and the World Religions: Paths of Dialogue with Islam, Hinduism and Buddhism* (London, 1993; first published 1986). Originally published as *Christentum und Weltreligionen* (Munich, 1984), xix.

164. B. S. Yadav, "Vaishnavism on Hans Küng: A Hindu Theology of Religious Pluralism," in P. F. Griffiths, *Christianity through Non-Christian Eyes* (New York, 1994), 234–47, esp. 242.

165. Ibid., 243.

166. Ibid.

167. K. Pathil, "Preface," in *Religious Pluralism: An Indian Christian Perspective*, ed. K. Pathil (Delhi, 1991), viii.

168. I. Puthiadam, "Theology of Religions in the Indian Context," 228–29.

169. R. Panikkar, "Indian Christian Theology of Religious Pluralism from the Perspective of Interculturation," in *Religious Pluralism*, ed. Pathil, 252–300, esp. 273.

170. Dupuis, *Jesus Christ at the Encounter of World Religions,* 11.

171. Ibid., 247.

172. S. Anand, "Universally Unique and Uniquely Universal," *Vidyajyothi Journal of Theological Reflection* (1991): 393–424.

173. Ibid., 422, 423.

174. Cited by J. Pathrapankal, *Text and Context* (Bangalore, 1993), from S. Athappally, "The Scandalon of the Uniqueness of Jesus Christ: Some Critical Reflections," *Christian Orient* 11 (1990): 103–19.

175. F. X. D'Sa, "The Dharma of Religion," in *Quest for an Indian Church*, ed. K. Kunnumpuram and L. Fernando (Gujarath, 1993), 65–95, esp. 89.

176. Ibid.

177. A. Amaladoss, "An Emerging Indian Theology, II, Some Exploratory Reflections," *Vidyajyothi Journal of Theological Reflection* 58 (1994): 572–600, esp. 572.

178. F. Vineeth, "Theology of Religions from the Perspective of Inter-religious Dialogue," in *Religious Pluralism,* ed. Pathil, 229–52, esp. 249.

179. Ibid.

180. V. F. Vineeth, "Theology of World Religions and the Church's Relation with the Religious Traditions of Mankind," in D. S. Amalorpavadass, *Indian Christian Spirituality* (Bangalore, 1982), 120–24, esp. 124.

181. D. S. Amalorpavadass, *Inculturation Is Not Hinduisation but Christianization* (Bangalore, 1985), 3–6.

182. Panikkar, *Unknown Christ of Hinduism*, 4ff.

183. R. Panikkar, *A Dwelling Place for Wisdom* (Louisville, Ky., 1993), 152–53; originally published as *Der Weisheit eine Wohnung bereiten* (Munich, 1991).

184. B. Griffiths, *A New Vision of Reality: Western Science, Eastern Mysticism and Christian Faith* (London, 1989), 111–21; *The Cosmic Revelation: The Hindu Way to God* (Bangalore, 1985), 76.

185. Abhishiktananda, *Saccidananda: A Christian Approach to Advaitic Experience* (Delhi, 1984).

186. Panikkar, *A Dwelling Place for Wisdom*, 149.

Conclusion

1. See HW; SW, 15; HW 1941, 15; HW 1963, 20.
2. See HW; SW, 20, 21; HW 1941, 18; HW 1963, 23, 24.
3. See HW; SW, 23–25; HW 1941, 20, 21; HW 1963, 26.
4. See HW; SW, 26, 27; HW 1941, 23; HW 1963, 29.
5. See Congregation for Clergy, *General Directory for Catechesis* (Vatican City, 1997), 106–8.

Index